MW01138357

Additional Praise for

Distress Investing: Principles and Technique

"*Distress Investing: Principles and Technique* presents a concise, practical description of the restructuring process, the various players in the process and the constraints and incentives motivating their actions, as well as the institutional and economic forces impacting the process. The power of this holistic view is demonstrated in many actual distressed investing situations. Without the wisdom in this book anyone investing in distressed securities runs the risk of becoming a distressed investor!"
> —STAN GARSTKA
> Deputy Dean and Professor in the Practice of Management, Yale School of Management

"Marty Whitman and Fernando Diz have produced an extraordinary guide to today's world of distressed investing. Drawing on Whitman's 50+ years of successful experience in the field, they have explained in straightforward terms how an investor can construct a portfolio of distressed investments within today's complex variety of different securities. While there are no guarantees of ultimate investment performance, following these principles will enhance the probability of above average portfolio returns."
> —JOSEPH W. BROWN
> CEO, MBIA Inc.

"In a world puzzled about the reasons for the collapse of our economy, we are fortunate to have two gifted observers, the authors of this book, who understand the elusive intricacies of the problem and explain their details so effectively."
> —WILLIAM BAUMOL
> Academic Director, Berkley Center for Entrepreneurship Studies, New York University

"A very comprehensive and thorough analysis of a timely and interesting topic. Filled with exciting and sometimes provocative insights, this is a must-read for the uninitiated as well as those deeply immersed in the topic."
> —ANDREW DeNATALE
> Partner, White & Case LLP

Distress
Investing

Founded in 1807, John Wiley & Sons is the oldest independent publishing company in the United States. With offices in North America, Europe, Australia, and Asia, Wiley is globally committed to developing and marketing print and electronic products and services for our customers' professional and personal knowledge and understanding.

The Wiley Finance series contains books written specifically for finance and investment professionals as well as sophisticated individual investors and their financial advisors. Book topics range from portfolio management to e-commerce, risk management, financial engineering, valuation, and financial instrument analysis, as well as much more.

For a list of available titles, visit our Web site at www.WileyFinance.com.

Distress Investing

Principles and Technique

MARTIN J. WHITMAN
FERNANDO DIZ

WILEY

John Wiley & Sons, Inc.

Published by John Wiley & Sons, Inc., Hoboken, New Jersey.
Published simultaneously in Canada.

For general information on our other products and services or for technical support, please contact our Customer Care Department within the United States at (800) 762-2974, outside the United States at (317) 572-3993 or fax (317) 572-4002.

Wiley also publishes its books in a variety of electronic formats. Some content that appears in print may not be available in electronic books. For more information about Wiley products, visit our web site at www.wiley.com.

Library of Congress Cataloging-in-Publication Data:

Whitman, Martin J.
    Distress investing : principles and technique / Martin J. Whitman, Fernando Diz.
        p.   cm. – (Wiley finance series)
    Includes bibliographical references and index.
    ISBN 978-0-470-11767-5 (cloth)
        1. Investments.   2. Business cycles.   I. Diz, Fernando, 1956-   II. Title.
    HG4521.W4742 2009
    332.6–dc22
                                                                    2008054928
    ISBN 978-0-470-11767-5

10   9   8   7   6   5   4   3   2   1

To my wife Lois

To my children and spouses and companions—
Jim and Sara; Barbara and Dave; Tom and Mira

To my grandchildren—
Daniel, Will, Nathaniel, Lucien, Raphael, and Rosalie

Martin J. Whitman

To my parents, Alfonso and Lelia,
for their unwavering support

To Pepa for her patience

To Claudia, Emmett, Mateo, and Patricia

Fernando Diz

Contents

Foreword

Today, one only needs to read the press or view the media to see how most people are struggling to understand the problems brought on by the deepest financial crisis that our country has seen in decades.

Even the very people we trust are struggling to find solutions to these problems. The current financial crisis has made it extremely important for all market participants, and the public alike, to better understand our nation's reorganization and liquidation processes.

Renowned distress investor Martin J. Whitman and Professor Fernando Diz do just that in this volume. In layman's terms, they walk the reader through the various processes that companies in financial distress use to either reorganize as going concerns or to liquidate. In doing so, they map the risks, rewards, conflicts of interests, and communities of interest faced by all participants in such processes: creditors, managements, control investors, passive investors, shareholders, professionals, employees, government, and the company itself. The book includes relevant discussions about the external forces, in today's environment, imposing or not imposing discipline on market participants. These discussions should prove very helpful to policy makers trying to find solutions for the diverse constituencies involved.

During the current financial crisis, the U.S. government has become the credit enhancer of last resort and policy makers are now struggling to decide where and how such power should be used. The contents of this book should provide a roadmap for deciding where such enhancements may prove helpful and where they will not. Throughout the book the authors highlight the notion of a business as a going concern and how this notion is at odds with current mark-to-market accounting for the types of businesses that are at the heart of the current financial crisis. As politicians and government officials debate the "good bank/bad bank" and/or "buying toxic assets" ideas, it is clear that they are trapped in liquidating concepts of insolvency rather than the more realistic "going concern" concepts. This confusion has made it more difficult to change accounting rules that are unrealistic for many businesses and create regulatory insolvencies that have paralyzed such businesses.

Many of the ideas in the book are also quite helpful to private equity investors who will undoubtedly play an important role in the solution of this crisis.

This is a one-of-a-kind book, a must read if you truly hope to understand many of the problems that businesses face in today's financial environment.

DANIEL D'ANIELLO
Co-founder and Managing Director
The Carlyle Group

Preface

This book is an outgrowth of annual seminars the two of us taught together at Syracuse University's Martin J. Whitman School of Management for the past seven years. The subject matters of these seminars were distress investing and value investing. We hope that many of the teachings in this volume will be helpful not only to the distress investor and the value investor, but also to the control investor and other parties interested in corporate restructurings. There are many investors who deploy funds away from cashlike investments only into situations where they have, or believe they can get, elements of control over a going concern and/or the reorganization or liquidation processes for troubled companies. In 2008 and 2009 it seems obvious that an important future activity will be obtaining control of both reorganization processes and troubled companies that are being reorganized.

One area that this book hardly touches on is the trading environment for distress credits. That is not where our talents or interests lie. Rather, the book is about buy-and-hold investing in distressed credits. Most distressed credits are likely to be performing loans or reinstated issues in the event an issuer has to be reorganized. Reinstatement means that the contract rights inherent in the credit instrument are restored. Principal is paid in accordance with the terms described in the bond indenture or loan agreement, as are contracted-for premiums, if any, as well as interest and interest on interest if there are any nonpayments during the reorganization period. If the analyst managing a debt portfolio is right in postulating that a performing loan will remain a performing loan, or that in the event of reorganization the loan will be reinstated, then the analyst doesn't ever have to worry about market prices. At this writing, for example, the Forest City Enterprises $3^5/_8$ percent senior unsecured debentures due October 15, 2011, are selling to afford the investor an approximate yield to maturity of 28 percent. If the analysis is correct that this performing loan will remain a performing loan, then the debenture holder, holding this issue to maturity, will garner an annual return of approximately 28 percent. In owning debt instruments that are likely to be performing loans or to be reinstated, we are perfectly content to be passive investors, and our relevant measures of return are yield to maturity, yield to an event, and current yield.

Where a security is likely to participate in a reorganization, either out of court in a voluntary exchange or as part of a Chapter 11 proceeding, we usually seek to have elements of control over the reorganization process and even sometimes elements of control of the reorganized company, as was the case for Nabors Industries, Mission Insurance Group, Home Products International, and Kmart. In these cases, returns are measured essentially by dollar price paid as compared to estimated workout values in an estimated time period. Whether owning a performing loan or an issue that will participate in a reorganization, this book gives very little weight to interim market prices or market price fluctuations.

Very little in distress investing lends itself to certainty. Rather, the investor always deals in probabilities. In the case of the Forest City debentures, it is our view, after thorough analysis, that the probabilities are 90 percent that the $3^5/_8$s will be a performing loan and only 10 percent that the $3^5/_8$s will participate in Chapter 11 reorganization. Further, it is our opinion that if Forest City Enterprises has to reorganize, the reorganization value attributable to the $3^5/_8$s will be well north of the current dollar price of 53. There is no Forest City parent company debt outstanding that is senior to the $3^5/_8$s, and the $6.8 billion of secured obligations outstanding are all non-recourse debt issued by Forest City subsidiaries, not the parent company. In other words, a creditor owning subsidiary-issued debt can look only to the individual property for repayment, not to any assets of Forest City as a parent company. So in effect, the $3^5/_8$s become a blanket second mortgage where to be a performing loan, not all, but only a number of Forest City's vast empire of prime real estate assets has to throw off cash to the parent company. It is possible that Forest City as a parent company could incur new debt that would be senior to the $3^5/_8$s. This could be a problem, but it is lessened by the probability that Forest City as a parent would receive the cash generated by the incurrence of this new debt, and that such cash would be invested profitably. We discuss many of these distress investing risks in Chapter 12.

We feel strongly that understanding distress investing is extremely helpful to analysts deciding to focus on common stock value investing. It is essential when investing in common stocks to learn to benefit from the use of disclosure documents, to understand capitalizations, and to appreciate the fact that, certainly in 2008 and 2009, common stocks can have little value regardless of price if they are issued by companies that are not creditworthy. Interestingly enough, even the best of value investing literature (e.g., the 1963 edition of *Security Analysis: Principles and Technique* by Benjamin

Graham and David Dodd with Sidney Cottrell) leave much to be desired in terms of credit analysis. Further, Franco Modigliani and Merton Miller, two eminent economists, received a Nobel Prize for postulating, "Assuming that managements work in the best interests of stockholders, corporate capitalizations are a matter of indifference." What utter nonsense! This book, we hope, has lessons for value investors who invest only in the common stocks of strongly capitalized companies.

Probably the most striking thing about the distressed area is that so many of the operative facts in distress are 180 degrees opposite from what the conventional wisdom says the facts are, even among sophisticated professionals without any distress background. In 1979, one of us served as financial adviser to the Kemeny Commission on the accident at Three Mile Island, a nuclear facility in Pennsylvania. Subsequently, that same author was retained by Long Island Lighting to explore bankruptcy scenarios for that troubled electric utility. In 1985 he wrote a paper about what would happen if an electric utility actually filed for bankruptcy relief. In that paper he compared what was likely to happen (correctly, as it subsequently turned out) with what the conventional wisdom was (and unfortunately still seems to be), as postulated at that time by Arthur Young & Company, a public accounting firm; Morgan Stanley & Company, an investment bank; and Milbank, Tweed, Hadley & McCloy, a law firm. The wrong postulates of the conventional wisdom as put forth by these professionals at the time were about as follows. The three institutions wrongly believed that:

- There would be a loss of tax revenues for state and local governments.
- There would be a loss of state pension fund investments in securities of the affected utility.
- There would be higher levels of unemployment in the state.
- There would be a loss of business confidence in the state.
- There would be uncertainty as to future levels of service by a bankrupt utility.
- There would possibly be increased rates for utility customers over the long term.
- There would be an increase in the costs of capital for other utilities in the state.
- A trustee would replace management.
- Operating costs would go up.
- Investors would shun acquiring the securities of a bankrupt utility after it was reorganized.

It seems to us that the 1985 conventional myths are being reiterated at the end of 2008 in looking at the proposed government capital infusions into the automotive Big Three—General Motors, Ford, and Chrysler. In order to be viable, these companies have to be able to sell cars and trucks. Their current levels of financial distress, widely publicized, have already tainted these companies in the eyes of the consumers who are potential car buyers. It seems a stretch that Chapter 11 filing would realistically cause the taint to be greater that it already is. Further, the three have experienced dramatic losses in market share over the past 30 years. With or without Chapter 11, the Big Three already suffer from the stigma of being so poorly financed that many people avoid their products because they believe the companies may lack staying power. Why would filing for Chapter 11 relief increase the stigma over and above what it already is? A basic problem seems to be that neither corporate management nor governmental authorities have much of a conception of what Chapter 11 involves. General Motors and Chrysler already appear to be toast because they can't sell cars and trucks and there seems to be little evidence that they will be able to compete effectively when the economy turns up. If the companies are to be feasible businesses, the advantages of making them feasible in Chapter 11, as discussed in this book, probably outweigh by a large margin the disadvantages of a Chapter 11 reorganization.

As part of distress investing, we pretty much reject, or largely modify, certain common beliefs held by economists and financial people. For example, it is not useful to state that a company or institution is "too big to fail." Rather, a more productive view is that a company or institution can be "too big not to be reorganized." Perhaps in this situation failure might be defined as having the old common stock interests become valueless. But the large company will not become valueless; it will be recapitalized and/or its assets will be put to other uses or other ownership.

Very often conventional wisdom stands in the way of understanding these real problems, and in Chapters 2 and 6 we lay out the foundation for a pragmatic understanding of many such problems. Economists all seem to say, "There is no free lunch." More useful, though, especially if one is to participate in reorganization negotiations, is the view that "Somebody is going to have to pay for lunch." In distress we do not consider general risk. For us, risk exists only where preceded by an adjective describing the specific risk. There is market risk, investment risk, credit risk, leverage risk, reorganization risk, failure to match maturities risk, commodity risk, hurricane risk, and so on. Also, there is no risk-reward ratio in distress investing. Rather, the lower the price, the less the risk of loss and the greater the potential for gain.

There are many other simple rules detailed in the book that are essential to be aware of if you are to enjoy success as a distress investor. Among these simple rules are the following:

- As a practical matter, in the United States no one can take away a creditor's contracted-for right to a money payment unless that individual creditor so consents or the debtor obtains relief from a duly constituted governmental authority, usually a Chapter 11 bankruptcy court.
- Reorganizations can be voluntary or mandatory. In a voluntary exchange, each creditor makes up his or her mind whether to exchange the securities owned for a new consideration. In a mandatory reorganization, the creditor is required to take the new consideration, provided there is the requisite vote of each class (in Chapter 11, the required vote for participants in a reorganization is, of those creditors voting, two-thirds in amount and one-half in number), or there is a court-ordered cram-down Chapter 11 plan.
- It is hard for voluntary exchange offers to succeed. The purpose of the voluntary exchange offer is to credit-enhance the company. In order to succeed, the exchange offer has to result in specific classes of nonexchanging creditors being credit degraded. This can't always be accomplished.
- Noncontrol participants in reorganizations need a cash bailout. For noncontrol participants, cash bailouts can come from only two sources: payments by the company or sale to market. Payments by a company to creditors take the form of principal, premium if any, and interest. Payments by the company to equity holders consist of dividends and/or share repurchases.
- Distress investors are by and large without political clout. The Internal Revenue Code in particular treats harshly investors who buy credits at a discount and also severely restricts the ability of most troubled companies to use favorable tax attributes created by past losses.
- Investing for cash return, especially in performing loans, tends to have different dynamics than investing for total return (i.e., income plus price appreciation).
- U.S. Chapter 11, which encourages corporate reorganization, seems to be a sounder law for troubled companies than that which exists in most other countries.
- Whereas individual debt obligations mature, aggregate indebtedness for companies, governments, and most individuals is almost never retired. Rather, it is normally refinanced and, as an entity progresses, expanded in size.

- The worldwide 2007–2008 financial meltdown is unprecedented. Many unknowns will be worked out in distress markets with at this time unknowable results. Even the best companies can be, and frequently are, denied access to capital markets in 2008.
- Accounting under generally accepted accounting principles (GAAP) can never give investors more that objective benchmarks. In one or more specific contexts, GAAP is almost always misleading.
- Some markets tend to become efficient. Some markets tend toward efficiency but never arrive there. Some markets are inherently inefficient.
- Reorganization of troubled companies is a very expensive process, whether undertaken out of court or in a Chapter 11 reorganization, or in liquidation proceedings in Chapter 7 or Chapter 11.
- Management entrenchment, management compensation, and corporate governance postreorganization are important issues in assessing troubled companies.
- From the point of view of participants in reorganizations, the form of consideration (new senior debt versus, say, common stock) is frequently as important as the amount of consideration.
- Distress investing really revolves around four different businesses:
  1. Performing loans likely to stay performing loans.
  2. Small reorganizations or liquidations.
  3. Large reorganizations or liquidations.
  4. Making capital infusions into troubled companies.
- There are four avenues used to create corporate wealth:
  1. Discounted cash flow (DCF).
  2. Earnings, with earnings defined as creating wealth while consuming cash.
  3. Asset and liability redeployments, including changes in control.
  4. Super-attractive access to capital markets.

The word *bailout* has pejorative connotations. It is more productive to look at capital infusions and credit enhancements by the government as necessary sources of financing for essential institutions at a time when all other sources of access to outside capital for these institutions have disappeared. It is our view that for delivering such capital infusions or credit enhancements, the government should seek, and be entitled to, reasonable profits. The elements of control given the government in return for its capital infusion or credit enhancement ought to be limited. It seems as if the terms of the Troubled Asset Relief Program (TARP) capital infusions ought to come close to achieving the two objectives the government ought to have of (1) prospects for a reasonable profit plus (2) limited control over the businesses receiving the capital infusions. The government, however, in making capital injections ought to avoid making deals on terms that amount to the expropriation of private property without fairly compensating the former owners of that property. This is what seems to have happened when the government took 80 percent equity interests in American International Group (AIG), Fannie Mae, and Freddie Mac. The theoretical standard for fair compensation revolves around the old Internal Revenue Code standard—"the terms, including price that would be arrived at in negotiations between a willing buyer and a willing seller, both with knowledge of the relevant facts and neither under any compulsion to act." In fact, AIG, Fannie Mae, and Freddy Mac were not willing sellers. They were, on behalf of their shareholders, coerced sellers faced with a compulsion to act in order to avoid draconian consequences.

Adam Smith described the "invisible hand" of the marketplace that will direct the allocation of resources to their most efficient use without government interference. This type of invisible hand does not exist in the United States. Instead, government will always have a huge role to play in how resources are allocated by the private sector. Activists in the U.S. private sector are very efficient in reacting quickly and powerfully to government actions in regard to tax policies, credit granting, credit enhancement, and, to some extent, direct subsidies. The rules of Chapter 11 have an important bearing on what "invisible hand" incentives participants will react to. For example, trade vendors unwilling to grant trade credit prepetition may become anxious to ship goods after a Chapter 11 filing occurs and they become postpetition creditors.

Finally, this Preface would be incomplete if the authors did not state that despite all its warts and problems, Chapter 11 seems to have been rather productive in permitting troubled companies to reorganize as feasible entities contributing to the general economic well-being of our nation. Chapter 11 seems to have a dual goal: (1) to result in the reorganized debtor becoming feasible so that it is unlikely to have to go through the reorganization process again, and (2) to deliver to claimants and parties in interest an approximation of the maximum present value to which they are entitled, all in accordance with a strict rule of absolute priority. At least in dealing with companies that have publicly traded securities, and where the businesses are reorganizable, we believe that Chapter 11 meets these goals at least approximately, much more often than not.

MARTIN J. WHITMAN
FERNANDO DIZ

Acknowledgments

Over the years, we had frequently talked about the extremely narrow and limited understanding that academic finance has about the very real issues faced by investors investing in the common stocks and/or credit instruments or claims of troubled corporations. The tangible result of our dissatisfaction with traditional academic finance was the creation of the Distress Investing Seminar at Syracuse University, which has been in operation since 2002. It was not until the 2007–2008 financial meltdown started to unravel companies that we realized how little people in the media, political decision makers, and the general public knew about the reality of corporate restructurings. Until then, the material in this book had been confined to the classroom at Syracuse University, and seminars at a few other universities. Early in 2007 we decided that the time was ripe for us to make a small contribution outside of the classroom to the understanding of the many issues faced by companies, creditors, managements, investors, and other constituents before and during corporate restructurings; this book is the end result.

The names of people who have helped us in various capacities are too numerous to mention, but our thanks go to all of them—family members, friends, students, colleagues, Wall Street professionals, guest speakers at the Distress Investing Seminar at Syracuse University, accountants, and restructuring lawyers.

Among the people who deserve special mention are Beth Connor at Third Avenue Management and Betty Ross at Syracuse University, who have kept us on track throughout this highly demanding period. We are grateful to Emilie Herman, Kate Wood, and Pamela van Giessen at John Wiley & Sons, Inc., for helping us make this project happen.

Errors and shortcomings belong to us alone.

One

The General Landscape of Distress Investing

1

The Changed Environment

Three earthshaking events have resulted in a markedly changed financial environment since the late 1980s and early 1990s: first, financial innovation; second, new laws and regulations; third, the 2007–2008 financial meltdown. The past three decades have witnessed a tremendous amount of financial innovation that has led to significant changes in the levels of debt, the types of credit market instruments, and the overall capital structures of nonfinancial U.S. corporations. These changes accelerated after the late 1980s. Such innovation has also been responsible for the acceleration of the claims' transformation process—loans into securities issued by structured investment vehicles (SIVs) like collateralized loan obligations (CLOs), for example—that has had important effects on the traditional roles of financial intermediaries and the creation of new credit markets.

After the 1999 Gramm-Leach-Bliley Act and prior to the 2008 financial meltdown, commercial banks tended to act more like underwriters and distributors than like financial intermediaries and investors. These banks no longer take the credit risks that they used to take in the 1970s and early 1980s, albeit they switched to instruments with vastly increased credit risk for their portfolios of consumer loans, including residential mortgages and consumer credit card debt. The development of securitization and financial derivatives markets has contributed to a major transfer of credit risk from commercial banks to other types of market participants, who have assumed active and growing functions in new markets for claims that were the traditional realm of regulated banks. New derivatives markets include credit default swaps (CDSs), which are bets, mostly by speculators, on the probabilities of money defaults on individual debt issues. Before the financial meltdown of 2007–2008, and even after, hedge funds speculated on the credit quality of an issuer using credit default swaps with very large amounts of leverage, and literally influenced market perceptions of the creditworthiness of issuers even though they might have been less knowledgeable than a bank or a credit rating agency making such assessments.

Another outcome of innovation was the development of new primary and secondary markets that have improved the liquidity for traditional and transformed claims. The creation of the original-issue below-investment-grade bond market in the 1980s and early 1990s and of the leveraged loan markets are but two examples of such transformation. With increased participation by nontraditional market participants, more liquid, efficient, and potentially unstable secondary markets have also developed. As an example of increased efficiency, back in early 1980s one could buy secured loans of distressed companies at about 40 cents on the dollar, whereas after the early 1990s and before the 2007–2008 financial meltdown one would have to pay 85 or 90 cents on the dollar for the same loans. As an example of the potential funding instability, almost 70 percent of the par value outstanding of leveraged loans is held by nonbank institutions like hedge funds, collateralized debt obligation (CDO) trusts, and the like.

Financial innovation has not been the only driver of change in the distress investment environment. The legal environment for reorganizations has also changed with the passage of the Bankruptcy Abuse Prevention and Consumer Protection Act of 2005 (BAPCPA), which made changes to the Bankruptcy Reform Act of 1978. Among the many changes with respect to business bankruptcy reorganizations, the 2005 Act has imposed new time limits on the debtor's exclusive right to file a Plan of Reorganization (POR), has shortened the time period during which debtors can decide whether to assume or reject nonresidential real estate losses, has attempted to limit executive compensation paid under key employee retention plans (KERPs), and has enhanced the rights of trade vendors. The administrative costs of a Chapter 11 reorganization have become quite onerous to many estates, and as a consequence we see a larger number of prepackaged and/or prenegotiated filings today.

These are just a few of the important forces that have shaped and continue to shape today's distress investment environment. In this chapter we try to give the reader a broad perspective on some of these trends and changes both during the period from 1990 up until 2007 and after the 2007–2008 financial crisis.

TRENDS IN CORPORATE DEBT GROWTH AND LEVERAGE BEFORE THE FINANCIAL MELTDOWN OF 2007–2008

Over the past 60 years, U.S. nonfinancial corporate credit market debt outstanding grew, on average and in real terms, faster than the gross domestic product (GDP). Corporate debt grew at an annual real rate of 4.1 percent, whereas GDP grew at an annual real rate of 2.7 percent for the same period. Growth was volatile and generally tied to the business cycle (see Exhibit 1.1),

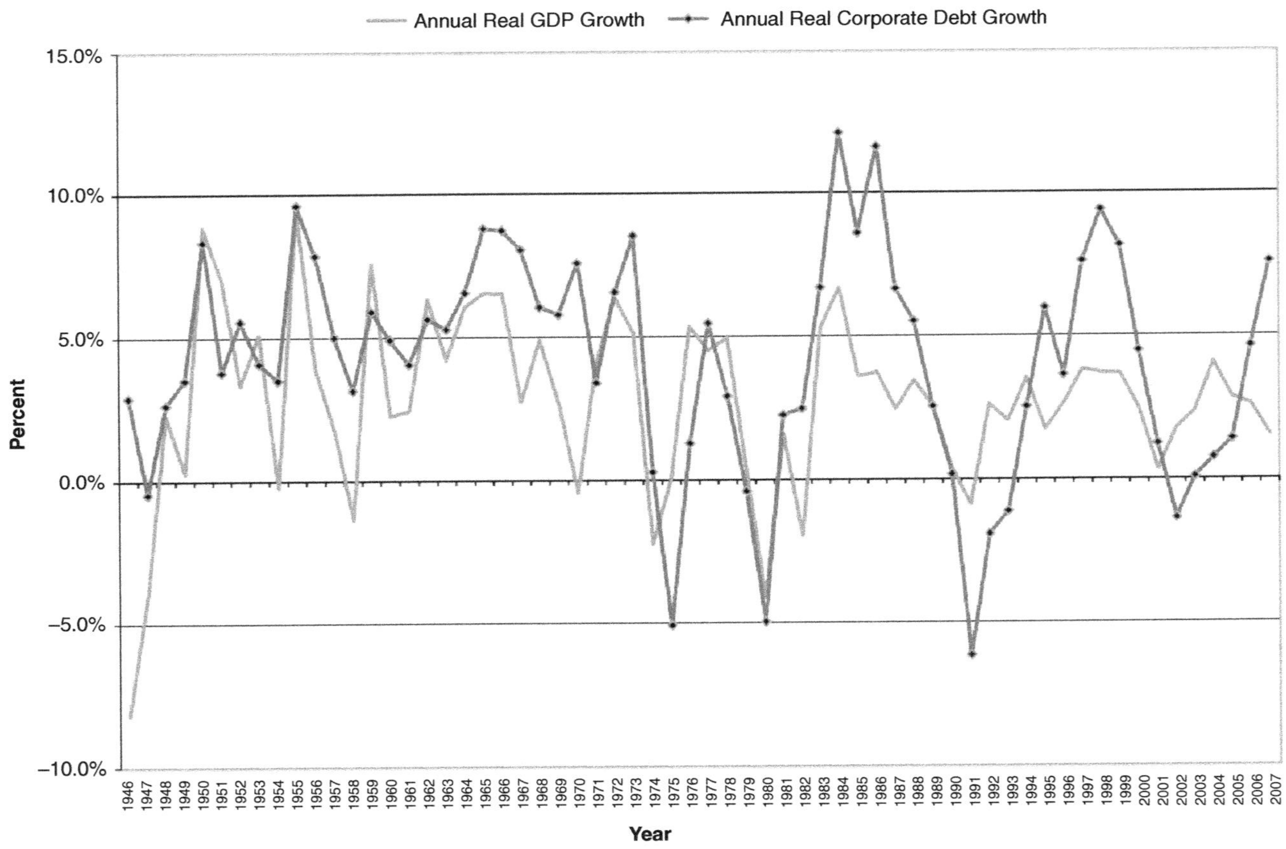

EXHIBIT 1.1 Annual GDP Growth Rate versus Corporate Credit Market Growth Rate, 1946–2007

but in the last 30 years the credit cycle became considerably more volatile than it had been in the previous 30 years.

For the 1945–1969 period, the volatility of the real rate of growth in GDP and corporate debt measured by their standard deviations were 4.00 percent and 2.39 percent respectively, whereas comparable numbers for the 1970–2007 period were 2.37 percent and 4.45 percent. Today, larger credit contractions are associated with much shallower slowdowns than in the past. The increased levels of leverage used by corporations brought about this larger volatility in the corporate credit cycle. In 1979, credit market debt at nonfinancial corporations was only 17.8 percent of assets, but by the end of 1990 it had grown to represent 26.2 percent of assets, surpassing the previous high level of 24.4 percent in 1970 (see Exhibit 1.2).

Increased levels of leverage were made possible by easier access to credit markets, which in turn resulted in an overall deterioration of creditworthiness. Understanding how these new levels of leverage came about is quite important to understanding the current distress investing environment. At the heart of this change in financial leverage was an unprecedented amount of financial innovation and regulatory change.

JUNK BONDS AND THE LEVERING-UP PERIOD

The leveraged restructuring movement and the development and growth of the original-issue below-investment-grade bond market played a major role in the levering-up process of the 1980s. The highly successful going-private transaction of Gibson Greetings, Inc. in 1982 and the astonishingly quick placement of $1.3 billion of junk bonds for Metromedia in 1984 signaled the beginning of a trend. From 1984 to 1989, use of proceeds for share purchases accounted for more than 80 percent of the net issuance of corporate bonds and bank loans put together.[1] Although below-investment-grade bonds had been around for a long time, a large proportion of the amount outstanding during the 1970s was investment-grade debt that had been downgraded to below investment grade—fallen angels—and represented only a small fraction of the total corporate bond debt outstanding.

Junk bonds are generally unsecured obligations (debentures), with covenants that are much less restrictive than those of bank loans. Primary offerings come to market either as registered issues or under the exemption of Rule 144A that allows public companies to issue quickly and avoid the delays of a public registration.[2] Deals that do not have registration rights are usually exchanged for an identical series of registered paper, which enhances their liquidity. Typical holders of this paper include mutual funds, pension funds, insurance companies, collateralized debt obligation (CDO) structured

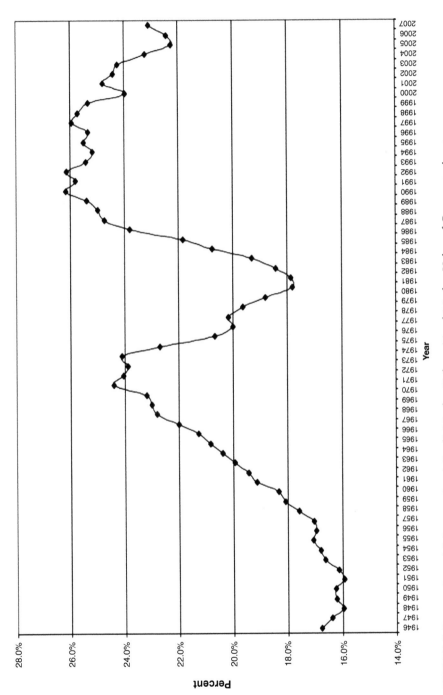

EXHIBIT 1.2 Nonfinancial Corporations' Credit Market Debt to Total Market Value of Corporate Assets, Based on Federal Reserve Data

7

vehicles, and hedge funds. Many of the junk bonds are subordinated issues that rank junior to senior unsecured debt. In bankruptcy, senior unsecured debentures are always put into a class of unsecured claims with payment priority below bank loans and other secured senior debt to the extent of the value of the security behind the secured debt. By the early 1980s, the junk bond market had become the preferred financing mechanism for leveraged buyouts (LBOs) and other mergers and acquisition (M&A) activities. By 1989, junk bonds represented 20 percent of the total amount of bond debt outstanding at U.S. nonfinancial corporations.

A parallel development to the growth of the junk bond market was the development of its younger cousin, the mezzanine finance market. Companies that were too small to tap the bond market became the users of mezzanine debt. Mezzanine debt issues are much smaller and are almost always privately placed, highly illiquid, and bought with the expectation of being held to maturity. Like junk bonds, mezzanine paper is unsecured and virtually always subordinated in right of payment to bank loans and other senior debt.

Two other phenomena occurred during the levering-up decade: the substitution of junk bond debt for bank lending, and the easing of credit underwriting standards. By the end of 1990, outstanding bank debt stood at 21.5 percent of total credit market debt, a substantial decrease from 26.2 percent at the end of 1985 (see Exhibit 1.3). This decrease was matched by an increase in total credit market debt represented by bond debt, most of which was below investment grade. By 1990, outstanding bond debt had grown to 39.8 percent of total credit market debt from a low of 35.7 percent in 1985, while total credit market debt represented by both bank lending and bond debt remained virtually unchanged in 1985 and 1990.

The substitution appears even more dramatic when one looks at the net issuance of credit market debt for the two five-year periods ending in 1985 and 1990 shown in Exhibit 1.4. Net new bank loans represented only 13.2 percent of total credit market debt issuance during the 1985–1990 period, compared with a 27.4 percent figure for the 1980–1985 period.

Although outstanding bank debt grew in excess of 5 percent per year, its share of the corporate capital structure declined. These statistics show an aggregate picture for the U.S. nonfinancial corporate sector. Confirming this aggregate trend, an influential study of buyouts in the 1980s showed that while bank debt represented upwards of 70 percent of all debt used in such transactions during the first half of the 1980s, it represented only 55 percent by the end of the decade.[3]

The reduced participation of bank lending in corporate capital structures was a result of the competitive pressures faced by banks in the past two decades. The role of commercial banks in channeling deposits to

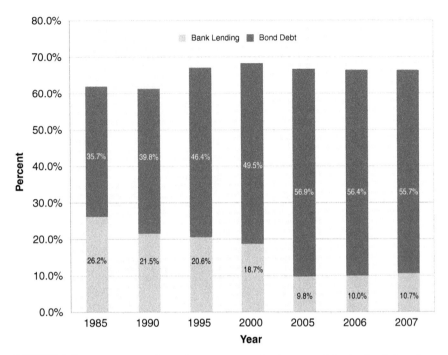

EXHIBIT 1.3 Percentage of Total Corporate Debt Accounted for by Bank Lending and Corporate Bond Debt, Based on Federal Reserve Data

corporations was being eclipsed by lower-cost funding alternatives. On the liability side, both deregulation and the emergence of money market funds largely eliminated large banks' ability to fund themselves at below-market rates. On the asset side, large corporate borrowers started to reach investors directly through the commercial paper market and the public market for below-investment-grade issues. As we shall discuss later in this chapter, the principal role of many commercial banks started to shift from that of a financial intermediary and investor to that of an underwriter and distributor.

At the time when U.S. corporations were levering up their balance sheets and substituting junk bond debt for bank debt, credit underwriting standards were easing considerably in the below-investment-grade market. One sign that standards were loosened was the emergence of financial innovations designed to reduce cash interest payment burdens. One such innovation was the payment in kind (PIK) bond, or bunny bond, which reproduced itself instead of paying cash interest. Another sign of such deterioration in credit standards was the reduction in the required cash flow support per dollar of debt, which translated to much higher ratios of debt per dollar of cash flow

EXHIBIT 1.4 Composition of U.S. Nonfinancial Corporate Credit Market Net Debt Relative Issuance, Based on Federal Reserve Data

	1975–1980	1980–1985	1985–1990	1990–1995	1995–2000	2000–2005	2005–2006
Total Credit Market Net Debt Issuance (billions)	$338.9	$707.7	$917.9	$388.6	$1,630.2	$718.6	$422.4
Net Debt Issues Accounted for by:							
Bank Loans	25.6%	27.4%	13.2%	14.5%	15.4%	−47.1%	13.1%
Bonds	33.0%	30.1%	46.8%	89.8%	55.0%	103.5%	50.5%
Loans from Finance Companies	12.2%	8.0%	11.6%	7.7%	8.5%	2.9%	4.0%
Commercial Paper	5.4%	6.2%	4.9%	10.4%	7.4%	−25.7%	5.5%
Other Loans	5.7%	11.6%	12.4%	−19.9%	−0.2%	11.1%	−7.7%
Asset-Backed Loans	0.0%	0.0%	0.5%	6.5%	3.7%	−0.2%	0.4%
Tax-Exempt	11.6%	11.5%	−1.3%	5.0%	1.2%	3.1%	2.7%
Mortgages	6.5%	5.2%	11.9%	−14.8%	9.0%	55.9%	25.2%

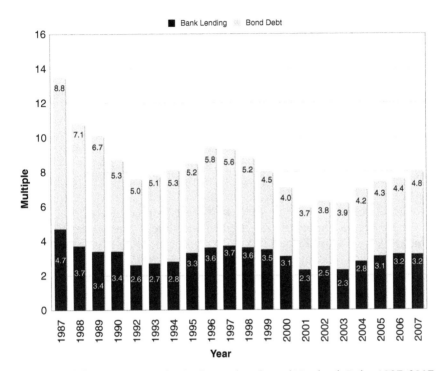

EXHIBIT 1.5 EBITDA Multiples for Bank Debt and Nonbank Debt, 1987–2007

measured by earnings before interest, taxes, depreciation, and amortization (EBITDA). In Exhibit 1.5 we show the average EBITDA debt multiples prevalent for bank and nonbank lending (mostly subordinated bond debt) for the 1987–2007 period. The very high multiples of the late 1980s are a very clear indication of the easing of underwriting standards.

It turned out that the levering-up trend of the 1980s, coupled with the substitution of high yield debt for bank lending brought about by relaxed underwriting standards, created the stage for the large supply of distressed credits of the early 1990s. Although there is controversy about all the factors that ultimately contributed to the sharp decline of liquidity in the high yield market, McCauley et al. in 1999 suggested the following as the plausible contributors:[4]

- Bank regulators' policies frowned on highly leveraged transactions at the end of 1988 and beginning of 1989.
- Passage of the Financial Institutions Reform, Recovery and Enforcement Act (FIRREA) forced savings and loans to liquidate their portfolios of junk bonds in late 1989. The Resolution Trust Corporation (RTC) rapidly disposed of junk bonds in 1990.

- Junk bond mutual funds investors redeemed about 5 percent of investments in such funds in September and October 1989.
- Campeau Corporation defaulted on an interest payment on its Federated Department Stores junk bonds in September 1989.
- RJR Nabisco's bonds were downgraded.
- Drexel Burnham Lambert bankruptcy in early 1990 removed a major source of liquidity from the market.

The final onset of the early 1990s recession brought about a very sharp increase in the default rates for high yield debt. A much deeper recession in 1980 had brought about substantially lower default rates in the below-investment-grade bond market, a sign that the creditworthiness of issuers was much higher in 1980 than in the 1990s (see Exhibit 1.6).[5]

From 1990 on, the levering-up trend abated and debt-to-asset ratios remained relatively stable (around 25 to 26 percent) until 2001 when leverage started to decline, reaching a low of 22 percent in 2005. The rapid growth trend of the high yield market had subsided during the early 1990s recession but promptly resumed after 1992.

However, unlike the 1980s when the bulk of junk bond issuance went to finance acquisition-related activities, in the 1990s these bonds were used for other purposes, including the refinancing of previous junk bond issues. By the end of 2005, junk bonds represented almost 36 percent of the corporate bond debt outstanding held by nonfinancial corporations.

The financial innovations of the 1980s facilitated the levering up of the capital structures of nonfinancial corporations, and this process resulted in a marked change in the composition of their credit market debt. Junk bond debt began to represent an ever-increasing mezzanine portion of the capital structure of U.S. nonfinancial corporations. Increased leverage and relaxed credit standards contributed to the deterioration of creditworthiness of the late 1980s that brought about the large supply of distressed credits we saw in the early 1990s. Moreover, financial innovation facilitated the shifting of credit risks from banks to other less regulated market participants who had become large providers of credit. The fundamental reasons responsible for the increased volatility of the credit cycle were in place throughout the 1990s and remain in place today.

THE SYNDICATED LOAN MARKET AND LEVERAGED LOANS

The trend toward further substitution of bond debt for bank debt did not abate until the end of 2005 when corporate bonds represented 56.9 percent

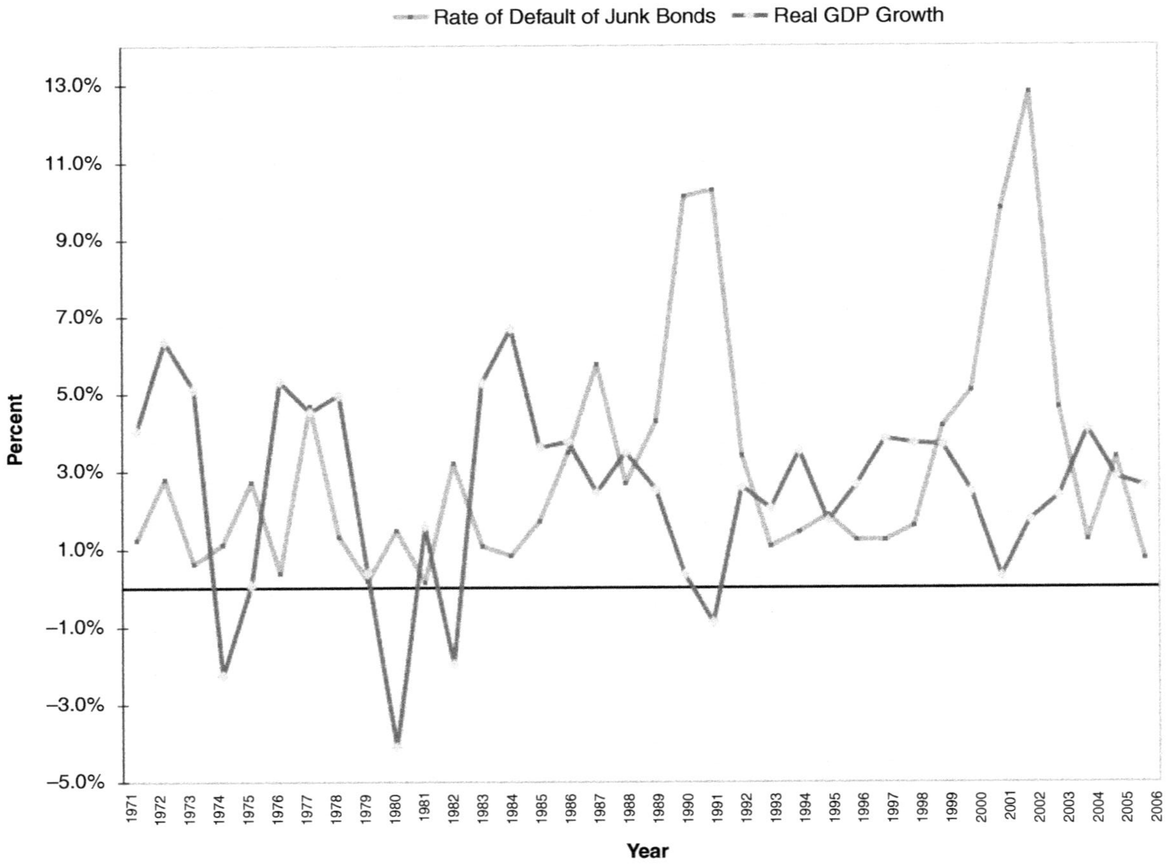

EXHIBIT 1.6 Relationship between Real GDP Growth and Default Rates on Junk Bonds

of the outstanding credit market debt and bank loans were only 9.8 percent (see Exhibit 1.3). The apparent disintermediation was simply a reflection of the fact that commercial banks gradually stopped taking the credit risks that they had taken in the seventies and the eighties. The below investment grade portion of corporate capital structures was abandoned by banks and taken over by mutual funds, pension funds, insurance companies, and other institutional investors, but it took two decades for banks to effect such transformation and at its heart was the emergence of the syndicated loan market.

Syndications had been around for a while. Syndicated lending in the 1970s and early 1980s consisted of loans extended by large commercial banks to sovereign borrowers. The large number of sovereign defaults following Mexico's default in 1982 effectively closed the syndicated market to emerging market borrowers. The essential change between syndications and the newer syndicated loan market was the role of the lead agent bank. Historically, the lead agent was a representative of the bank group and it negotiated terms and conditions on behalf of the other banks.[6] This role changed with the development of the syndicated loan market where the lead agent began to act more like an investment bank, viewing the issuer as the client and lenders as investors.

The syndicated loan market represents the bridge between the private and public debt markets, providing corporate borrowers with an alternative to high yield bonds and illiquid loans. It also allowed borrowers to access a larger pool of capital than any single lender would be prepared to make available. The boom in leveraged buyouts (LBOs) and mergers and acquisitions (M&A) of the mid-1980s drove the development of this market. Syndicated loans became a way to raise senior financing for LBO transactions that were far too large for any one bank to fund. During the credit crunch of the early 1990s, banks sought to reduce their exposure and sold off both performing and nonperforming distressed loans. Selling some of their loan exposures to other intermediaries was a means of keeping their credit and liquidity exposures manageable, keeping their capital requirements down, retaining the lion's share of structuring and underwriting fees, and getting a portion of the credit spread. This was the birth of the syndicated loan secondary market.[7] By 1997, 25 dealers were actively trading loans, Standard & Poor's (S&P) had started rating them, the Loan Syndication and Trading Association had been created, and dealer mark-to-market pricing was available.

Syndicated loans usually are floating-rate instruments with payments set at a spread over a benchmark rate like the London Interbank Offered Rate (LIBOR).[8] This spread compensates the syndicate members for the liquidity and credit risks assumed. The main two types of loan facilities are revolvers, where borrowers have the right to draw some portion of a credit line, and term loans, which are loans for a specified amount with a fixed repayment schedule. These loans can be either secured or unsecured and contain more numerous and stricter covenants than bonds.

Based on either credit ratings or the loan's initial rate spread over LIBOR, syndicated loans are classified as either nonleveraged or leveraged. For example, leveraged loans are defined by the Loan Pricing Corporation (LPC) as those with BB, BB/B, B, or lower bank loan ratings. Other organizations (e.g., S&P) define leveraged loans as those with spreads of 125 basis points or higher.[9] The overwhelming majority of the volume in the secondary market is accounted for by leveraged loans.

The primary syndicated loan market has grown from roughly half a trillion dollars in commitments in 1989 to a peak of two and a quarter trillion dollars in 2007.[10] In the beginning, primary participants were foreign banks; next came insurance companies, and by the late 1980s other institutional investors joined the market.

These institutions that are lenders not affiliated with banks, such as CLOs, CDOs, mutual funds, and hedge funds, have taken on larger positions in the syndicated loan market. They have increased their share of total commitments to 15.9 percent or $548 billion in 2007 compared to only 2 percent or $14 billion in 1996 and held almost 70 percent of the syndicated loans par value outstanding, the bulk of which was in leveraged loans (see Exhibit 1.7).[11] These nonbank institutions tend to hold the poorest credit quality paper also. According to Federal Reserve National Shared Credit data, nonbank institutions held 56 percent of nonaccrual loans in 2006, with U.S. banks holding only 16 percent. This is just another indication that banks' corporate loan portfolios are of much higher credit quality than those held by nonbank institutions.

Throughout the past two decades, commercial banks have gradually abandoned participation in the riskiest portions of the U.S. nonfinancial corporate capital structures. Such lending and the risks thereof have been shifted to the public and nonbank financial institutions through the below-investment-grade bond market, the mezzanine market, and the high-leverage syndicated loan markets. At the heart of this large credit risk shift has been the relentless process of financial innovation through which new investment vehicles and markets were created that greatly improved access and liquidity for lenders and borrowers alike. The preeminent lenders in these markets have been nonbanking institutions like mutual funds, insurance companies, pension funds, CDO trusts, CLO trusts, and hedge funds. These new developments have introduced the likelihood of larger degrees of volatility in funding in the face of normal credit cycles since these sources of funding are seen as less stable than traditional ones.

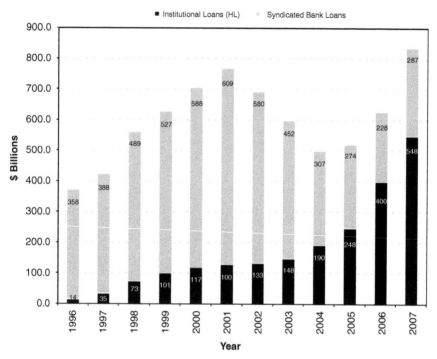

EXHIBIT 1.7   Syndicated Loan Outstanding Amounts by Institution

Banks, however, have continued to lend to the most senior part of the corporate capital structure and have become the originators and distributors of the lower-quality credits to institutional investors.

FINANCIAL MELTDOWN OF 2007–2008

The earthshaking consequences of the current financial crisis have altered dramatically not only the market for distressed securities but also the operations and feasibility for various companies that need access to capital markets either to refinance existing obligations or to raise funds for expansion. Put simply, the capital markets had frozen up as of late 2008. Access from conventional sources became unavailable. The U.S. government has become virtually the only source of access to capital markets for most U.S. financial institutions and the three U.S. auto assemblers: General Motors, Ford, and Chrysler.

Going concerns, whether they prosper or suffer losses, rarely pay off debts as they mature in any dynamic sense. While an individual debt issue does mature, the going concern retires that debt by refinancing rather than reducing the amount of debt on its balance sheet. For prosperous, expanding businesses, increased earning power permits the company to carry increasing amounts of debt.

The 2007–2008 financial meltdown brought this corporate ability to refinance old debt or to incur new debt to a screeching halt. The capital markets froze up. Thus almost any company needing relatively continuous access to capital markets, even ones only seeking to refinance, found itself in deep trouble. This included good companies as well as less well-managed companies. In the fall of 2008, the list of companies in trouble because of lack of access to capital markets, as well as those that either liquidated or had to be rescued on bases that massively diluted existing stockholders, included those found in Exhibit 1.8.

The problems of lack of access to capital markets in 2007–2008 have been exacerbated by the growing strength of bear raiders (i.e., short sellers), who probably have never been as powerful as they are now, even compared with the pre-1929 era. The problems have also been further exacerbated by certain aspects of generally accepted accounting principles (GAAP), which, under rules promulgated by the Financial Accounting Standards Board (FASB), require investors in credit instruments and creditlike instruments (e.g., credit default swaps) to use mark-to-market accounting under FASB 133 and FASB 157.

EXHIBIT 1.8 Companies in Distress Because of Lack of Access to Capital Markets in 2008

Good Companies	Deeply Troubled Companies
Ford Motor Credit	AIG
General Electric	Bear Stearns
Goldman Sachs	CIT
JPMorgan Chase	Citigroup
Merrill Lynch	Fannie Mae
Morgan Stanley	Freddie Mac
	General Motors Acceptance Corp.
	Lehman Brothers Holdings
	Reserve Funds
	Wachovia Bank
	Washington Mutual

Bear raiders now have more weapons than they have ever had before to bankrupt or near-bankrupt companies needing continual access to capital markets, and where customers and counterparties can withdraw business from a target company at no cost or at low cost. Five weapons available to the bear raiders are:

1. Lack of an uptick rule on the New York Stock Exchange since 2007. This seems relatively unimportant.
2. Well-developed options markets permit short sellers to establish positions at little or no cost: buy put options (i.e., options to sell securities at a fixed price) and collect a premium by selling call options (i.e., options to buy securities at a fixed price).
3. Another relatively new short technique is to buy credit default swaps and go short the underlying common stock. As CDS prices rise (i.e., spreads widen), the market sends a message that the probabilities of money defaults on a company's credit instruments have increased. Buying CDSs, of course, increases their price. As the implied probability of a money default increases, the price of the underlying common stock tends to decline.
4. Indexes can be used as a low-cost method of going short.
5. The Internet and business television can be used to broadly air opinions as well as unfounded rumors and all types of analysis. While corporate managements are restricted by securities laws in what they can say and when they can say it, bear raiders are not subject to these disciplines.

These relatively new forms of communication seem to be the most important reason why bear raiders are so much more powerful now than they have ever been heretofore.

Bear raiders are not content merely to condition markets. They also try to ruin businesses as going concerns. Bear raiders will try to get customers and counterparties to flee from troubled issuers, as was the case for Bear Stearns and Lehman Brothers Holdings. The bear raiders also will exert as much pressure as they can on rating agencies and regulatory authorities to drive companies out of business. For example, in the case of monoline insurer MBIA, Inc., the bear raiders attempted to convince the Securities and Exchange Commission that MBIA should be prohibited from publicly marketing new securities issues; attempted to convince the New York State Insurance Department that MBIA was insolvent; and attempted to convince (apparently with some success) the rating agencies—Moody's Investors Service, Standard & Poor's, and Fitch Ratings—that MBIA and Ambac Financial Group, Inc. ought to lose their AAA credit ratings.

Mark-to-market accounting is wholly appropriate when appraising a group of common stocks held in a trading portfolio. Here market prices, or models based on simulated market prices, are the best single measure of what the portfolio of securities that might be sold at any time is worth; and changes in market prices are the best measure of portfolio performance. However, mark-to-market accounting is utterly inappropriate for portfolios of performing loans that are likely to continue to be performing loans and are held in portfolios where the intent is to collect interest income from the particular instruments until maturity. This is what most financial institutions do—depository institutions, insurance companies, finance companies, and pension plans.

As is noted in the following discussion, two of the performing loans recommended by the authors are MBIA 14 percent surplus notes selling around 49, and affording a yield to call at January 15, 2013, of 39.9 percent; and Forest City Enterprises $3\,^5/_8$ percent senior unsecured notes due on October 15, 2011, selling around 53, and affording a yield to maturity of 28.0 percent. The authors believe after careful analysis that the great weight of probability is that both instruments will remain performing loans. MBIA is extremely well capitalized after receiving capital injections of around $2.8 billion in 2007 and early 2008. Forest City enjoys cash flow of well over $600 million per annum from the ownership and management of high-quality office buildings, shopping centers, and apartment residences. These cash flows exceed by a comfortable margin debt service requirements and corporate overhead. If this analysis that the loans will remain performing loans is correct, market prices can be completely ignored in appraising what the future performance of these securities will be as long as the holder is not dependent on borrowed money for which these securities are collateral, and the holder is not forced to sell the security prior to maturity or call. The return will be in the neighborhood of, say, 37 percent to 38 percent for the MBIA notes and 26 percent to 27 percent for the Forest City notes. The reason the effective returns are less than the yield to call or the yield to maturity is that both yields assume that interest received will be reinvested at the 39.9 percent and 28.0 percent rates; this seems unrealistic. If the MBIA notes are not called in 2013, we will rely on the current yield, which is 28.6 percent. However, after the 2013 call date, the interest payable on the MBIA surplus notes becomes a floating rate of three-month LIBOR (3.42 percent at the time of this writing) plus 11.26 percent. This high rate of interest after the call date gives us confidence that MBIA will use maximum efforts to have the surplus notes called. Efficient market theorists justify mark-to-market accounting by stating that it is the best measure of both the probability of default and how the issuer will fare in a reorganization or liquidation in the event of default. There is virtually no evidence of which we are aware attesting to the validity of this efficient market theory view of securities markets, especially distressed debt securities markets.

The U.S. government capital infusion into companies denied access to capital markets became absolutely essential in 2008 as the financial crisis unfolded. The terms by which the government is buying $700 billion of securities from these issuers under the Troubled Asset Relief Program (TARP) seems quite reasonable: 5 percent preferred stocks, which step up to 9 percent after five years, plus 10-year warrants that allow the government to invest 15 percent of the amount of preferred stocks purchased at a price equal to market value on the date of the transaction. However, some of the pre-TARP transactions seemed to be at exploitive prices, to wit JPMorgan Chase acquiring 100 percent of the equity of Bear Stearns at a price of $10 per share. After collecting huge commitment fees and selling preferred stock with a double-digit dividend rate to AIG, Fannie Mae, and Freddie Mac, the government reserved for itself 80 percent of the equity of each company. The U.S. government, of course, was absolutely within its rights to seize private property. The question, though, is should the government be required to pay a fair price, not a price unilaterally determined by the government? This issue may very well surface after the present financial crisis has passed. There is also the issue of how much control the U.S. government ought to exercise over those financial institutions in which it has invested. Under TARP, there seems to be little in the way of elements of control for the government. The 5 percent/9 percent preferred stocks are plain-vanilla instruments allowing the government to elect two directors if quarterly dividends go into arrears for six quarters.

During past financial crises (the late 1980s and early 1990s), most performing loans have remained performing loans. This is likely to be the case in the current financial crisis. However, distress investors want to be able to feel that they will fare reasonably well if the debt instrument becomes nonperforming and the investor as a creditor participates in a reorganization or, less likely, a liquidation. Insofar as the distress investor owns a performing loan, the investor measures the return by current yield, yield to an event, and yield to maturity. If the investor is to participate in a reorganization or liquidation, return is measured by the dollar price of the security as a percentage of the dollar value of the perceived workout in the reorganization or liquidation in an estimated time period. In our three recommended securities, the authors believe there is a 70 percent to 90 percent probability that each loan will continue to be a performing loan. If participating in a reorganization, it is hoped that our credit instruments will be converted largely into the common stocks of companies that will be well financed and might even have attractive tax attributes in the form of a long-lived net operating loss (NOL) carryforwards. General Motors Acceptance

Corporation (GMAC), which we also recommend, would be a reorganized finance company or depository institution regulated as a commercial bank; MBIA would be a reorganized insurance vehicle (one of the authors reorganized Mission Insurance Group in the early 1990s and it is now Covanta, the nation's leading converter of waste to energy); and Forest City would be a reorganized real estate investment builder.

With lack of access to capital markets for GMAC and lack of access to an AAA rating for MBIA, both companies are effectively in runoff; that is, their assets are being converted to cash. The key to the runoffs in terms of the remaining performing loans can be found in the question: "Will the cash being generated in the runoff exceed by enough margin the losses to be realized on bad assets so that the loans can be paid at maturity or call?" The authors think this is the likely case. An additional problem in GMAC may be that the company is providing support for Rescap, its troubled mortgage-lending subsidiary (GMAC is mostly auto finance). GMAC seems to be providing such support on arm's-length terms. Insofar as GMAC may be, in effect, providing subsidies to Rescap and receiving in return inadequate or no consideration, GMAC creditors appear to have a cause of action against GMAC under the fraudulent transfer statutes. Counterbalancing this possible negative for the GMAC senior unsecureds is the probability that GMAC will be eligible to receive from the U.S. government a TARP investment in GMAC preferred stock. The relevant statistics for the three distressed issuers in October 2008 are shown in Exhibit 1.9.

The current financial meltdown seems to offer compelling evidence that unless financial markets and financial institutions are strictly regulated, fraud, corruption, and incompetence seem inevitable. The authors can only speculate on what the new regulatory schemes will encompass.

Interestingly, in the 1950s one of the authors wrote a master's thesis in which the gravamen was that trading on the floor of the New York

EXHIBIT 1.9 Relevant Statistics for Distressed Issuers in 2008

Issue	Current Price Percent of Par	Current Yield	Yield to Maturity	Yield to Event
Forest City $3^5/_8$% Due 10/15/2011	53	6.8%	28.0%	NM
GMAC $7^3/_4$% Due 1/19/2010	62	12.5%	54.1%	NM
MBIA 14% Surplus Notes Due 1/15/2033	49	28.6%	28.6%*	39.9%

*Assumes a 14 percent interest rate after the 2013 call date.

Stock Exchange does, in fact, simulate the conditions necessary for pure and perfect competition. Transactions take place at the price where the demand and supply curves intersect; there are myriad participants in the market, none of whom by themselves can influence prices; and all participants have access to the same information. The thesis then went on to state that, in actuality, this simulation of pure and perfect competition could be achieved only by erecting a draconian police state where there were comprehensive regulations overseen not only by government agencies but also by private self-regulatory organizations.

PRINCIPAL PROVISIONS OF THE 2005 BANKRUPTCY ACT AS THEY AFFECT CHAPTER 11 REORGANIZATIONS OF BUSINESSES

By far the most important and far-reaching impact of the Bankruptcy Abuse Prevention and Consumer Protection Act of 2005 (BAPCPA) affects individuals seeking relief under Chapter 7 or Chapter 13 of the bankruptcy code. An extended discussion of the effect on individuals of BAPCPA is beyond the scope of this volume. Suffice to say, BAPCPA for individuals is far wide of the mark sought to be achieved for businesses seeking relief under Chapter 11 or Chapter 7 of the bankruptcy code. The general aim of Chapter 11 for businesses is to make the debtor feasible within the context of maximizing present value for creditors, who receive such value in accordance with a rule of absolute priority where no creditor of a class is given priority over other creditors in that class unless such other creditors so consent. In contrast, BAPCPA for individuals seems designed to maximize return for creditors while paying minimal attention to making the debtor feasible. Various provisions speak to the belief that the individual debtor is unintelligent (needs counseling) and neither the debtor nor his or her attorney is to be trusted (required filings and attestations). Most provisions of BAPCPA went into effect on October 17, 2005—both business and individual.

The 13 principal provisions of BAPCPA as they affect businesses are:

1. Period of exclusivity:
   - The debtor's exclusive right to file a plan of reorganization (POR) may not be extended beyond 18 months, and the exclusive right to solicit acceptances for a POR may not be extended beyond 20 months.
   - Under the old law, there was a 120-day exclusive period for a debtor to file a POR and a 180-day exclusive period to solicit acceptances. These periods were routinely extended. In Chapter 11 cases such as

Johns Manville and McCory Corporation, exclusive periods lasted seven or eight years.

2. Prepackaged plans:
   ▪ Solicitations commence prior to filing for Chapter 11 relief may continue postfiling.
   ▪ Under the old law, solicitations of votes had to be completed prior to the commencement of a case. Section 1125 prohibited postpetition solicitation of votes until a disclosure statement was approved.

3. Executory contracts and unexpired leases:
   ▪ Assumption of an executory contract or unexpired lease by a debtor requires three elements:
     1. Cure of defaults (clarified under BAPCPA).
     2. Compensation for actual monetary losses (clarified under BAPCPA).
     3. Assurance of future performance.
   ▪ Rejection of an executory contract or unexpired lease is treated as a prepetition breach by the debtor. Damages are generally treated as a prepetition, unsecured claim. There are certain limitations on rejection damages.
   ▪ Under BAPCPA, the deadline for the assumption of nonresidential real property leases is 210 days. Under the old law, the debtor had 60 days to assume or reject a nonresidential real property lease, but this was usually extended indefinitely.
   ▪ Under BAPCPA, if there is a subsequent rejection of a previously assumed lease, the lessor may claim two years' rent as an administrative claim. Damages in excess of two years' rent are treated as general unsecured claims limited to the greater of one year's rent or 15 percent of the remainder of the lease, not to exceed three years' rent.

4. Employment contracts—one year's salary.

5. Preferences:
   ▪ Under BAPCPA, transfers in payment of debts incurred in the ordinary course of business will be excluded from avoidance if (1) made in the ordinary course of business or (2) made according to ordinary business terms.
   ▪ Under the old law, exclusion from avoidance depended on the transfers being (1) made in the ordinary course of business and (2) made according to ordinary business terms.
   ▪ Under BAPCPA, a transfer cannot be considered avoided with respect to a noninsider. (If a transfer is avoided, the consideration received from the debtor has to be returned.)
   ▪ Under BAPCPA, purchase money security interests are deemed perfected contemporaneously with the granting of a security interest if

perfected within 30 days after the debtor obtained possession of the underlying property. Previously, there had been 20- and 10-day periods rather than 30 days.

6. Fraudulent transfers:
   - Under BAPCPA, there is now a two-year look-back period rather than one year.
   - Under BAPCPA, the constructive fraudulent transfer definition has been expanded to include transfers and obligations incurred for less than a reasonably equivalent value to or for the benefit of an insider under an employment contract and not in the ordinary course of business.

7. Key employee retention plans (KERPs)—No KERP payments are permitted unless:
   - The executive has a bona fide job offer from another company at the same or greater compensation.
   - The executive's services are essential.
   - The compensation is not greater than 10 times the mean retention amount paid to nonmanagement employees, or if no such payments were made, no more than 25 percent of similar payments made to the executive during the prior year.
   - Any severance payments to insiders have to be part of a program generally applicable to all full-time employees and must be no greater than 10 times the mean severance payment given to nonmanagement employees.
   - The restrictions imposed on KERPs have been easily evaded by executives of companies in Chapter 11 by substituting "incentive plans" for "KERPs."

8. Tax claims:
   - Interest on tax claims is determined under applicable nonbankruptcy law. Priority tax claims must be paid in regular installment payments not to exceed five years from the commencement of the case. Previously, there had been a "six-year stretch."

9. Creditor committees:
   - Under BAPCPA, the creditor committee must provide nonmembers in the class access to information, and must solicit and obtain comments from such parties.

10. Investment bankers as disinterested persons:
    - Under BAPCPA, an investment banker who advised the debtor on a prepetition basis can be retained postpetition as an adviser who is a disinterested person. Under the old act such retention was not possible.

- Under BAPCPA, the investment banker need only demonstrate that it does not hold an interest adverse to the debtor on the matter for which the investment banker is to be retained.
11. Reclamation claims:
    - Under BAPCPA, the seller of goods to a debtor (a debtor is defined as a firm that has secured Chapter 11 relief), or soon-to-be debtor, has reclamation rights allowing the undoing of a transaction by having the debtor return goods received. The seller now enjoys a reclamation period for goods received up to 45 days prior to the Chapter 11 filing date, with an additional 20 days after the filing date if the 45-day period expires after the commencement of the debtor's case. If the seller fails to provide notice of its reclamation claim, the seller still may assert an administrative expense claim for the value of the goods received by the debtor within 20 days prior to the commencement of a case.
    - Under the old law, a seller of goods could assert a reclamation claim within 10 days after a debtor's receipt of goods, unless the 10-day period expired after the commencement of a Chapter 11 case, in which case the seller had 20 days after the debtor's receipt of goods to assert a reclamation claim.
12. Adequate assurance to utilities:
    - Under BAPCPA, there exists a specific listing of six steps a debtor may take to establish adequate assurance of payment of a utility during the pendency of a case:
    1. Cash deposit.
    2. Letter of credit.
    3. Certificate of deposit.
    4. Surety bond.
    5. Prepayment of utility consumption.
    6. Mutually agreed-upon security.
13. Ancillary and cross-border cases—new Chapter 15:
    - The new Chapter 15 supplants the former Section 304 of the bankruptcy code. Chapter 15 incorporates into federal bankruptcy law the Model law on Cross Border Insolvency drafted by the United Nations Commission on International Trade Law (UNCITRAL). Foreign proceedings are classified as either foreign main proceedings or foreign nonmain proceedings. Foreign main proceedings exist in the debtor's center of main interests. Upon recognition of a foreign main proceeding insofar as U.S. property is concerned:
    - The automatic stay will apply.
    - Adequate protection rules will apply.

- Rules governing postpetition transfer of property and the postpetition effects of prepetition security interests will apply.
- Unless the court rules otherwise, foreign representatives may operate the debtor's business and use, sell, or lease property of the estate like a U.S. debtor.
- In its discretion the court may grant virtually all other relief available to a debtor in a typical Chapter 11 case, other than the ability to invoke U.S. avoiding powers. Under old Section 304, the court did not have the power to authorize asset sales or financing, reject contracts and leases, issue securities without a registration statement, or invoke U.S. avoiding powers.
- Under BAPCPA, the recognition of a foreign nonmain proceeding does not result in the granting of any automatic relief. However, all of the relief available in a case ancillary to a foreign main proceeding is available in a nonmain proceeding, at the discretion of the court.
- The court must ensure that relief relates to assets that should be administered in the foreign nonmain proceeding or relates to information required in that proceeding.

2

The Theoretical Underpinning

Conventional wisdom is generally very bad wisdom when it comes to understanding value investing in general and distress investing in particular. For example, the conventional thinking is that if a borrower defaults on the payment of either interest or principal and files for Chapter 11 relief, the game is over for both the borrower and the lender. It is assumed that the borrower will cease operations and that the best the lender can do is to sell the loan or passively wait for something to happen. This is an utterly unrealistic view with respect to larger companies that have issued publicly traded securities. In all likelihood these companies will continue operating. Lenders do not get wiped out, but either their claims are reinstated or they participate in the reorganization process and receive value in the form of cash and/or new securities.

The preceding is but one example of how the conventional wisdom stands in the way of clearly understanding many of the issues that are important to both value investing and distress investing. In this chapter we introduce those important areas where the conventional view introduces more noise than clarity in achieving such understanding.

WHAT MARKET?

Probably the worst misconceptions about dealing with troubled issuers in general and about Chapter 11 reorganizations in particular are promulgated by the academic literature on the subject. One such area is the definition of a market. Most academicians seem to define a market as either the New York Stock Exchange, NASDAQ, or some other forum populated by outside passive minority investors (OPMIs). For the purposes of our discussion it is helpful to provide a general definition of a market:

*A market is any financial or commercial arena where partici-
pants reach agreement as to price and other terms, which each
participant believes are the best reasonably achievable under the
circumstances.*

Myriad markets exist and include the following:

- OPMI markets such as the New York Stock Exchange, NASDAQ, and
  the various commodity and option exchanges.
- Markets for control of companies.
- Markets for consensual reorganization plans in Chapter 11.
- Institutional creditor markets.
- Markets for executive compensation.

For the past 40 years, financial academics have mostly operated on
the assumption that financial markets are highly efficient. In a highly efficient market, the price of a common stock multiplied by the amount
of shares outstanding reflects the underlying equity value of the company issuing that common stock. This is embodied in the efficient market hypothesis (EMH). Recently, behaviorists have challenged EMH based
on the theory that investors sometimes make emotional, irrational, and
stupid decisions. But even behaviorists seem to concede that if investors
were rational, financial markets would be highly efficient. We disagree.
Certain markets always will be inefficient versus EMH standards of
efficiency.

A basic problem faced by financial academics, whether efficient market theorists or behaviorists, is that they are strictly top-down—studying
economies, markets, and prices, not the underlying bottom-up fundamentals that really determine what a business might be worth and what are
the characteristics of the securities issued by that business. Put simply,
the academics are best described as chartist-technicians with PhDs. Insofar as academics try to be value investors, they seem to believe to
a man (or woman) that value is measured only by predictions of future discounted cash flow (DCF). They don't grasp the fact that most
firms and market participants have an overriding interest in wealth creation, not DCF, and DCF is only one of several paths usable to create
wealth.

In bottom-up analysis, conclusions are drawn based on detailed analyses of individual situations—securities, commodities, companies—to ascertain whether gross mispricing exists or persists. As a general rule, such

mispricings can arise out of one or more wealth-creation factors that are sometimes interrelated:

- Discounted cash flow.
- Earnings, defined as creating wealth while consuming cash. For most firms (and governments), earnings can have long-term value only insofar as they are combined with reasonable access to capital markets.
- Asset and/or liability redeployments via mergers and acquisitions (M&A), contests for control, asset redeployments, refinancings, capital restructurings, spin-offs, and/or liquidations.
- Access to capital markets on a super-attractive basis such as selling common stock issues into a superheated initial public offering (IPO) market or having access to long-term, nonrecourse debt financing at ultralow interest rates.

TOWARD A GENERAL THEORY OF MARKET EFFICIENCY

Markets run an efficiency gamut. Some markets tend toward instantaneous efficiency, thereby comporting with the standards that are the essence of the EMH. Other markets tend toward a long-term efficiency but may never actually reach EMH efficiency. As a subset of this, it should be noted that a price efficiency in one market, say the OPMI market, is usually, per se, a price inefficiency in another market, say the takeover market. Some markets are inherently inefficient. Or to put it in another context, an efficient market in these situations means that certain market participants are virtually assured of earning very substantial excess returns on a relatively continual basis.

Four characteristics determine whether a market will tend toward EMH-like instantaneous efficiency on the one hand or it will tend to be inherently inefficient by EMH standards on the other hand, or something in between.

Characteristic I: Market Participant

Insofar as the market participant is unsophisticated about value analysis, financed with borrowed money, and lacks inside information, that participant will face a market tending strongly to instantaneous, EMH-like efficiency. Insofar as an investor is well trained, well informed, and not influenced by day-to-day or short-run price fluctuations, that investor avoids being subject to an EMH-like efficiency.

Characteristic II: Complexity

How complex, or simple, is the security or other asset that is the object of the market participant's interest? Insofar as the security is simple (i.e., it can be analyzed by reference to a very few computer-programmable variables), the asset pricing will reflect a strong tendency toward instantaneous, EMH-like efficiency. A further condition for EMH-like efficiency is that there be a precise ending date, such as when indebtedness matures, options expire, or a merger transaction is consummated. EMH-like efficiencies cannot exist if one concentrates on analyzing the common stock of a going concern with a perpetual life, or if one analyzes a troubled debt issue that will participate in a reorganization and the timing on the completion of such reorganization is relatively unknowable. Insofar as securities are concerned, three types of issues tend to be characterized by instantaneous, EMH-like efficiencies:

1. Credit instruments without credit risk (e.g., U.S. Treasuries).
2. Derivatives, including options, warrants, and convertibles.
3. Risk arbitage; that is, situations where there are relatively determinate workouts in relatively determinate periods of time, as, for example, tend to exist after merger transactions are announced publicly.

Insofar as the analysis of the security entails complexity, EMH-type efficiencies tend to become unimportant factors.

Characteristic III: Time Horizons

If the participant is an OPMI involved in day-to-day trading, that participant will, in all probability, be faced with EMH-like efficiencies. If, however, the participant is a manager of a well-financed company and has a five-year time horizon during which time the company might choose to access capital markets (credit markets or equity markets), that participant will be involved in a market that is inherently inefficient by EMH standards. The manager who can control timing of when to access capital markets over a five-year period knows that there will be times when credit markets are very attractive for the company (i.e., interest rates are ultralow), and there will be times when it will be ultra-attractive to issue new equity in public offerings and/or mergers (i.e., an IPO boom).

EMH efficiencies exist only for participants in outside passive non-control markets who are heavily involved in daily, and even hourly, price movements of securities. The basic EMH concept is that market prices at any time reflect equilibrium. The old equilibrium changes to a new equilibrium only as a market absorbs new information. Thus, even securities that are analyzable by reference to a few computer-programmable variables are not priced efficiently if those securities lack very early termination dates. No EMH efficiencies can exist for investors with a long-term time horizon.

Again, in an efficient market, market prices determine the value of the company for all purposes. It is as William F. Sharpe, a Nobel laureate and a typical efficient market believer, stated in his book *Investments*: that if you can assume an efficient market, "every security price equals its investment value at all times."[1]

Where there are no reasonably determinate termination dates, markets for securities can be grossly inefficient even though the analysis is simple and few variables are involved. A good example of this revolves around the common stocks selling at huge discounts from net asset value (NAV) of companies that are extremely well capitalized, highly profitable, and with glowing long-term records of increasing earnings, increasing dividends, and increasing NAVs. The principal assets of these simple-to-analyze companies consist of private equity investments, marketable securities, and/or Class A income-producing real estate. The market data in Exhibit 2.1 are as of September 30, 2008.

The same analysis seems pertinent for certain distressed securities as of September 30, 2008, albeit that analysis is not as simple as that which exists for the high-quality common stocks just cited. The authors' analyses indicate strongly that the probabilities are that both General Motors Acceptance Corporation (GMAC) senior unsecured loans and MBIA Insurance Corp. surplus notes are likely to remain performing loans. If not, upon reorganization or rehabilitation, the holder of these obligations likely will receive the common stocks of, by then, a well-capitalized finance company or bank holding company, or an insurance company.

EXHIBIT 2.1 Simple-to-Analyze, Extremely Well-Capitalized, and Highly Profitable Companies Selling at Discounts from NAV

Issuer	U.S. Dollar Price 9/30/08	Per Share Latest Reporting Date NAV*	NAV Discount from Market
Henderson Land Development	$4.38	$7.27	40%
Investor AB	$17.67	$24.61	28%
Wharf Holdings	$24.73	$43.81	44%
Wheelock & Co.	$1.80	$3.88	54%

*At the latest reporting date.

GMAC notes due in 15 months were selling at 60, at a current yield of 13 percent and a yield to maturity of 55 percent. The MBIA surplus notes were selling at 53 and afforded a current yield of 27 percent and yield to call of 38 percent. In the cases of GMAC notes and MBIA surplus notes, it is important to mention that market price is unimportant for a holder who has not borrowed money to carry the securities. To earn excess returns here, all the analyst has to do is be right that the great weight of probabilities is that both instruments will be performing loans.

Characteristic IV: External Forces

How powerful are the external forces seeking to impose disciplines on the market participants and on the companies that are securities' issuers? Insofar as the external forces are very powerful, prices will tend toward EMH-like instantaneous efficiencies. Competition among market participants, such as exists on the floor of the New York Stock Exchange or on NASDAQ, represents powerful external forces imposing restraints on OPMI day traders so that their returns will likely reflect EMH-like efficiencies. Insofar as the external forces are weak, markets will be inherently inefficient. Boards of directors are an external force imposing discipline on the compensation of top management executives. Boards tend to be weak, and thus corporate executives tend to earn excess returns consistently. Indeed, when external forces are weak, certain market participants (not only corporate executives) will earn excess returns consistently. This is part and parcel of the definition of a market where each participant strives to achieve the best returns reasonably achievable under the circumstances.

EXTERNAL FORCES INFLUENCING MARKETS EXPLAINED

Markets and market participants are very much influenced by external forces that impose disciplines on stockholders, companies, and management. The principal ones are:

- Competitive markets.
- Regulatory agencies:
  - Governmental.
  - Financial Industry Regulatory Authority (FINRA), a self-regulatory organization.
- Tax system.

- Creditors.
- Control stockholders.
- Boards of directors.
- Rating agencies.
- Communities.
- Labor unions.
- Plaintiffs' bar.
- Federal and state courts.
- Passive stockholders.
- Auditors.
- Corporate attorneys.

When external forces impose very strict disciplines (e.g., government regulators, senior creditors, credit rating agencies, and the plaintiffs' bar), such strict regulation or control tends to stifle innovation and productivity. It is important to note that government does not have a monopoly on actions that stifle innovation and productivity. The same disease exists in the private sector, where, say, financial institutions follow overly strict lending practices.

When external forces impose little or no discipline (e.g., boards of directors rubber-stamping top management compensation and entrenchment packages or passive shareholders' proxy votes), there tends to be created an environment that will be characterized by corporate inefficiency, frauds, and a gross misallocation of resources.

Who can deny that there is a need for balance in the imposition of disciplines? They should be neither too strict nor too soft. There is a school of thought stating that government regulation is ipso facto nonproductive and that private sector regulation is ipso facto productive (except for the plaintiffs' bar). Nothing could be further from reality than such beliefs. Certain government actions have been extremely productive for the U.S. economy; for example, the GI Bill of Rights gave the country not only a highly educated populace but also a first-rate university system. Certain private actions, such as giving top corporate executives a free ride in the form of multimillion-dollar annual compensations and entrenchment without having to meet any performance standards, certainly have been counterproductive for the U.S. economy. Also counterproductive for the economy have been the exorbitant fees paid to professionals, mostly attorneys and investment bankers, involved in restructuring or liquidating troubled companies both out of court and in Chapter 11.

Put otherwise, actions or expenditures by governments are not necessarily unproductive, and actions or expenditures by the private sector are not necessarily productive. Actions and expenditures ought to be gauged for usefulness on a case-by-case basis. Government roles seem to encompass the following:

- Regulator.
- Tax collector.
- Provider of direct subsidies.
- Provider of loans.
- Provider of credit enhancements.
- Insurer.
- Direct payer.
- Police and the military.
- Customer.
- Competitor.
- Direct service provider, infrastructure and other.

Some of these governmental activities are useful, even essential. Others are wasteful. On balance, though, it will likely prove highly damaging to the U.S. economy if government activities are cut back severely, or eliminated, so that the U.S. government restricts itself to "delivering the mail and defending our shores."

WHAT RISK?

Risk is not a meaningful concept unless modified by an adjective. There exist market risk, investment risk, Chapter 11 reorganization risk, credit risk, failure to match maturities risk, hurricane risk, terrorism risk, and so forth; but it is not really useful to look at general risk. When risk is discussed in conventional academic finance, the subject is almost always market risk (i.e., fluctuations in market prices). Beta, alpha, and the capital asset pricing model (CAPM) are based on market prices. We ignore market risk and focus on investment risk, especially in distress investing (i.e., the probabilities of something going wrong with the company and/or the securities issued by the company).

For us there is no risk-reward ratio. A risk-reward ratio exists where price is in equilibrium. In that instance risk and reward for securities are measured by two variables:

1. Quality of the issuer.
2. Terms of the issue.

The higher the quality and the more senior the terms, the less the risk and the smaller the potential for gain. Introducing price turns the risk-reward ratio on its head. The lower the price, the less the risk of loss and the greater the prospect for gain.

In the book *The Great Risk Shift* (Oxford University Press, 2006), Jacob S. Hacker, a political science professor at the University of California, discusses how in recent years various risks—job risk, family stability risk, retirement risk, and health care risk—have been shifted increasingly from corporations and governments onto the backs of individuals. The raison d'être for the Great Risk Shift is to foster the creation of an ownership society where the beneficiaries of, say, pension plans and health plans take the risks that go with ownership by being responsible for investing funds with no guarantees of minimum returns. What the proponents of this type of ownership risk fail to recognize is that the most successful owners don't take risks. They lay off the risks onto someone else. Put simply, the vast majority of great individual fortunes built in this country, especially by Wall Streeters and corporate executives, were not built by people who took investment risks. Rather, the secret to building a great fortune is to avoid, as completely as possible, the taking of any investment risk. Investment risk consists of factors peculiar to a business itself or to the securities issued by that business. Investment risk is a risk separate and apart from market risk. Market risk involves fluctuations in the prices of securities and other readily tradable assets. A directory of those in the financial community who build great fortunes by avoiding risk includes the following:

- **Corporate executives who receive stock options or restricted stock.** If the common stock appreciates, the executive builds a substantial net worth. If the common stock does not appreciate, the executive loses nothing; indeed, the executive may obtain new options at a lower strike price or new restricted common stock.
- **Members of the plaintiffs' bar who bring class action lawsuits in order to earn contingency fees.** The expenses involved in financing such lawsuits are minimal, and it is seldom that plaintiffs' attorneys ever incur costs for sanctions or for paying a defendant's costs and fees. The fee awards obtained tend to be huge upon settlement of such lawsuits or, less frequently, upon obtaining a favorable verdict for the plaintiff after trial.
- **Initial public offering (IPO) underwriters and sales personnel.** If you run a promising private company and desire to go public, you will find that many potential underwriters will compete for your business. However, as a general rule they won't compete on price. The price will be a 7 percent gross spread plus expenses. Thus, on a $10 IPO, the gross spread will be $0.70 per share. In contrast, to buy a $10 stock in

a secondary market like the New York Stock Exchange, a customer can negotiate a commission rate of, say, $0.02 to $0.05 per share.

■ **Bankruptcy professionals—lawyers and investment bankers.** Chapter 11 is now set up so that bankruptcy professionals have to be paid in cash, on a pay-as-you-go basis (with only minor holdbacks); such payments are given a super-priority so that these professionals very rarely have any credit risk at all. Attorneys' fees billed at up to $900 per hour and investment banking fees of over $300,000 per month (plus success fees) are not uncommon; see Chapter 4 in this volume.

■ **Money managers, mutual fund managers, private equity and hedge fund managers.** Normal fees might range from 1 percent of assets under management (AUM) to 2 percent of AUM plus 20 percent of annual realized or unrealized capital gains (after a bogey of, say, 6 percent paid or accrued to limited partners). These fees are paid to entities that receive the cash fees without incurring any credit risk in business entities that have few physical assets and very little necessary overhead. Most hedge funds are limited partnerships where the money manager is the general partner (GP) and outside passive minority investors (OPMIs) are the limited partners (LPs). A limited partnership has been waggishly described as a business association where at the beginning the GP brings experience and the LPs bring money. At the end of the business association, the GP has the money and the LPs have the experience.

■ **Venture capitalists.** These people finance a portfolio of start-ups, and then are able to realize astronomical prices on some of the portfolio companies when there occurs, as it always seems to do from time to time, an IPO speculative boom.

■ **Real estate entrepreneurs, especially investment builders.** Two keys to making fortunes in large-scale real estate projects are the availability of long-term, fixed interest rate, nonrecourse financing and an income tax shelter.

In terms of understanding corporate finance, economists have it all wrong when they say, "There is no free lunch." Rather, the more appropriate comment ought to be "Somebody has to pay for lunch—and it isn't going to be me." The methods by which OPMIs can attempt to alleviate investment risk are:

■ **Buy cheap.** Warren Buffett, the chairman of Berkshire Hathaway, describes his investment technique as trying to buy good companies at reasonable prices. Buffett, however, is a control investor, and while a reasonable price standard has worked remarkably well for Berkshire Hathaway, that standard is not good enough for OPMIs. OMPIs have to try to buy at bargain prices (i.e., cheap). The definition of cheap in acquiring common stocks in the vast majority of cases is to acquire issues at prices that reflect substantial discounts from readily ascertainable net asset values (NAVs), and such NAV is likely to increase by not less than 10 percent per year. Readily ascertainable NAVs means that most OPMI common stock portfolios will to a large extent be concentrated in financial institutions and companies involved with income-producing real estate. Control investors can afford to pay up versus OPMIs, because they are in a position to undertake financial engineering and to cause management changes. OPMIs pretty much have to leave companies as-is, and therefore place particular efforts into buying into well-managed businesses with stable, but clearly superior, managements. In investing in distressed debt, too, the OPMI investor has to buy cheap. For the authors there are two rules of thumb in 2008: If the analysis indicates the probabilities are that a loan will be a performing loan, the minimum return sought is a 25 percent yield to maturity or yield to an event. Coupled with this is the requirement that if the loan does not remain performing and participates in a reorganization, the loss to the investor should be minimal. If it seems likely that the performing loan will default, the distress investor participating in a reorganization ought to look for an internal rate of return (IRR) well north of 30 percent.

- **Buy equity interests only in high-quality businesses or well-positioned debt instruments.** One reasonable rule for OPMIs is to not knowingly acquire the common stock of any company unless that company enjoys a superstrong financial position. If a company does not enjoy strong finances, be a creditor owning well-covenanted debt instruments. Also try as an OPMI to buy into reasonably well-managed companies. Any relationships between OPMIs and corporate managements combine communities of interests and conflicts of interest. Diligent OPMIs try to restrict themselves to situations where the communities of interest seem to outweigh the conflicts of interest. Restrict common stock investments to companies whose businesses are understandable to the portfolio manager and where there exists full documentary disclosure, including audited financial statements. In distress investing, the creditor has only contract rights. These contract rights ought to be strong enough to preclude or at least discourage management overreaching.
- **Ignore market risk.** Fluctuations in market prices are mostly a random walk, with changes in market prices not in any way a measure of long-term investment risk or investment potential. It is as Benjamin Graham used to say: "In the short run the market is a voting machine. In the long run the market is a weighing machine." Most competent control

investors—again Warren Buffett—pretty much ignore market risk also, in that little or no weight is given to daily, or even annual, marking to market for portfolio holdings.

- **If dealing in equities, buy growth but don't pay for it.** In the financial community, *growth* is a misused word. Most market participants do not mean growth, but rather mean generally recognized growth. Insofar as growth receives general recognition, a market participant has to pay up. Cheung Kong Holdings, Forest City Enterprises, Covanta, and Toyota Industries Corporation are growth companies. None of these issues seemed to enjoy general recognition as having growth potential in the fall of 2008.

- **It is usually a good idea to be a buy-and-hold investor.** Although an entry point into a common stock is a bargain price, one can continue to hold a security where the portfolio manager believes that the business has reasonable prospects that it can over the long run increase annual NAV by a double-digit number, and where the portfolio manager does not believe he or she made a mistake. Mistakes are measured by beliefs that there has occurred a permanent impairment in underlying value or financial position. Sell if there is a belief that the security is grossly overpriced. Also sell for portfolio considerations—that is, where there are massive enough redemptions of funds under management so that liquidity is threatened. Most sales in most well-run portfolios will occur because the portfolio companies are taken over. Investing in distressed credits, however, involves having some idea of a termination date. If a loan is to remain a performing loan, the instrument will contain payment schedules and a maturity date. If the distressed credit is to participate in a reorganization, there will be an estimated reorganization date; and if the debtor is to be liquidated, there will be an estimated payment date.

CAPITAL STRUCTURE AND CREDIT RISK

The issue of credit risk and how capital structures allocate such risk is quite important to the distress investor. Unlike the conventional academic view, we are of the opinion that capital structure arises out of a process that involves meeting the needs and desires of a multiplicity of constituencies, including various creditors, regulators, rating agencies, managements and other control groups, OPMIs, and the company itself.[2] Out of this process, one important way in which a particular capital structure allocates credit risk is through payment priority mechanisms. Liens and rights of setoff that give rise to secured claims have payment priority over unsecured claims, both prepetition and postpetition, since such liens and rights generally survive during the pendency of a Chapter 11 case, as do subordination agreements. In large part these mechanisms control the operation of the "fair and equitable" standard of Section 1129(b) of the Bankruptcy Code.[3] Under this section, a plan of reorganization (POR) can be confirmed only if it is "fair and equitable" with respect to each class of claims or interests whose rights are impaired under the plan. With respect to a dissenting class of unsecured claims, the standard is satisfied when "the holder of any claim or interest that is junior to the claims of such class will not receive or retain under the plan on account of such junior claim or interest any property" (Section 1129(b)(2)B). This is also known as the rule of absolute priority.

Whether or not a company in distress files for bankruptcy protection, the rules of Chapter 11 will weigh heavily in any attempt at a reorganization. For all practical purposes, a distress investor is better off assuming that a Chapter 11 filing will take place and analyzing the investment strategy from that perspective. In doing so, it is helpful to keep in mind that the bankruptcy code deals with "claims," not creditors or specific credit instruments, and that Section 1123 requires that such claims be categorized into classes. Classification of claims is quite important since it will affect who gets what under the plan of reorganization. Section 1122(a) provides that the test for whether claims can be included in the same class is that they are "substantially similar," even though it does not define what substantially similar means. In determining whether claims are substantially similar, the courts have focused primarily on legal rights. Thus, a claim arising from a credit instrument "A" that is subordinated to another credit instrument "B" is likely to be placed in a different class of claims, and since subordinating agreements survive in Chapter 11 under Section 510 of thebankruptcy code, the class containing "B" type claims will have payment priority over the class containing "A" type claims. The point is that the name of a credit instrument means little when it comes to appraising its true credit risk and or its investment value in a distressed situation. The relevant appraisal of the value of a claim or interest in a distressed situation where the credit will participate in a reorganization will have more to do with the investor's cost and the percentage of claim that might be paid on such class of claims or interests under a plan of reorganization and/or whether the class will participate in a reorganization.

VALUATION

Distress investing analysis, whether for reorganization or for liquidation of companies, is almost the same as for leveraged buyouts (LBOs) or management buyouts (MBOs). First, one needs to determine a value for the enterprise and its probable dynamics before looking at the cost of capital. To do this, forecast operating income; earnings before interest and taxes (EBIT); earnings before interest, taxes, depreciation, and amortization (EBITDA); and the value of separable and salable assets.

Second, to the aforementioned apply an appropriate capitalization. In an LBO or MBO analysis, leverage up the capitalization; in distress investing, leverage down the capitalization.

Access to new capital for distressed companies tends to be much, much easier in Chapter 11 than out of court. Most distressed companies, but not all, need such access to new capital.

There are eight analytic differences between distress investing and LBO investing:

1. In distress investing, it may be harder to analyze the business, especially pre–Chapter 11.
   - Frequently, there is no chance to undertake a due diligence investigation.
   - Companies are generally weaker.
   - There are fewer well-managed companies.
2. In distress investing, it may be harder for the security holder and the company to borrow funds, with the exception that in Chapter 11, debtor-in-possession (DIP) financing is very safe and very attractive for postpetition lenders.
3. In distress investing, reorganization risks, separate and apart from business risks, are always an important consideration.
4. In distress investing, adequately secured lenders may receive adequate protection payments during the pendency of a proceeding or the "indubitable equivalent" thereof.
5. In distress investing, a creditor is much less likely to be wiped out if things do not go well than is the case for an LBO equity investor, especially a noncontrol investor.
6. In distress investing, securities laws may be considerably less onerous than is the case for owners of voting securities, such as common stocks.
7. In distress investing, it frequently is not necessary to pay up versus OPMI market prices in order to establish security positions that will allow the holder to have an influential voice in the reorganization. In LBOs and MBOs, premiums over OPMI market prices almost always have to be paid.
8. In distress investing, it is much tougher to use the Internal Revenue Code advantageously than is the case for LBOs and MBOs.

THE COMPANY AS A STAND-ALONE ENTITY

A company is a separate entity that has relationships with many constituencies, including its public owners and creditors. This fact is not clearly understood by academics who implicitly assume a consolidation of interests between the company and its public owners, treating them as one and the same for all practical purposes. The recent controversy over stock options as to whether they ought to be expensed using the "fair value method" (FASB 123) or the "intrinsic value method" (APB 25) sheds much light on the prevalent confusion that exists on this point.

First, stock options are a stockholder problem, not a company problem. Stock options cause dilution of the existing ownership. Viewing the company as a stand-alone entity, the cost to the company of issuing stock options equals the present value of the net cash drain from future cash payments to the common stock to be issued on the exercise of these options, and also the present value of the expected reduced access to capital markets that the company might have because of the stock options. Both of these costs seem difficult to measure. From a creditor's point of view there can be, and there usually is, a world of difference in the creditworthiness of an issuer between one that pays out, say, $200 million per annum in cash for executive compensation and one that issues stock options on a non-dividend-paying common stock with a fair value of $200 million.

As to that fair value of $200 million for stock options, it is a pretty ludicrous number if the company is viewed as a stand-alone entity. There seems to be no rationale whatsoever for equating the value of a noncash benefit to a recipient (i.e., a corporate executive receiving a stock option) to the real cost to the company to bestow that benefit. It seems doubtful that the real cost to the company for issuing the stock option benefit is measurable, while the value of the benefit to the recipient does seem measurable by fair value techniques. Why saddle the company with such a fictitious cost from a company perspective where the company is a stand-alone entity?

Fitch Ratings published an interesting article on April 20, 2004, in which it recognized that stock options were basically a stockholder problem, not a creditor problem; but then it went on to state, "Because of their dilutive effect, many companies have a high propensity to repurchase shares issued upon exercise of employee stock options. In this context, from a bondholder perspective, employee options have a true cash cost and can be thought of as a form of deferred compensation, which has the effect of reducing available cash to service debt and increasing leverage." Fitch Ratings seems to be involved in overkill. First, most companies issuing stock options probably do not have stock repurchase programs. Second, any company making cash distributions to shareholders for any reason, whether such cash distributions are in the form of dividends or share repurchases, "has the effect of reducing available cash to service debt and increasing leverage." Indeed, from a creditor's point of view, cash distributions to shareholders are helpful only insofar as they enhance the debtor's access to capital markets. Third, share repurchases are strictly voluntary and thus do not have as adverse a credit impact as do required cash payments to creditors for interest, principal, or premium. Finally, some share purchases can be beneficial to creditors and companies if the common stock being repurchased pays an ultrahigh cash dividend.

The FASB 123 versus APB 25 dispute is strictly about form over substance. Companies that had used APB 25, the intrinsic value method, were required under GAAP in financial statement footnotes to disclose the far greater expense of the fair value method as contained in FASB 123. The whole dispute revolves around whether disclosure of an ephemeral expense ought to be made in the income account or in the footnotes to the financial statements. The question for the serious investor who is not a short-run stock market speculator is: "Who cares?" An exception might be that in an overall appraisal of management by a trained analyst, information about management attitudes could be gleaned by looking at management opting either for FASB 123 or for APB 25.

CONTROL AND ITS VITAL IMPORTANCE

There is no more important topic in finance. Certain investors invest only for control, or elements of control, whether those investors hold common stocks or debt instruments issued by troubled companies. In the case of troubled companies, debt holders may seek elements of control over the reorganization process, the company, or both. For our purposes, control securities are different securities from noncontrol securities even though the rights attaching to each security, say a common stock, are identical. One of the characteristics of control, or elements of control, is that the participant gets a voice in negotiations and decisions. It is important to be conscious of the fact that each and every constituency involved in finance has both communities of interest and conflicts of interest with every other constituency. For example, in Chapter 11, do attorneys representing unsecured creditors, who are paid by the hour—without credit risk—have incentives to prolong bankruptcy cases that the unsecured creditor clients would like to see resolved expeditiously?

3

The Causes of Financial Distress

The theme of this book is that Chapter 11 bankruptcy is not the end of the game but the beginning of the game. When evaluating a potential investment in a distressed issue, as a norm, we assume the worst-case scenario of a potential Chapter 11 filing. Why? Because any resolution of a distressed situation, whether it happens out of court or in a bankruptcy proceeding, will be heavily influenced by the rules of Chapter 11. With that in mind, a question that bears asking is: Why would an investor care about understanding the causes of financial distress? If such an understanding helps us better estimate the workout potential for different credit instruments and/or security interests in Chapter 11, then such understanding is quite important to an investor. An example of when such knowledge may be of academic value only is the case of an adequately secured creditor. As long as the value of the collateral securing a creditor's secured claim is more than adequate (oversecured) prepetition, and will not diminish in value postpetition, such a creditor or an investor in such claims should not care much about the reasons why the firm is in distress. In all likelihood, these claims will be reinstated, paid in full or paid during the pendency of a Chapter 11 proceeding, and receive scheduled interest and principal payments as "adequate protection." The story changes for unsecured claims or security interests whose ultimate recoveries will depend on how the distressed situation unfolds: whether the company files for Chapter 11 reorganization, Chapter 7 liquidation, or does not file at all; whether the claim class will have payment priority over other classes of unsecured claims (their treatment under a plan of reorganization); and what the ultimate value or valuation of the estate will be after the value-draining process of a bankruptcy proceeding. The outcomes of many of these events are likely to be influenced by the factors that created the distressed situation in the first place.

Companies become financially distressed when their ability to meet either their current or their future financial obligations (an impending interest payment, a principal repayment, a refinancing, insurance claims, tort claims, etc.) becomes or is expected to become materially impaired. An issuer's actual, expected, or perceived inability to meet its financial obligations can be viewed as due to credit markets freezing up, a material deterioration in the value of a company's assets, a sudden ballooning of current or expected liabilities, or all of these causes. The factors leading to these situations are many and often interrelated, making the development of a detailed taxonomic classification of somewhat limited value. We illustrate what we believe are some of the common factors as they play an important role in specific distressed cases. Another evidence of financial distress can exist where the fair market value of a company's liabilities exceeds the fair market value of its assets. But this insolvency test is far less important, and far less meaningful, than the test of a company's ability to meet its obligations as they come due.

LACK OF ACCESS TO CAPITAL MARKETS

Lack of assess to capital markets seems likely to be the principal cause of distress in 2008 and 2009. There are plenty of examples of companies whose liquidity needs, growth potential, and ultimate survival as going concerns depend on recurrent access to capital markets. For these companies, not having access to capital markets when needed is a sure trip into financial distress. The reasons for this lack of access can range from a crisis of confidence to events in capital markets that are unrelated to the issuer in question. One such case was that of Drexel Burnham Lambert Group, Inc., the parent company of its broker-dealer subsidiary, Drexel Burnham Lambert, Inc. The parent company was forced to file for Chapter 11 on February 13, 1990, because of its inability to raise funds to refinance $30 million of commercial paper coming due. In the months leading to its filing, the parent company had been getting cash from its broker-dealer subsidiary to meet its financial obligations until the Securities and Exchange Commission (SEC) insisted that the parent borrow against its own assets, which consisted of a portfolio of then highly illiquid junk bonds. The parent company had been set up to have all the liabilities that were supported by what at the time were highly illiquid assets. Once banks pulled the parent company's lines of credit, a crisis of confidence ensued and institutions stopped doing business with the firm. That was the end of Drexel Burnham Lambert.

Lack of access to capital markets was the result of several interrelated factors. Drexel Burnham Lambert had a poorly designed corporate capital structure where the parent company carried all the liabilities but only the then less liquid assets.[1] The junk bond market had been in distress since early summer of 1989 but took a turn for the worse when Campeau

Corporation[2] missed an interest payment in September 1989 and eventually filed for bankruptcy protection under Chapter 11 in January 1990. Drexel Burnham Lambert Group's assets consisted of a portfolio of junk bonds of uncertain value. The SEC intervention effectively shut off its ability to tap liquidity from its broker-dealer subsidiary, and lenders were unwilling to lend unless they were provided with a backstop guarantee from the Federal Reserve—which at the time was highly unlikely to happen against the background of the turmoil in the savings and loan industry and a guilty plea to six felony counts by Michael Milken, an important Drexel Burnham executive who ran Drexel's junk bond operations. These factors rendered Drexel Burnham Lambert noncreditworthy and resulted it the loss of access to the capital it needed to remain a viable going concern.

A more recent distressed situation similar to the Drexel Burnham Lambert one is the case of Bear Stearns and Company. The events that precipitated Bear's difficulty accessing capital markets were similar in that the crisis developed on the perception that Bear was not creditworthy. The questionable assets this time were not junk bonds but mortgage-backed securities and other debt-backed securities. In June 2007 there were reports that Merrill Lynch had seized collateral from Bear's High-Grade Structured Credit Fund, a hedge fund heavily invested in mortgage- and loan-backed securities managed by Bear Stearns Asset Management. By the end of June the company had committed $1.6 billion in secured financing to the fund and continued to work with creditors and counterparties of a second such fund[3] to facilitate its orderly deleveraging. By August 1, 2007, both funds had filed for bankruptcy protection and the company had frozen the assets in a third fund. By the beginning of 2008 the mortgage-related credit crunch had worsened, and on March 10 market rumors spread that Bear might not have enough cash to do business. The rumors implied that Bear had lost access to capital markets. Over the weekend of March 15, the boards of JPMorgan, Chase, and Bear agreed to a reorganization plan whereby JPMorgan would buy all the common stock of Bear in a stock swap transaction and the Federal Reserve would provide short-term financing to JPMorgan secured by Bear's assets. This was the case of an out-of-court reorganization where the Federal Reserve provided debtor in possession (DIP) equivalent financing to maintain the going-concern value of Bear while the reorganization took place. It was highly unlikely that Bear would have survived as a going concern had it not been able to access capital with the help of an implicit guarantee from the Fed; banks were not willing to lend to Bear on the perception that it was not creditworthy.

Both cases highlight how important having access to capital markets is for companies whose business model relies on having continuous access to such capital. Neither Drexel nor Bear was insolvent, but that did not prevent these companies from falling into distress rather rapidly only because they both lost access to capital markets when they needed it.

DETERIORATION OF OPERATING PERFORMANCE

The deterioration of operating performance is a common reason for companies going into financial distress. The reasons that lead to such a deterioration are many and include but are not limited to cyclical economic downturns, cost inflation, competition, regulation/deregulation, uncompetitive product or service, unrealistic business plan, or poor management. It is seldom the case that only one of these factors is responsible for the deterioration of operating performance. More frequently it is a combination of these factors that leads to such deterioration, which in turn ends in financial distress. In the example that follows we show how the deterioration of operating performance is a combination of several factors that include an economic downturn, foreign competition, raw materials inflation, and a failed growth strategy combined with an unfeasible capital structure.

A Combination of Factors: Home Products International, Inc.

The retail environment of 1994, 1995, and 1996 was quite difficult, as evidenced by large numbers of retail chains seeking relief from creditors by filing under either Chapter 11 or Chapter 7 of the bankruptcy code. Such high-profile filings included names like Caldor Corporation, Bradlees Inc., Jamesway Corporation, and Barney's Inc. In 1994, Selfix, Inc., an international consumer products company specializing in the design, manufacture, and marketing of quality plastic products for home use, appointed a new CEO to improve the profitability of the company. In early 1997, Selfix, Inc. embarked on a growth by acquisitions strategy, adopting the holding company form of organization and changing its name to Home Products International, Inc. (HPI). The core of HPI's growth strategy was outlined in the company's 10-K filing for 1996:

> *The housewares industry segment, including plastic products, is highly fragmented. Over the past several years, retailers have consolidated rapidly, with mass discounters such as Wal-Mart, Kmart, and Target capturing increasingly larger shares of the market. Management believes that as these retailers consolidate, they are actively seeking to reduce the number of suppliers from whom they source*

product. As a result, management believes that larger housewares manufacturers with focused product lines covering entire categories (such as Storage Containers or Bath/Shower Organization) will capture increasingly larger market shares at the expense of smaller manufacturers with limited product offerings. The Company intends to continue to focus on the entry-level price segment and to grow by expanding its offerings within existing product categories, by making selective acquisitions which management believes offer synergistic opportunities, and by capitalizing on established distribution channels to increase international sales.

As expected, the acquisition strategy brought increased sales to HPI, and management correctly forecast that mass discounters would seek to reduce the number of suppliers from whom they sourced products. HPI financed the acquisition strategy almost entirely with debt. The increased sales and debt levels are shown in Exhibit 3.1.

What management could not accurately foresee back in 1997 was the insidious margin erosion over the next few years due to increased raw material costs, competition from foreign imports, and an increased dependence on the three top customers. Exhibit 3.2 shows such deterioration over time.

Several company attempts to restructure and reduce costs came to an end in November 2006 when the company missed an interest payment on its $9^5/_8$ percent senior subordinated notes and entered into negotiations together with the majority shareholder and Third Avenue Management, LLC (the majority note holder) to effect a financial reorganization. HPI filed a prepackaged Chapter 11 shortly thereafter.[4]

The HPI case shows how a strategy that might have seemed warranted back in 1997 led to filing for bankruptcy protection in 2006. HPI's strategy of growing through acquisitions led the company to take on levels of debt that turned out to be unsustainable for a business facing a relentless deterioration in gross margins due to foreign competition, increasing costs

EXHIBIT 3.1 Home Products International, Inc., Operating Results in Thousands for 1995–1998

	1995	1996	1997	1998
Net Sales	$41,039	$38,200	$129,324	$252,429
Gross Margin	37.4%	39.8%	31.3%	33.0%
Total Debt	$ 7,914	$ 7,650	$ 34,550	$223,085
Interest Coverage	1.5	5.1	3.6	2.9
Debt/EBITDA	6.0	2.1	1.9	4.9

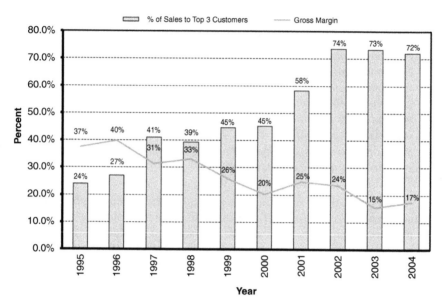

EXHIBIT 3.2   Home Products International, Inc., Gross Margins versus Sales to Top Three Customers, 1995–2004

of raw materials, and selling almost exclusively to the largest three discount retailers. What in hindsight appears obvious was not that obvious at the time these decisions were made.

DETERIORATION OF GAAP PERFORMANCE

Financial accounting under generally accepted accounting principles (GAAP) is a system in which reports are made following a rigid set of rules whose descriptions of reality are limited and in many instances unrealistic. The focus of conventional equity analysts is on what the GAAP numbers *are*, whereas in distress or value investing the focus is on what the numbers *mean*. The following example shows how focusing on the GAAP numbers contributed to the development of a distressed situation.

Mark-to-Market Losses: MBIA, Inc.

MBIA, Inc.[5] is in the business of providing financial guarantee insurance and other forms of credit protection to public finance and structured finance issuers, investors, and other capital market participants. The company conducts its financial guarantee business through its wholly owned insurance subsidiary, MBIA Insurance Corporation.

MBIA's original structured finance business provided credit enhancement to bonds issued by securitization vehicles, and in the early 1990s the company began writing more business with financial institution customers with loan assets on their balance sheets that were not destined for securitization vehicles. These financial institutions sought to hedge the default risk of these assets (i.e., reduce the risk of loss of the assets without selling them), and one way of doing this was to buy a financial guarantee insurance policy from MBIA. The accounting for these assets involves fair value accounting, where the assets are recorded on the balance sheet at the price at which they can be sold, and changes to the fair value of those assets are recorded on the income account. A traditional financial guarantee policy effectively hedges the credit risk of these assets but does nothing about the mark-to-market effects on the reported performance of the financial institution holding these assets. To address the need of these financial institution clients to reduce the reported earnings' volatility created by fair value accounting and at the same time hedge the default risk of those assets, the financial guarantors, including MBIA, started insuring a special breed of credit default swap (CDS) that is a highly modified version of the standard CDS used by investment banks and reads more like a financial guarantee policy.[6] Since insurance regulations allow only financial guarantors to guarantee the performance of a contract, MBIA does not enter into the CDS directly; a number of special purpose entities (SPEs) or affiliate companies created for the specific purpose of transacting with these financial institutions transact the CDS, and MBIA in turn provides a financial guarantee on the performance of these entities for the benefit of the counterparty.

In a CDS, the financial institution client transfers credit risk to a counterparty—an affiliate of the financial guarantor or an SPE—without the legal transfer of the underlying assets. These highly modified CDS contracts do not have collateral posting or payment acceleration provisions, are generally limited to payment shortfalls of interest and principal on a pay-as-you-go basis, and are held to maturity. One thing that they have in common with the standard CDS is that they are subject to derivatives accounting under Statement of Financial Accounting Standards (SFAS) 133 and have to be accounted for on a mark-to-market basis.[7]

The mark-to-market accounting provides the accounting that the financial institution wants for the financial guarantee, and the end result of these transactions is that the financial institution gets credit default protection *and* the accounting it needs to reduce reported earnings volatility. The drawback for MBIA is that the arrangement transfers the mark-to-market volatility from its clients' books onto MBIA's books. Even though the mark-to-market

EXHIBIT 3.3 MBIA, Inc., Condensed Revenue Results for the Insurance Segment, Year-to-Date Results as of June 30, September 30, and December 31, 2007 ($ in Thousands Except EPS)

	June 30 6 Months	September 30 9 Months	December 31 12 Months
Net Premiums Earned	$431,165	$ 634,358	$ 855,624
Net Investment Income	$292,291	$ 437,749	$ 571,207
Fees, Reimbursements, and Realized Gains or Losses	$ 46,846	$ 58,136	$ 72,883
Revenue before Mark-to-Market Effect	$770,302	$1,130,243	$1,499,714
Net Gains or Losses on Financial Instruments at Fair Value	–$ 12,211	–$ 347,528	–$3,618,258
Revenue after Mark-to-Market Effect	$758,091	$ 782,715	–$2,118,544
Earnings per Share	3.07	2.84	–15.22

Data from press releases, 10-Q and 10-K reports.

effect on earnings does not reflect the economics of the business, it can, and indeed did, result in large GAAP losses on MBIA's books. Exhibit 3.3 shows how dramatic the reported mark-to-market losses were in fiscal year 2007. To the unsuspecting reader who judges performance only through what the GAAP numbers are, the dramatic change in revenue and earnings per share after the mark-to-market changes was shocking. These mark-to-market adjustments were largely irrelevant to the economics of MBIA's business. Far from representing actual gains or losses, the adjustments only represented changes in the market or model value of derivative instruments that were held to expiration,[8] and in the absence of any credit event these adjustments would revert to zero at expiration. Market participants interpreted these mark-to-market adjustments as signs of impending massive losses in MBIA's insured portfolio even though the company had separate estimates of such potential credit losses and had appropriately reserved for them.[9]

Against this background, credit rating agencies raised concerns that MBIA Insurance Corporation might fall short of the required capital cushion to maintain its triple-A credit rating, and bear raiders were very effective in painting a gloom-and-doom scenario that suggested that MBIA was not creditworthy and that it would not be able to meet policyholders' claims in the future. The end result of all of these events was that MBIA, Inc. was forced to access capital markets to raise the additional capital required by credit rating agencies to maintain its insurance subsidiary's credit rating. The fulcrum security[10] in this de facto reorganization was the common stock, and MBIA successfully effected such reorganization by raising $1.5 billion through the issuance of MBIA, Inc. common stock and an issue of $1 billion of MBIA Insurance Corporation surplus notes.[11]

LARGE OFF-BALANCE-SHEET CONTINGENT LIABILITIES

Off-balance-sheet contingent liabilities are liabilities that sometimes can materially affect the prospects of a company surviving as a going concern. The nature of these liabilities ranges from contingent tort claims to liability arising from fraud, liabilities related to special purpose entities (SPEs) or structured investment vehicles (SIVs), and those arising from complex derivative transactions and other contracts. The damaging effect of these types of liabilities can be unexpected and very sudden. Part of this category might also include massive long-term liabilities for employee and retiree health costs as well as long-term liabilities for employee-defined benefit retirement plans.

Large Potential Tort Liabilities: USG Corporation

Throughout 2000 and 2001, a large number of companies that were defendants in asbestos personal injury cases, including Armstrong World Industries, W.R. Grace & Company, Owens Corning, and others, filed for bankruptcy. Following the bankruptcy filings of these companies, plaintiffs substantially increased their settlement demands to U.S. Gypsum Company. In response to these increased settlement demands, U.S. Gypsum attempted to manage its asbestos liability by contesting, rather than settling, a greater number of cases that it believed to be nonmeritorious. On June 25, 2001, USG Corporation and its major domestic subsidiaries filed a voluntary petition for reorganization under Chapter 11 of the U.S. bankruptcy code to manage the litigation costs of its U.S. Gypsum Company subsidiary. Clearly, what put USG Corporation in a distressed situation was the real potential for an uncontrolled growth in its asbestos liabilities.

Commenting on the company's operations at the time of filing for Chapter 11, William C. Foote, chairman, president, and CEO, explained,[12]

> *Today's filing is not about restructuring our Company's operating units or dealing with a liquidity crisis. Rather, the Chapter 11 process was the only alternative to prevent the value drain that has been occurring as U.S. Gypsum was forced to pay for the asbestos costs of other companies that have already filed for Chapter 11.*

At the time of filing, USG Corporation was a well-capitalized company, with no operating problems. Filing for Chapter 11 reorganization appeared to be the most efficient way (perhaps the only way) to manage the significant liabilities arising from asbestos-related claims.

Understanding the interrelated factors leading a company into financial distress is important in the analysis and development of an investment strategy, but by no means it is the only consideration; it is only a starting point. If the cause of financial distress is an inadequate capital structure but the fundamentals of the business are sound, one is likely to start the analysis from the perspective that a reorganization may be likely and feasible. If the soundness of the business is in question, assuming the worst-case scenarios of either a Chapter 11 liquidating plan or a Chapter 7 liquidation filing may be a safe assumption to start the analysis. If the distressed situation was generated by the sudden ballooning of liabilities due to unexpected tort or bad contract claims, one may safely assume the worst and focus only on issues that are likely to be reinstated in a Chapter 11 reorganization or paid in full in a Chapter 7 liquidation.

Recognizing the factors leading to financial distress is an important step in the multistep process of investing in distressed issues.

4

Deal Expenses and Who Bears Them

Unlike in many other financial arenas, the administrative expenses of a bankruptcy proceeding are paid by the estate. These expenses are largely comprised of fees and expenses paid out to professionals, mainly attorneys and financial advisers, who will perform services for both the debtor in possession (DIP) and the committees formed pursuant to Section 1102 of the bankruptcy code. Although there is usually one committee of creditors holding unsecured claims, Section 1102 gives the U.S. Trustee the power to appoint additional committees of creditors or of equity security holders as the U.S. Trustee deems appropriate. The complexity of the capitalization structure of a debtor will be one likely determinant of the number of committees that will be formed.

Section 503(b)(4) of the bankruptcy code gives professional fees and expenses the legal status of an administrative expense of the case. This legal status is important because Section 507(2) gives administrative expenses super-priority in payment over any other unsecured claim; that is, professional fees and expenses are paid before any unsecured claim gets paid. Moreover, while unsecured creditors must wait to the end of the case to find out how much they will recover on their claims and in what form, professional fees and expenses are paid in cash, on a pay-as-you-go basis, and with very modest holdbacks. Even though most professionals will work in what they perceive to be a client's best interest in deciding whether to compromise with others or to be aggressive, the tilt will often be in the direction that will prolong a case. Later in this chapter we discuss statistical results that support this observation.

Since professional fees and expenses are paid in cash and on a pay-as-you-go basis, they are a drain on the estate that can also affect the feasibility of a debtor as a going concern. The effect of these cash costs on feasibility is quite important for companies with small reorganization values (i.e., less than $300 million as a rule of thumb), where they can wipe out the estate and unsecured creditors with it. In large cases, professional costs may not detract from feasibility because such cash expenses can be frequently offset, wholly or in great part, by the suspension of all cash payments to unsecured claims pursuant to the automatic stay and/or by the availability of super-priority postpetition financing in the form of DIP loans. Either way, it is indisputable that these expenses come out of the hides of unsecured and not adequately protected creditors, and that in small cases they can wipe out the estate and unsecured creditors with it.

No one should question that professionals are essential to the reorganization or liquidation process either out of court or in Chapter 11 or Chapter 7. Reorganizations and liquidations would be very chaotic without the involvement of skilled professionals. However, uncontrolled professional costs can materially detract from unsecured creditor recoveries and in extreme cases might detract from the feasibility of the debtor as a going concern. Both parties in interest and holders of unsecured claims will be rather sensitive to the size of these expenses since they are the constituents that ultimately pay for them. These are important enough reasons to further understand some of the elements that determine the amount of professional compensation in large Chapter 11 cases.

ATTORNEYS AND FINANCIAL ADVISERS' COMPENSATION STRUCTURE AND THE DISTRIBUTION OF THE FEE PIE

Attorneys and financial advisers (primarily investment bankers and tax advisers) represent the bulk of the administrative expenses of large Chapter 11 cases. Although there is wide variation on a case-by-case basis, on average, attorneys and financial advisers share almost equally in the fee pie. Exhibit 4.1 shows the results of the examination of a sample of 48 bankruptcy cases for which detailed information on professional fees and expenses was available.[1] For this group of cases, attorneys' fees and expenses represented on average 55 percent of the professional costs to the estate while financial advisers accounted for 45 percent of such costs. The distribution of the fee pie between attorneys and financial advisers appears to be invariant to whether a Chapter 11 case is filed as a conventional case or a preplanned one.

Both attorneys and financial advisers are paid on a time basis, either hourly or monthly. Exhibits 4.2 and 4.3 show retention summaries for both

EXHIBIT 4.1 Average Dollar Amount of Fees and Expenses Charged to the Estate by Attorneys and Financial Advisers in Chapter 11 Cases by Type of Plan

	Attorneys	Conventional Chapter 11s Number of Cases = 30 Financial Advisers	Case
Average Fees and Expenses	$9,881,535	$ 7,872,579	$17,754,114
Fees and Expenses as % of Total Professional Costs	55.80%	44.20%	
Minimum Fees and Expenses		$ 909,533	$ 819,651
Maximum Fees and Expenses		$48,791,466	$43,523,086

	Attorneys	Prepackaged and Prenegotiated Number of Cases = 18 Financial Advisers	Case
Average Fees and Expenses	$2,221,639	$1,785,729	$4,007,368
Fees and Expenses as % of Total Professional Costs	54.60%	45.40%	
Minimum Fees and Expenses		$ 303,960	$ 0
Maximum Fees and Expenses		$6,324,733	$7,553,788

A list of the bankruptcy cases is provided in the appendix at the end of this chapter. The fee data is part of a database provided by Professor Lynn M. LoPucki.

attorneys and financial advisers. Unlike attorneys, who get compensated on an hourly basis, financial advisers' compensation structure includes monthly payments and bonuslike components known by names like "restructuring fee," "consummation fee," "incentive fee," "transaction fee," or "success fee," to name a few. These bonuslike fees are time independent, represent an important portion of the advisers' total compensation, and are usually tied to the completion of a transaction or just the completion of a case, whatever its outcome. Exhibit 4.4 presents a summary of some of these arrangements for Chapter 11 cases in 2003 and 2004.

It is clear that one important determinant of the total amount of fees and expenses paid by the estate is the duration of a case. This factor is likely to play a more important role in the accruing of legal fees and expenses since attorneys' total compensation is uniquely time dependent in bankruptcy cases. In Exhibit 4.5 we show the average and median lengths of Chapter 11 cases since 1980.

EXHIBIT 4.2 Hourly Rates for Different Professionals in Different Chapter 11 Cases, 2003–2004

Filing Date	Company Filing	Firm to Be Retained	P,P,SMD	MD	D,OC	SM	M,V	SA	A	AnJA	PP
07/10/03	Acterna Corp.	Ernst & Young Corporate Finance LLC		$550–$595	$475–$545		$375–$440		$320–$340	$275	$140
04/22/04	Adelphia Communications Corp.	Foley & Lardner LLP	$385–$775		$195–$550			$220–$435			$85–$205
07/15/03	Adelphia Communications Corp.	BDO Seidman, LLP	$375–$475				$250–$350		$80–$250		
01/31/03	American Commercial Lines LLC	Huron Consulting Group LLC		$400–$500	$350–$450		$310–$350		$250–$310	$175	
02/02/04	Atlas Air Worldwide Holdings Inc.	Ernst & Young LLP	$726–$759			$655	$545	$347			$187–$248
02/02/04	Atlas Air Worldwide Holdings Inc.	KPMG LLP	$540–$600			$450–$510	$360–$420	$270–$330	$180–$240		$120
08/25/03	DVI Inc.	AP Services LLC	$420–$670					$325–$495	$275–$390	$150–$180	$105–$110
04/05/03	Fleming Cos. Inc.	FTI Consulting Inc.	$500–$595					$150–$325	$150–$326		$75–$140
03/03/04	Footstar Inc.	Weil Gotshal & Manges LLP	$450–$800	$325–$490	$325–$490				$240–$505		$125–$225
02/13/04	Heilig-Meyers	Capstone Corporate Recovery LLC									
07/16/03	Loral Space and Communications Ltd.	Key Consulting LLC	$500								
06/14/04	Maxim Crane Works LLC	Kirkland & Ellis LLP	$425–$950		$325–$740				$235–$540		$90–$280
06/15/04	Maxim Crane Works LLC	Pepper Hamilton LLP			$160–$550						$65–$110
07/19/04	Maxim Crane Works LLC	KPMG LLP	$590–$650		$480–$570		$390–$450	$300–$360	$190–$270		$140
04/20/04	Mirant Corp.	Energy & Environmental Engineering	$350–$400					$200–$330			$50–$150
04/20/04	Mirant Corp.	New Energy Associates	$440		$350			$180–$320			$85–$125
07/22/03	Mirant Corp.	Charles River Associates Inc.	$525–$550	$325–$450	$250	$360–$645					$95
08/22/03	Mirant Corp.	KPMG LLP	$600–$800		$360–$645	$350	$360–$645	$180–$585	$150–$275		$60–$120
09/09/03	Mirant Corp.	Risk Capital Management Partners	$500–$750					$200–$300			$150
09/11/03	Mirant Corp.	Huron Consulting Group LLC							$250	$175	
09/18/03	NorthWestern Corp.	Alvarez & Marsal		$600	$450		$350	$275–$350		$175–$250	
05/14/03	NRG Energy Inc.	PricewaterhouseCoopers LLP	$490–$690	$500–$650	$350–$450		$325–$550	$150–$325	$150–$325		$75–$140
05/14/03	NRG Energy Inc.	Leonard LoBiondo LLC	$650	$325–$550	$325–$550		$225–$600				
05/14/03	NRG Energy Inc.	Kroll Zolfo Cooper LLC	$550				$225–$600				$50–$225
02/24/04	Oglebay Norton Co.	Ernst & Young LLP	$545–$1,025			$400–$600	$320–$485	$215–$395			$150–$260

Date	Company	Firm							
03/25/04	Oglebay Norton Co.	Stroock & Lavan LLP	$500–$750				$205–$600		$150–$260
04/08/04	Parmalat USA	BDO Seidman	$335–$675				$100–$205		$95–$195
06/02/04	Pegasus Satellite Television Inc.	Bernstein Shur Sawyer	$155–$400		$230–$510	$210–$345	$150–$255		$60–$115
06/02/04	Pegasus Satellite Television Inc.	Sidley Austin Brown & Wood LLP	$425–$775				$170–$435		$50–$190
06/26/03	Philip Services Corp.	KPMG LLP	$450–$600	$330–$510	$330–$510	$175–$330			$120
05/27/04	RCN Corp.	Swindler Berlin Shereff Friedman LLP	$540				$180		$135–$175
05/27/04	RCN Corp.	Pricewaterhouse Coopers LLP	$743–$900		$517–$662	$319–$389	$187–$273		
05/27/04	RCN Corp.	Skadden Arps Slate Meagher & Flom LLP	$495–$760				$280–$485		$80–$195
06/25/04	RCN Corp.	AP Services LLC	$540–$690	$475–$575		$430–$520	$300–$400	$225–$280	
03/17/03	Spiegel Inc.	Alvarez & Marsal Inc.	$370	$350–$450			$275–$350	$175–$225	
03/19/04	Spiegel Inc.	Sheppard Mullin Richter & Hampton LLP					$260		$150–$190
04/24/04	Spiegel Inc.	FTI Consulting Inc.	$550–$625	$425–$525	$350–$405		$360–$550		$165–$325
08/07/03	Texas Petrochemicals L.P.	KPMG LLP	$540–$650		$360–$550	$360–$550	$150–$350		$120
07/16/03	Touch America Holdings Inc.	PricewaterhouseCoopers LLP	$400–$500		$205–$280	$205–$280	$85–$180	$85–$180	$60–$65
07/16/03	Touch America Holdings Inc.	PricewaterhouseCoopers LLP	$488		$311–$466	$311–$466	$311–$466	$135–$255	$135–$255
09/23/03	Trenwick Group Ltd.	Ben S. Branch	$600						
09/22/03	Trenwick Group Ltd.	Ernst & Young LLP	$520–$740		$385–$415	$320–$360	$140–$260		
09/22/03	Trenwick Group Ltd.	PricewaterhouseCoopers LLP	$520–$740		$385–$415	$320–$360			
01/30/03	UAL Corp.	KPMG LLP	$540–$600		$360–$420	$270–$330	$180–$240		$75–$150
03/19/04	UAL Corp.	FTI Consulting Inc.	$525–$625	$450–$510			$175–$345		$120
03/08/04	UAL Corp.	Leaf Group LLC	$200–$800	$370–$525					
07/03/03	UAL Corp.	Cognizant Associates Inc.	$700						
06/01/03	WestPoint Stevens Inc.	Ernst & Young Corporate Finance LLC	$575–$595	$475–$545	$375–$440	$375–$440	$320–$340	$275	$140
06/01/03	WestPoint Stevens Inc.	Ernst & Young LLP	$500–$751	$445–$646	$343–$522	$252–$408			$180–$338

P, P, SMD = Partners, principals, senior managing directors; MD = Managing directors; SM = Senior managing director; D,OC = Director, of counsel; M,V = Managing director; M,V = Associate directors, vice presidents; SA = Senior associate; A = Associate; AnJA = Analyst, junior attorney; PP = Paraprofessionals.

EXHIBIT 4.3 Retention Summaries for Financial Advisers Where There Is a Monthly Fee Involved

Retention Filing Date	Company Filing	Firm to Be Retained	Monthly Fee
12/26/02	Encompass Services Corp.	Chanin Capital Partners LLC	$117,000
01/29/03	Conseco Inc.	Raymond James & Associates Inc.	$175,000
01/31/03	American Commercial Lines LLC	Richard Weingarten & Co.	$ 55,000
03/06/03	Ntelos Inc.	UBS Warburg LLC	$160,000
03/17/03	Spiegel Inc.	Alvarez & Marsal	$100,000
03/27/03	UAL Corp.	Saybrook Restructuring Advisors LLC	$250,000 1–6, $200,000 after
04/05/03	Fleming Cos. Inc.	Gleacher Partners LLC	$200,000
04/30/03	DirecTV Latin America LLC	Huron Consulting Group LLC	$165,000
07/14/03	WestPoint Stevens Inc.	Rothschild Inc.	$200,000
07/15/03	Loral Space & Communications Ltd.	Conway Del Genio Gries & Co.	$250,000
07/17/03	Mirant Corp.	Blackstone Group L.P.	$225,000
08/07/03	Texas Petrochemicals L.P.	Petrie Parkman	$150,000 1–3, $100,000 after
08/18/03	Penn Traffic Co.	Ernst & Young Corporate Finance LLC	$175,000 1–3, $150,000 after
08/20/03	Trenwick America Corp.	Greenhill & Co.	$175,000
09/11/03	Mirant Corp.	Miller Buckfire Lewis Ying & Co. LLC	$150,000
09/16/03	WestPoint Stevens Inc.	Lehman Brothers Inc.	$ 75,000
09/17/03	NorthWestern Corp.	Lazard Freres & Co. LLC	$200,000
09/19/03	Loral Space & Communications Ltd.	Jefferies & Co.	$150,000
02/02/04	Atlas Air Worldwide Holdings Inc.	Lazard Freres & Co. LLC	$250,000
02/13/04	Solutia	Houlihan Lokey Howard & Zukin Capital	$150,000
02/24/04	Oglebay Norton Co.	Cobblestone Advisors	$ 10,000
02/24/04	Oglebay Norton Co.	Lazard Freres & Co. LLC	$200,000
02/27/04	Rouge Industries Inc.	Development Specialists Inc.	$ 50,000
03/29/04	Footstar Inc.	Credit Suisse First Boston LLC	$150,000 1–3, $125,000 4–6, $100,000 after
05/27/04	RCN Corp.	Blackstone Group L.P.	$200,000
06/04/04	Cornerstone Propane Partners LP	Greenhill & Co.	$175,000
06/15/04	Maxim Crane Works LLC	CIBC World Markets Corp.	$150,000

EXHIBIT 4.4 Bonuses for Financial Professionals: Retention Summaries
for 2003 and 2004

Filing Date	Company	Firm to Be Hired	Bonus Potential
01/29/03	Conseco Inc.	Raymond James & Associates Inc.	Not applicable.
01/31/03	American Commercial Lines LLC	Richard Weingarten & Co.	Richard Weingarten will be entitled to a $420,000 success fee after negotiating and closing a restructuring agreement between the company, its senior lenders and senior noteholders, and parent company Danielson Holding Corp.
03/06/03	Ntelos Inc.	UBS Warburg LLC	If asked to render a fairness opinion, the firm will receive an opinion fee equal to $1.25 million. The firm will also be entitled to a restructuring transaction fee of at least $2 million, potentially higher depending on the terms of the transaction and whether the firm assists in the modification to the covenants of the company's senior credit facility.
03/17/03	Spiegel Inc.	Alvarez & Marsal	The company has agreed to pay the firm incentive compensation under the agreement. The firm expects that the incentive compensation amount will be consistent with amounts awarded to it in cases of similar size and complexity—between $2 million and $5 million.
03/27/03	UAL Corp.	Saybrook Restructuring Advisors LLC	If either a plan is confirmed and becomes effective in the company's bankruptcy case or a sale transaction (as defined in the agreement) closes, the firm will be entitled to an incentive fee. The fee will be measured based on the percent, if any, by which the value of consideration issued to bondholders under a restructuring increased over

(Continued)

EXHIBIT 4.4 (*Continued*)

Filing Date	Company	Firm to Be Hired	Bonus Potential
			the median value of the bonds on Dec. 30 (based on a median trading price of 9.83 cents for every dollar of principal amount outstanding). The incentive fee is capped at $7.5 million. The firm will be entitled to an incentive fee of $7.5 million for a 50% increase above the baseline trading price. To the extent that the increase is between 0% and 50%, the firm will be entitled to a prorated fee calculated to the nearest $10,000. If the firm doesn't earn an incentive fee under this formula, the panel may elect to pay a discretionary incentive fee not to exceed $3.5 million. The amount of the earned incentive fee (not the discretionary incentive fee) will be reduced by the total amount of all monthly advisory fees paid to the firm after the sixth month.
04/05/03	Fleming Cos. Inc.	Gleacher Partners LLC	The firm will be entitled to an additional amendment fee of $2 million payable in cash upon the execution of an amendment (as defined in the agreement). The firm will also be entitled to a restructuring fee of $10 million, payable in cash upon the completion of a restructuring (as defined in the agreement). However, if an amendment and restructuring are both executed, the total amount of both fees won't exceed $10 million. The firm will be entitled to an arrangement fee, payable in cash upon the consummation of any new debt or equity raised by the company. Finally, the firm will be entitled to an additional divestiture

EXHIBIT 4.4 (*Continued*)

Filing Date	Company	Firm to Be Hired	Bonus Potential
			fee, payable in cash upon the consummation of any sale or divestiture by the company. However, half of any divestiture fees paid by the company will be credited against any restructuring fees.
04/30/03	DirecTV Latin America LLC	Huron Consulting Group LLC	Not applicable.
05/14/03	NRG Energy Inc.	Leonard LoBiondo LLC & Zolfo Cooper LLC	The firm will be entitled to a consummation fee of $6,000,000 in cash at the earlier of a court order entered approving the company's reorganization plan or a court order approving the sale of substantially all of the company's assets. The firm will also be entitled to a financing fee payable in cash upon the consummation of a financing, as defined in the agreement. The fee will be equal to 1% of the total amount of the maximum amount of permanent financing available under the financing facility.
06/09/03	Penn Traffic Co.	Ernst & Young Corporate Finance LLC	Not applicable.
07/14/03	WestPoint Stevens Inc.	Rothschild Inc.	A completion fee of $10,000,000 would be paid in cash when a confirmed Chapter 11 plan for the company takes effect or when the company completes a sale of its assets, whichever is earlier. If the company asks Rothschild to perform additional services not addressed in the employment agreement with Rothschild, the additional fees would be mutually agreed upon by Rothschild and the company, in writing, in advance.

(*Continued*)

EXHIBIT 4.4 (*Continued*)

Filing Date	Company	Firm to Be Hired	Bonus Potential
07/15/03	Loral Space & Communications Ltd.	Conway Del Genio Gries & Co.	Not applicable.
07/17/03	Mirant Corp.	Blackstone Group L.P.	The firm will be entitled to an additional restructuring fee of $7 million. The restructuring fee shall be deemed earned when the company first sends definitive offer documents seeking to refinance, restructure, repurchase, modify, or extend in a material respect a substantial portion of its existing credit facilities, existing notes, bonds, or debentures that mature prior to 2006 pursuant to terms approved by the board.
08/07/03	Texas Petro-chemicals L.P.	Petrie Parkman	$500,000.
08/20/03	Trenwick America Corp.	Greenhill & Co.	The firm will be entitled to a $1 million restructuring transaction fee payable when a reorganization plan in the company's Chapter 11 case is consummated.
08/25/03	DVI Inc.	AP Services LLC	The firm will be entitled to a contingent success fee of $4 million, whichever of the following occurs first: (1) effective date of a confirmed plan, (2) transfer of a substantial portion of its assets as a going concern, or (3) sale of a majority of DVI's assets.
09/11/03	Mirant Corp.	Miller Buckfire Lewis Ying & Co. LLC	Upon restructuring (as defined in the engagement letter), Miller Buckfire will be entitled to a transaction fee of $2.5 million. The firm also reserved the right to seek further compensation after plan confirmation based on, among other things, recoveries to unsecured creditors and the timing of the company's case.

EXHIBIT 4.4 (*Continued*)

Filing Date	Company	Firm to Be Hired	Bonus Potential
09/16/03	WestPoint Stevens Inc.	Lehman Brothers Inc.	On the day a plan for the company becomes effective, the firm will be entitled to a $100,000 cash fee.
09/17/03	NorthWestern Corp.	Lazard Freres and Co. LLC	The firm will be entitled to a restructuring fee of $5.5 million. In the event of any sale (as defined in the agreement) the company will pay the firm a fee to be calculated based on the amount of consideration involved in the transaction. One-half of any bonus fee paid under a sale will be credited against any restructuring fee.
09/19/03	Loral Space & Communications Ltd.	Jefferies & Co.	The firm will be entitled to a completion fee equal to the greater of $1 million or 1% of the total consideration received by unsecured creditors between $500 million and $700 million plus 1.75% of total consideration over $700 million.
02/02/04	Atlas Air Worldwide Holdings Inc.	Lazard Freres & Co. LLC	The firm will be entitled to a $5 million restructuring fee payable in cash upon the consummation of a restructuring, as defined in the agreement. The firm will also be entitled to a financing fee representing a placement fee or underwriting spread as a percentage of the total gross proceeds raised in a financing, as defined in the agreement.
02/13/04	Solutia	Houlihan Lokey Howard & Zukin Capital	Upon the closing or consummation of a transaction, the firm will be entitled to a base fee of $1 million plus an incentive fee (collectively, the transaction fee). The incentive fee is equal to 1% of general unsecured creditor recoveries greater than 35% of their allowed claims. The entire transaction fee is payable in cash.

(*Continued*)

EXHIBIT 4.4　(*Continued*)

Filing Date	Company	Firm to Be Hired	Bonus Potential
02/24/04	Oglebay Norton Co.	Cobblestone Advisors	Cobblestone Advisors will be entitled to a closing fee at closing of a transaction (as defined in the agreement) equal to the sum of $375,000, plus 3.5% of the amount of the total purchase price that is between $10 million and $14 million, plus 7.5% of the amount by which the total purchase price exceeds $14 million.
02/24/04	Oglebay Norton Co.	Lazard Freres & Co. LLC	The firm will be entitled to an additional restructuring fee equal to $2 million upon consummation of a restructuring. If the company consummates a sale transaction that includes all or a majority of its assets or equity securities, the firm will be paid a sales transaction fee to be determined by a formula that takes into consideration the size of the asset transaction.
02/27/04	Rouge Industries Inc.	Development Specialists Inc.	Not applicable.
03/29/04	Footstar Inc.	Credit Suisse First Boston LLC	Sale fee, if sale is consummated, payable upon closing and calculated as: 1.5% of the aggregate consideration up to $200 million, plus 1% of the aggregate consideration between $200 million and $500 million, plus 0.75% of the aggregate consideration, if any, in excess of $500 million.
05/27/04	RCN Corp.	Blackstone Group L.P.	Restructuring fee of between $6 million and $8 million upon consummation of a restructuring and a 2% of transactions consideration fee, the sum of the two not exceeding $10.5 million.

EXHIBIT 4.4 (*Continued*)

Filing Date	Company	Firm to Be Hired	Bonus Potential
05/27/04	RCN Corp.	AP Services LLC	Contingent success fee: $5 million upon the completion of a restructuring, the sale of a majority of the company's assets, or confirmation of a plan prior to Sept. 15, 2004, or $4 million after Sept. 15 but before Feb. 15, or $3 million after Feb. 15, 2005.
06/04/04	Cornerstone Propane Partners LP	Greenhill & Co.	If a restructuring is consummated, transaction fee of $4.55 million less 50% of the monthly advisory fees received during the fourth through twelfth month of the firm's engagement.
06/15/04	Maxim Crane Works LLC	CIBC World Markets Corp.	If the company consummates a restructuring transaction (as defined in the agreement), the firm will be entitled to a cash restructuring transaction fee.

The bankruptcy amendments contained in the 2005 Bankruptcy Abuse Prevention and Consumer Protection Act (BAPCPA) cap the amount of time that a debtor has the exclusive right to propose a plan of reorganization and solicit votes at 20 months. This cap is representative of the average duration of a typical conventional Chapter 11 case, as shown in Exhibit 4.5. Although in theory this cap may reduce the duration of Chapter 11 cases, in practice cases may still be prolonged beyond the period of exclusivity by the introduction of competing plans by other constituents in the case. The jury is still out on whether the BAPCPA amendments will in fact reduce the duration of the average Chapter 11 case, even though it appears from the results in Exhibit 4.5 that the few cases post-BAPCPA have had shorter average duration.

Unlike attorneys, financial advisers' total compensation is less influenced by time since bonuslike fees often comprise an important proportion of their total remuneration. Most attempts at understanding, explaining, and/or predicting the professional costs of Chapter 11 cases treat these two categories of professionals as if they were one and the same. Since their compensation structures are so different, we focus on each of them separately.

EXHIBIT 4.5 Average and Median Duration of Chapter 11 Cases in Months, by Type of Filing, 1980–2007

| | | Pre-2005 BAPCPA | |
	Cases	Average	Median
Conventional	523	22	18
Prenegotiated	110	8	5
Prepackaged	63	2	2
		Post-2005 BAPCPA	
	Cases	Average	Median
Conventional	6	13	14
Prenegotiated	4	4	5
Prepackaged	2	2	2

TIME IN CHAPTER 11 AND NUMBER OF LEGAL FIRMS RETAINED

What are the reasons why some cases take longer to reach confirmation than others? Common sense points to the size of the case and/or its complexity as factors that may be associated with the amount of time that it takes to get a plan of reorganization proposed and confirmed.[2] The more complex the capital structure of a debtor, the more likely it is that it would take more time to sort out the conflicts between different classes of creditors and parties in interest and come up with a confirmable plan. We were surprised to find out that neither of these factors seems to have an effect on the duration of Chapter 11 cases.[3] Surprisingly, we found that the only factor that is statistically associated with the duration of a case is the number of professional firms retained by the various parties in the case (debtor, creditors' committee, etc.). We found a direct relationship between the number of firms retained and the duration of a Chapter 11 case. Moreover, when we separated the firms retained into those providing legal services and financial advisers, we found that the relationship remained strong but only for the number of law firms retained.

We have argued elsewhere[4] that even though most professionals undoubtedly do work in what they perceive to be their client's best interests, where questions exist as to whether to settle or be confrontational, the scale may tip toward prolonging cases. It turns out that a close examination of the data tends to support this view, which is the result of many years of experience in the field. Of course people could argue that the number of firms retained in a case is simply a proxy for its size and/or complexity. Again, we were surprised to find out that this was not the case, either. The number of firms retained had no relationship to the size of the debtor or the complexity of the debtor's capital structure as measured by the number of classes in its reorganization plan. The only factor that appeared to be associated with the number of professional firms retained was whether the case was filed as a conventional case or a preplanned one. Preplanned cases (prenegotiated and prepackaged) were found to retain fewer professional firms, and this was independent of their size and of the capital structure complexity of the debtors involved in those cases.

The preceding discussion suggests that the saying "A small town that cannot support a lawyer can support two" may be quite accurate when used to explain the length and legal costs of large Chapter 11 cases. The time a debtor stays in Chapter 11 appears to be a function of neither its size nor the complexity of its capital structure but a function of the number of legal firms retained on behalf of various claimants and parties in interest, and paid for by the estate.

DETERMINANTS OF LEGAL FEES AND EXPENSES

The amount of fees and expenses paid to law firms in a Chapter 11 case will be a function of the time a debtor stays in Chapter 11. In turn, as we discussed in the previous section, the time that a debtor stays in Chapter 11 will be, to a great extent, a function of the number of legal firms retained in the case. Retaining fewer legal firms is likely to reduce the amount of time that a debtor spends in bankruptcy. This result may follow because in retaining fewer legal firms debtors and creditors' committees are likely to retain larger firms, which may have the resources and the professionals that can handle numerous contested matters at once, thus reducing the amount of time that it takes to settle them.

However, the duration of a case is not the only determinant of the size of its legal bill. Two important factors adding to the bill are (1) the size of the debtor as measured by the book value of its assets and (2) the complexity of its capital structure as measured by the number of classes in the plan of reorganization. These two factors are likely to be related to the amount of effort or hours billed to the estate. The larger or more complex the debtor, the higher the likelihood that more hours will be billed to the estate per billing cycle. The effect of these two factors is independent of the number of legal firms retained in the case. The confluence of size, complexity, and duration of a case makes the size of the legal bill to the estate quite predictable.

DETERMINANTS OF FINANCIAL ADVISERS' FEES AND EXPENSES

Although financial advisers' compensation structure includes time-dependent fees (i.e., monthly fees), an analysis of the 48 cases that we study shows that their total remuneration is entirely unrelated to the time a debtor spends in Chapter 11. Moreover, their compensation is related to neither the size nor the complexity of the debtor's capital structure. All the factors that are strongly associated with fees and expenses paid to lawyers have no bearing on the amount paid to financial advisers. It is also worthwhile to note that financial advisers' total bill is much less predictable than that for attorneys, and given that they seem to consistently represent almost half of the fee pie, this maybe the area where most control should be exercised. The only factor strongly associated with the size of their bill to the estate is the number of financial adviser firms retained in the case. Unlike fees and expenses for attorneys, the costs of financial advisers are more difficult to predict.

CAN PROFESSIONAL COSTS BE EXCESSIVE?

Without the help of professionals, reorganizations would be extremely chaotic and expensive. On the one hand, professionals may reduce the feasibility of the debtor because they represent a cash drain on the estate. On the other hand, professionals may enhance feasibility by facilitating a recapitalization that makes the debtor more valuable as a going concern. On balance, professional services will be beneficial to the estate because the increased feasibility they help create more than outweighs the cost of their services. That said, more and more anecdotal evidence is coming in that professional costs can be excessive in some cases; that is, the cash drain on the estate does not contribute to increasing the feasibility of the debtor. In September 2003 the U.S. Trustee in the Fleming Companies, Inc. Chapter 11 case filed a report and objections to the pending fee applications of several of the professionals involved in that case. This filing prompted the issuance of an opinion by the bankruptcy judge in the case where the bankruptcy court found that two firms had rendered services that unnecessarily generated litigation and did not benefit the estate.[5] The court also found that the hourly rates of one of the firm's practitioners were higher than the hourly rates charged by similarly experienced attorneys in other practice areas within the same firm. To the extent possible, courts and the U.S. Trustee have explored approaches to the issue of fee review, including the appointment of fee examiners or fee review committees. Their focus, however, is not whether the benefits of professionals outweigh their costs but rather compliance with the bankruptcy code. Unsecured and undersecured creditors and parties in interest who are the ultimate payers of these fees and expenses focus more on increased feasibility and whether their recoveries will be enhanced when they assess whether professional costs are excessive. Models for predicting professional fees like those proposed by LoPucki and Doherty[6] or by the authors of this book may serve as benchmarks for what constitutes an expected amount of professional fees that will not detract from feasibility.

APPENDIX

Companies Used in Fee Study*

Alliance Entertainment Corp.	Leasing Solutions
American Banknote Corp.	Levitz Furniture, Inc.
APS Holding Corp.	Loewen Group International
Boston (Market) Chicken, Inc.	Medical Resources
Bradlees Inc.	Montgomery Ward Holding Corp.
Breed Technologies	Oxford Automotive
CellNet Data Systems, Inc.	Paging Network
Cityscape Financial Corp.	Pegasus Gold, Inc.
Comdisco, Inc.	Philip Services Corp.
ContiFinancial Corp.	Plaid Clothing Group, Inc.
Creditrust	Prime Succession, Inc.
Drug Emporium	Purina Mills, Inc.
Farm Fresh, Inc.	Salant Corp.
First Merchants Acceptance Corp.	Southern Pacific Funding Corp.
Fruit of the Loom	Stratosphere Corp.
Geneva Steel Co.	Sunterra Corp.
Golden Books Family Entertainment, Inc.	Talon Automotive Group
Grand Union	Trans World Airlines
Great Bay Hotel and Casino, Inc.	Unison Healthcare Corp.
Heartland Wireless Communications, Inc.	USInternetworking, Inc.
Home Holdings, Inc.	Venture Stores, Inc.
Imperial Sugar Co.	Vista Eyecare, Inc.
Kenetech Corp. (Windpower, Inc.)	Westbridge Capital Corp.
Key Plastics	Wireless One, Inc.

*The fee data was provided by Professor Lynn M. LoPucki.

5

Other Important Issues

MANAGEMENT COMPENSATION AND ENTRENCHMENT

Participants in any market, efficient or inefficient, will take advantage of the climate that exists in order to achieve returns that are the best reasonably achievable under the circumstances. The climate that exists in a Chapter 11 reorganization creates unusually good opportunities for managements of distressed companies to enjoy the benefits of very high compensation and very high degrees of retention, or the receipt of attractive termination packages if management is replaced:

- In Chapter 11, the debtor's management continues in place. It is relatively rare that a trustee or examiner is appointed.
- There is a need for speed in reorganization, especially in small cases where, if the company is not reorganized fast, expenses (especially for attorneys and investment bankers) will leave little or no assets for prepetition creditors.
- Key employee retention plans (KERPs), part of the 2005 Bankruptcy Abuse Prevention and Consumer Protection Act (BAPCPA) amendments, can easily be circumvented by, for example, incentive plans. Payoffs to departing Kmart executives are one example.

Management Continues in Place

As will be discussed in Chapter 9, after filing for Chapter 11 relief, management continues to operate the business under court supervision for activities outside the ordinary course of business. In theory, managements can be removed for cause (fraud, gross mismanagement) and replaced with a trustee, or can be supervised by an examiner. In practice this is rarely done. Section 1121 of the bankruptcy code gives the debtor in possession the exclusive right to propose a plan of reorganization for 120 days up to a maximum of 18 months, and since management to a large extent controls most companies, exclusivity gives management considerable advantages over creditors. The result is that managements can extract very large benefits from exclusivity, including entrenchment, compensation, and restrictions on newly issued securities. These benefits continue to exist notwithstanding the amendments brought about by the 2005 BAPCPA.

Need for Speed in Reorganizations

The need for speed in Chapter 11 reorganizations cannot be overemphasized. Since professional fees and expenses are mainly a function of time,[1] the longer a case is pending, the greater the expense borne by the estate directly and in reality by unsecured creditors and undersecured creditors. The reader is also reminded that these expenses are paid in cash on a pay-as-you-go basis, which seem to frequently give professionals the economic incentives to prolong cases. Many, if not most, cases are prolonged unnecessarily even though most professionals will work in what they perceive to be their client's best interest. In deciding what is in the client's best interest, whether to compromise with others or to be aggressive, the tilt is often in the direction that will enhance the professionals' compensation (i.e., prolonging cases).

The need for speedy reorganizations is particularly important for smaller companies (i.e., those with reorganization values of under $300 million), since in a protracted Chapter 11, professional fees and expenses will detract mightily from feasibility and recoveries by prepetition creditors.

Given the period of exclusivity, management and/or a control group can delay a reorganization and greatly affect prepetition creditors' recoveries. This is a very important source of leverage that management has over creditors.

Key Employee Retention Plans

One of the amendments contained in the 2005 BAPCPA is the one relating to key employee retention plans (KERPs). Prior to BAPCPA, debtors implemented KERPs that typically provided for key executives to get paid a bonus to remain with the debtor throughout its reorganization or liquidation on the presumption that these employees were vital to the success of the debtor's bankruptcy. The statutory basis for such plans was Section 363 of the bankruptcy code, which only required that debtors demonstrate that the plans represented the reasonable exercise of their business judgment. The BAPCPA amendments of 2005 introduced Section 503(c)(1), which makes it (in theory) more difficult to approve these plans. Mindful of the new requirements of Section 503(c)(1), debtors have structured their plans as incentive plans instead, which are not covered in Section 503.

While it is dangerous to overgeneralize, it should be recognized that if there exists any one group that does not deserve generous compensation, generous entrenchment, or generous severance, it is those managements of corporations that either couldn't or wouldn't pay their bills. Those are the companies that sought, and seek, Chapter 11 relief. The bankruptcy code as written is far from perfect and never can be made perfect. The Chapter 11 climate is such that managements of these companies enjoy benefits that do not exist for similarly situated companies in most foreign jurisdictions. Yet, net-net, Chapter 11 seems to be far more beneficial for the U.S. economy than are systems in other countries where money defaults result in the required appointment of a shadow trustee to supervise, or take control from, incumbent management forthwith.

Maybe Chapter 11 can be improved by requiring the appointment upon filing of a Chapter 11 trustee who will observe management and recommend after, say, a six-month observation period whether to leave management in place, appoint a permanent trustee, or appoint an examiner.[2]

TAX AND POLITICAL DISADVANTAGES

The distressed creditor seems to be a constituency without any political clout, either Democratic or Republican. There has been a 20-year trend toward disadvantaging secondary creditors, as evidenced by the creation of cancellation of debt (COD) income for issuers, which results in the reduction of tax attributes for the company initially, but could in a few instances actually result in a tax payable; by the creation of original issue discount (OID) for holders of publicly traded credits, which results in the holders having to recognize phantom taxable income; and by the elimination of the stock-for-debt exception for "hot and new creditors," which limits the ability of reorganized companies to utilize net operating losses (NOLs).

There are three determinations that both creditors and debtors need to make to assess the tax consequences resulting from debt exchanges and/or debt modifications: (1) whether COD income will be created[3] and recognized by the debtor; (2) whether gains, losses, or interest income will be recognized by the creditor; and (3) whether OID will be recognized by either the creditor or the debtor. The answers to these questions hinge on whether the exchange constitutes a tax-free recapitalization or a taxable exchange, and whether the original debt is recourse or nonrecourse. Although it is beyond the scope of this book to thoroughly discuss the almost infinite and complex tax issues that arise in particular cases, we focus on some of the issues involved in tax-free recapitalizations, which are those most likely to be faced by purchasers of debt deemed securities for tax purposes.

Under IRC Sections 368(a)(1)(E) and 354 the exchange of new debt for old debt pursuant to a plan of reorganization is a tax-free recapitalization if both the new debt and the old debt are securities. Whether a debt instrument is a security for tax purposes is an inherently factual determination, but a useful rule of thumb is that debt instruments with original maturities of ten years or more tend to be viewed as securities for tax purposes.

Cancellation of Indebtedness Income

Cancellation of debt (COD) income arises where debt of the corporation is canceled or discharged for less that its adjusted issue price (usually its principal amount plus or less any unamortized premium or discount). The amount of COD generally equals the excess of the adjusted issue price over the consideration paid in the exchange, which could consist of cash (rarely), the market price of newly issued common stock, and the market price (or fair value) of newly issued debt instruments.[4]

Before the passage of the Revenue Reconciliation Act of 1990, IRC Section 1275(a)(4) provided a limitation on the creation of new OID in reorganization exchanges. This had the effect of eliminating the creation of COD income in debt exchanges. After the repeal of Section 1275(a)(4), debtors have to structure debt exchanges to minimize the creation of COD instead.

The tax treatment of COD is codified in IRC Section 108, which provides one set of treatments for taxpayers who are in bankruptcy or insolvent, and a very different one for those who are solvent. IRC Section 108(a)(1)(A) provides for an exclusion of COD income where the corporation discharges the debt in a bankruptcy case. The offset to this exclusion is provided by Section 108(b)(1), which requires the insolvent or bankrupt corporation to reduce various tax attributes by the amount of COD excluded from income after calculating its tax for the taxable year. There are two choices for reducing the tax attributes. The corporation can either opt to reduce the tax attributes in accordance with the order of reduction provided by Section 108(b)(2)—NOLs, general business credits, minimum tax credits, capital loss carryover, basis in the corporation's property, passive activity losses, passive activity credits, and foreign tax credits—or, alternatively, opt to reduce first its basis in its depreciable property pursuant to the election provided by Section 108(b)(5). Either way, whereas pre-1990 debtors did not create COD income, post-1990 they do, and even though COD income is excluded under bankruptcy, the exclusion is offset by what could be significant reductions in the debtor's tax attributes.

Original Issue Discount

The repeal of IRC Section 1275(a)(4) in 1990 removed the limitation on the creation of new original issue discount (OID) in reorganization exchanges. As a result, larger amounts of OID income can currently be created in debt exchanges. In a tax-free recapitalization, an exchanging bondholder will not recognize any gain or loss, except to the extent that the bondholder receives boot (i.e., cash or any other property received other than stock or a security of the debtor) and any excess of the adjusted issue price of the new debt over and above the adjusted issue price of the old debt security. However, in cases where the debt exchange is not a tax-free recapitalization, including voluntary exchanges, OID income is taxable.

OID is the most pernicious form of taxation: (1) the taxpayer pays tax at the maximum rate, (2) the taxpayer has no control over when the tax becomes payable (versus, for example, realizing capital gains); and (3) the event that gives rise to the tax OID does not also give rise to the cash with which to pay the tax.

Stock-for-Debt Exception

The stock-for-debt exception was the single most important exception to the creation of COD income before it was repealed in 1993. Before then, a debtor could issue stock in exchange for its old debt and not recognize any gain or loss as a result of the exchange. This exception was confined to debtors in bankruptcy or insolvent (to the extent that they were not rendered solvent by the exchange).

Today, the issuance by a debtor of stock in exchange for its debt will create COD income to the extent that the fair market value of the stock issued is less than the adjusted issue price of the old debt. Although COD income is excluded in tax-free recapitalizations, the required offsets can impair or even destroy a debtor's net operating losses (NOLs) and other tax attributes.

Preservation of Net Operating Losses

Companies attempting to reorganize in Chapter 11 by reworking their capital structure will try to preserve their NOLs as much as possible to reduce the future tax liabilities of the reorganized entity. The amount of NOLs that can be preserved by a debtor in bankruptcy will depend on how the debt is restructured and on how such restructuring affects its stock ownership.

As discussed in a previous section of this chapter, the way the debt restructuring is accomplished will affect the amount of COD income created, and this in turn will reduce important tax attributes including the debtor's

NOLs. A further attack on the preservation of NOLs is IRC Section 382 limitations that limit the annual amount of income generated by the new entity against which the NOLs can be used. This limitation is triggered upon an ownership change, which is a change of more than 50 percentage points in ownership of the value of the stock of the loss corporation[5] within a three-year period. The annual amount of income against which NOLs can be applied is limited to the product of the fair market value of the stock of the loss corporation prior to ownership change and the long-term tax-exempt bond rate.

IRC Section 382(5) provides an exception to the limitation if three conditions are met:

1. The loss corporation is in bankruptcy.
2. The shareholders and creditors of the old loss corporation own 50 percent of the stock of the reorganized debtor.
3. The stock transferred to a creditor shall be taken into account in the calculation only to the extent such stock is transferred in satisfaction of indebtedness and only if such indebtedness was held by the creditor at least 18 months before the date of the filing for bankruptcy ("old and cold"), or arose in the ordinary course of business.

The exception provided by IRC Section 382(5) allows a reorganized debtor to preserve its ability to use the NOLs after an ownership change that takes place as part of a plan of reorganization. However, if the company experiences another ownership change or it does not continue its business enterprise at all times during a two-year period after the ownership change, the corporation's NOLs are subject to complete disallowance.

These rules in general and the change in ownership rule in particular place a burden on the debtor that wants to keep its NOLs, and adds substantial risks to the noncontrol holder of common stock as a result of a plan of reorganization. The debtor needs to monitor the identity of its creditors and shareholders, and must seek court approval of procedures to restrict claims and equity trading if it wants to protect its NOLs. NOL preservation motions are becoming commonplace in Chapter 11 cases. These restrictions can deprive noncontrol holders of non-dividend-paying common stocks of a market out. Preserving NOLs is a bad idea: By preventing trading versus giving noncontrol claimants and parties in interest opportunities for a cash bailout by a sale to market, it gives rise to conflicts of interest between the corporation on the one hand and its noncontrol securities holders on the other. The noncontrol shareholders need a market out if, as a practical matter, they receive in a reorganization non-dividend-paying common stock.

6

The Five Basic Truths of Distress Investing

Distress investing is different from what most academic theorists and common stock investors are used to. Distress investing involves being a special sort of creditor. In contrast, modern capital theory (MCT), the principal academic discipline, looks at investing from the point of view of either the outside passive minority investor (OPMI) in common stocks or the common stockholder consolidated with the company itself. Both approaches clearly are irrelevant for distress investing, though many MCT concepts are very helpful—for example, an expanded view of the concept of net present value (NPV).

Most common stock investing involves trying to predict near-term market prices in most situations even where there are no reasonably determinate workouts. Weight to market is minimal in distress investing. Most credit analysis revolves around trying to predict whether there will be a money default. In distress investing we assume that there is some probability that there will be a money default. Distress investment analysis bottoms on figuring out what happens next, that is, after a money default occurs. Some senior creditors will be reinstated, and perhaps never even miss a contracted-for cash payment for interest, principal, or premium; some creditors will participate in a reorganization and receive a new package of securities (and maybe even some cash) in satisfaction of their claims; and some junior creditors and stockholders will be wiped out, receiving no value in the reorganization. Sometimes a company will be liquidated pursuant to Chapter 7 or a Chapter 11 liquidation plan. Proceeds from a liquidation will be distributed to claimants and parties in interest in accordance with the rule of absolute priority; that is, a senior class is to be repaid in full before anything is paid to a junior class. In distress investing, Chapter 11 is not an ending; rather, it is a beginning.

TRUTH 1: NO ONE CAN TAKE AWAY A CORPORATE CREDITOR'S RIGHT TO A MONEY PAYMENT OUTSIDE OF CHAPTER 11 OR CHAPTER 7

Outside of a court proceeding, usually Chapter 11, no one can take away a corporate creditor's right to a money payment for interest, principal, or premium unless that individual creditor so consents. Ignorance of this basic rule seemed evident in the airline bailout in the fall of 2001, which, among other things, was approved by a 96-to-1 vote in the U.S. Senate. Cash payments of $5 billion were made to the airlines, of which well over $2 billion was used in the subsequent 12 months to pay cash interest on already outstanding airline indebtedness. None of the funds dedicated to interest payments were used to enhance the efficiency or security of airline operations. Put otherwise, the bailout seemed to be a bailout of airline creditors in great part, rather than a bailout of the airlines.

What does it mean for a distress investor?

If a company is going to avoid Chapter 11, credit instruments with a short term to maturity give the distress investor de facto seniority. If a company is to be granted Chapter 11 relief, seniority of credit instruments will lie in their covenants and intercreditor agreements, and maturity dates for unsecured lenders become irrelevant. The authors took advantage of the right to money payments by acquiring General Motors Acceptance Corporation (GMAC) senior unsecured notes in late October 2008. The relevant data were:

- GMAC $7^3/_4$ senior unsecured notes, maturing 1/19/2010
- Amount issued: $2,500,000,000
- Current price: $62.00
- Yield to maturity (YTM): 53.42%
- Current yield (CY): 12.50%

Denied access to capital markets to refinance maturing obligations, the GMAC business was effectively in runoff in October 2008. GMAC had three types of assets that could be convertible to cash to meet maturing obligations:

1. Receivables and leases.
2. A 100 percent interest in a profitable property and casualty (P&C) insurance company that earned $400 million to $600 million per year and was probably worth a sizable premium over book value.

3. A one-third stock interest in GMAC Bank, much of whose assets might be in residential mortgages.

The three questions that a distress investor is likely to ask are:

1. Will the $7^3/_4$ notes remain performing loans?
2. Will the $7^3/_4$ notes participate in a Chapter 11 reorganization?
3. Will there be a voluntary exchange offer for the $7^3/_4$ notes run by Cerberus L.P., the principal owner of 51 percent of GMAC common stock?

Whether or not the $7^3/_4$ notes would remain a performing loan seemed to depend a lot on what the loss experience would be on the runoff of the receivables and lease portfolios. The authors did not know, but guessed there was a 70 percent to 75 percent probability that the runoff would be profitable enough to keep the $7^3/_4$ notes a performing loan through maturity. If this happened, the key performance measure for the distress investor would be yield to maturity (YTM) of 53.42 percent.

If the $7^3/_4$ notes were to participate in a Chapter 11 reorganization—a 25 percent to 30 percent probability, say—the investor would receive upon reorganization a new package of securities, probably including common stock, in what ought to become a conservatively financed finance company. Here the distress investor measures his return by the dollar price paid for the $7^3/_4$ notes and the workout value of the securities to be received in a reorganization (see Kmart case, Chapter 16 in this volume). Our guess was that such a workout value could be in a range of $60 to $90, but it was only a stab in the dark.

Cerberus could try a voluntary exchange offer for various GMAC senior unsecured notes, including the $7^3/_4$s. The exchange offer would probably propose that the $7^3/_4$s accept a new package of securities with stretched-out maturity dates that would have an expected market value of, say, $80 to $85. There was no way that such an exchange offer would be accepted by most holders of the $7^3/_4$s unless the holders could be shown some meaningful downside if they did not exchange. The one downside that we could think of that might have encouraged acceptances was that if an insufficient number of $7^3/_4$s were tendered, GMAC could file for Chapter 11 relief. Such a scenario seemed very unlikely. Cerberus, a GMAC stockholder, was not going to want to commit suicide, or even take a suicide risk, knowing what could happen to GMAC common stock in a Chapter 11 reorganization.

This requirement to pay cash in the absence of Chapter 11 relief will be the case as long as that creditor is a beneficiary of either U.S. securities law or the terms contained in virtually all bond indentures and loan agreements.

These rights to money payments for most publicly traded debt instruments exist because of the provisions of Section 316 of the Trust Indenture Act of 1939 (TIA), the provisions of the typical indenture issued for publicly traded bonds, and the provisions of typical loan agreements protecting institutional lenders such as commercial banks. Section 316(b) states in relevant part:

> Notwithstanding any other provision of the indenture to be qualified, the right of any holder of any indenture security to receive payment of the principal of and interest on such indenture security, on or after the respective due dates expressed in such indenture security, or to institute suit for the enforcement of any such payment on or after such respective dates, shall not be impaired or effected without the consent of such holder.

The TIA contains two exceptions to this right to payment, both of which seem minor.

The first exception is contained in Section 316(a)(2):

> The indenture to be qualified may contain provisions authorizing holders (except those known to the indenture trustee to be the debt issuer or insiders of the debt issuer) of not less than 75 percent in principal amount of the indenture securities or if expressly specified in such indenture, of any series of securities at the time outstanding to consent on behalf of the holders of all such indenture securities to the postponement of any interest payment for a period not exceeding three years from its due date.

The second exception is contained in the latter part of Section 316(b) of the TIA:

> [S]uch indenture may contain provisions limiting or denying the right of any such holder to institute any such suit, if and to the extent that the institution or prosecution thereof or the entry of judgment therein would, under applicable law, result in the surrender, impairment, waiver, or loss of the lien of such indenture upon any property subject to such lien.

A corporate issuer is required to comply with the TIA if $10,000,000 or more principal amount of debt instruments is to be marketed publicly by the issuer over a 36-month time span (Section 304(a)(9)). The TIA protection in the United States against depriving a creditor of rights to interest and principal payments does not necessarily apply in other jurisdictions, such as Canada.

The indenture for Home Products International, Inc. $9^5/_8$ percent senior subordinated notes is typical for credit instruments complying with the TIA.[1] Relevant language in the Home Products indenture follows:

> *Section 9.2. Amendments with consent of Holders: The Company, the Subsidiary Guarantors and the Trustee may amend this Indenture or the Securities without notice to any Security holder but with the written consent of the Holders of at least a majority in principal amount of the Securities. However, without the consent of each Security holder affected, an amendment may not:*
>
> *(1) reduce the amount of Securities whose Holders must consent to an amendment;*
> *(2) reduce the rate or extend the time for payment of interest of any Security;*
> *(3) reduce the principal of or extend the Stated Maturity of any Security;*
> *(4) reduce the premium payable upon the redemption or repurchase of any Security or change the time at which any Security shall be redeemed or repurchased in accordance with this Indenture;*
> *(5) make any Security payable in money other than that stated in the Security;*
> *(6) impair the right of any Holder to receive payment of principal of and interest on such Holder's Securities on and after the due dates therefore or to institute suit for the enforcement of any payment on or with respect to such Holder's Securities;*
> *(7) make any change to the amendment provisions which require each Holder's consent or to the waiver provisions.*

Typical language contained in a loan agreement for debt syndicated among commercial banks is contained in a 1996–1997 "Credit Agreement among Safelite Glass Corp., Various Lending Institutions and the Chase Manhattan Bank as Administrative Agent" and follows in "Section 12.12 Amendment or Waiver; etc.":

> *(a) Neither this Agreement nor any other Credit Document nor any terms hereof or thereof may be changed, waived, discharged or terminated unless such change, waiver, discharge or termination is in writing signed by the respective Credit Parties party thereto and the Required Banks, provided that no such change, waiver, discharge*

> *or termination shall, without the consent of each Bank (other than*
> *a Defaulting Bank) with Obligations being directly affected thereby*
> *in the case of the following clause (i), (i) extend the final sched-*
> *uled maturity of any Loan or Note or extend the stated maturity*
> *of any Letter of Credit beyond the Revolving Loan Maturity Date,*
> *or reduce the rate or extend the time of payment of interest or Fees*
> *thereon, or reduce the principal amount thereof, or amend, modify*
> *or waive any provision of this Section 12.12.*

This inability in the United States for anyone outside of a court proceeding to take away a creditor's right to a money payment unless the individual creditor consents is extremely important both to corporate managements and to creditors.

TRUTH 2: CHAPTER 11 RULES INFLUENCE ALL REORGANIZATIONS

In the reorganization of any publicly traded issuer, whether that reorganization takes place out of court or in Chapter 11, the rules governing a Chapter 11 reorganization will influence heavily the actual reorganization that eventually takes place. These rules include the "rule of absolute priority" and the "period of exclusivity" during which the debtor is the only party who can propose a plan of reorganization (POR).

If a financially troubled company, especially a large company with publicly traded securities, is required to recapitalize, it will have three choices:

1. **Voluntary exchanges.** The company may seek to exchange new and more liberalized securities for the outstanding securities. In connection with these voluntary exchange offers, the company frequently will seek consents from each creditor or security holder to delete or amend restrictive covenants in the indentures or agreements under which the instruments were issued. Exchange offers and consent solicitations rarely work satisfactorily. Exchange offers frequently fail because they are premised on the often fallacious assumption that creditors will accept an instrument with more immediate market value (as opposed to inherent or potential value) in exchange for outstanding debt securities that have a currently depressed market value (see earlier GMAC example). The one factor that frequently induces creditors to agree to voluntary exchanges is to show the creditors that there is a significant downside risk for them if they do not participate in the offer. This can often be made to be the case if exchanged debt instruments are granted se-

niority over nonexchanging debt instruments. Even if an original bond indenture prohibits the issuance of senior debt, that provision can be abrogated by the consent of the requisite amount of bonds: in the case of Home Products International, "the written consent of the Holders of at least a majority in principal amount of the Securities" (Section 9.2 of the indenture). Agreeing to the exchange offer can constitute a written consent.

2. **Conventional Chapter 11.** The company may first file a bankruptcy petition under the Bankruptcy Reform Act of 1978 (Chapter 11, Title 11 of the U.S. Code) and then attempt to recapitalize by soliciting acceptances of a plan of reorganization. This conventional approach to bankruptcy in most situations entails considerable risk and uncertainty for the company and its management. In a Chapter 11 bankruptcy, each of the company's creditors and stockholders is a party to the proceeding with standing to object to any and all transactions outside the ordinary course of business. These creditors and stockholders are represented by official committees having significant voice in the administration of the bankruptcy and are generally well represented by active and aggressive attorneys, accountants, and investment bankers. Each of these parties in interest will likely press its own agenda. In addition, the company will end up funding huge administrative expenses because it will be required to pay the fees and expenses of not only its own attorneys, accountants, and investment bankers, but also the attorneys, accountants, investment bankers, and other agents for various claimants and parties in interest. This tends to be the case whether the reorganization takes place in Chapter 11 or via voluntary out-of-court exchanges.

3. **Prepackaged of functionally equivalent filings.** Pursuant to Section 1126(b) of the bankruptcy code, the company may solicit requisite consents to its bankruptcy reorganization plan *before* filing for Chapter 11 relief. Such solicitations commenced prior to filing for Chapter 11 relief may now continue past the filing date based on the 2005 BAPCPA. If such consents are obtained, the company then will file for Chapter 11 for the limited purpose of getting the plan of reorganization confirmed by a bankruptcy court. Obtaining consents prior to filing for a Chapter 11 relief dramatically reduces the uncertainty, risk, and expense involved when a company attempts to recapitalize. Prepackaged bankruptcy reorganization is the ideal method for recapitalizing certain types of public companies. Good candidates are those troubled companies with relatively stable and predictable sources of operating income from core businesses and those with fairly simple capitalizations involving conventional debt and only small amounts of contingent liabilities.

Whether the company being recapitalized is healthy or financially troubled, the techniques used to recapitalize have to be either voluntary or mandatory. Voluntary techniques (such as exchange offers) are those where each security holder will make an independent decision whether to accept the offered recapitalization. If the security holder does not elect to accept the voluntary offer, there will be no change to the entitlements to interest and principal in accordance with the terms of his or her instrument. Mandatory techniques (such as freeze-out mergers in the case of healthy companies, and Chapter 11 bankruptcies in the case of financially troubled companies) involve a compulsory change to the instruments of dissenting security holders if the required threshold of acceptances is received. Mandatory techniques almost always entail use of the voting process and proxy machinery, which machinery is almost always within the absolute control of management when a healthy company is involved, but is rarely within the absolute control of management when a troubled company is involved.

Reorganization of a troubled company, whether through the voluntary exchange of securities or through relief under Chapter 11, involves, in the final analysis, recapitalizing a company. Successful recapitalizations invariably involve reducing, delaying, or eliminating contractual requirements that the company make cash interest or principal payments. Healthy companies also reorganize (i.e., recapitalize), even though such reorganizations/recapitalizations almost always involve increasing as opposed to reducing the company's obligations to make cash payments to creditors. Recapitalizations of healthy companies go under such names as leveraged buyout, management buyout, cash-out merger, purchase, and going private.

TRUTH 3: SUBSTANTIVE CHARACTERISTICS OF SECURITIES

John Burr Williams, an eminent economist, wrote in 1938, "Investment value is the present worth of the future dividends in the case of a common stock, or of the future coupons or principal in the case of a bond." Williams had it wrong in terms of analyzing distressed situations. Here, investment value is the present worth of a future cash bailout, whatever the source of that cash bailout.

A security gives a holder either rights to cash payments by a company or ownership rights in that company, present or potential. If the promise of cash pay as scheduled is legally enforceable, the security is a debt obligation or credit instrument. If the promise of cash pay as scheduled is not a legally enforceable right except in very limited circumstances (e.g., neither the declaration of a common stock dividend or repurchases of outstanding common stock can be made unless cash payments are first paid to a security with seniority over the common stock), the security is a preferred stock. If the security combines the promise of cash pay with ownership rights—present or potential—the security is a hybrid, either a convertible debt or convertible preferred, or a unit consisting of a credit instrument or preferred stock and detachable or nondetachable warrants or common stock. A security with ownership rights but no contractual or legal rights to receive cash pay is a common stock.

For a security to have value, it has to have the promise of delivering a cash bailout to a holder. Cash bailouts come from three disparate sources:

1. Payments by the company, whether for interest, principal, premium, dividends, or share repurchases.
2. Potential sale to some sort of a market, not just an outside passive minority investor (OPMI)—a market such as the New York Stock Exchange, but also other markets, such as takeover markets.
3. Control or elements of control of the company. Common stocks without economic value can sometimes have a governance value.

A common stock that does not pay a dividend has value to a holder only if it provides either a market-out or elements of control (also, but rarely, nuisance value). Many if not most recipients of common stocks upon the consummation of a plan of reorganization (POR) are passive rather than control investors. For example, commercial banks and insurance companies by definition are noncontrol investors. Frequently, they are required to take common stock in a POR, as was the case in the 1985 reorganization of Anglo Energy when they received 75 percent of the new Anglo common stock. Rule 1145 of the bankruptcy code prevents persons getting 5 percent or more of the common stock to be outstanding from selling those shares in public markets unless they are held, fully paid, for one year, after which common shares can be dribbled out weekly at the greater of 15 percent of the daily volume or 1 percent of the outstanding issue. Regulators and others promulgate Rule 1145 and others like it (SEC Rule 144) because they fear share price declines in common stock markets if blocks of common stock are dumped. This fear factor seems much worse in Japan than in the United States, where large amounts of cross-holdings, especially common stocks held by commercial banks, are frequently restricted from being sold in the open market. This seems mistaken policy. It is much more important to have PORs become feasible by giving noncontrol shareholders easy market-outs so that they become willing recipients of common stocks in PORs than it is to provide price supports for OPMI stock markets, which are bound to price securities capriciously in any event.

A disconcerting development revolves around bankruptcy court rulings that prohibit sales by creditors who are likely to receive common stocks in a reorganization in order to permit companies to preserve the value of net operating losses that would be compromised if, for purposes of Section 382 of the Internal Revenue Code, there were to be a change of ownership. One example is the 1994 Phar-Mor Chapter 11 case heard in the Northern District of Ohio. For noncontrol shareholders owning non-cash-pay securities, those securities have little or no value unless the security holder is provided with a market-out sooner or later, preferably sooner.

Control securities are a different commodity from passive securities from an economic point of view even though they are indistinguishable in legal form. As an example, a security with no apparent value to a holder would be a nonmarketable, non-dividend-paying, minority-interest common stock where the holder has no nuisance potential. A similar situation where there is apparent value to a holder is that of a security that is a deeply underwater common stock where the holder is the debtor in possession (DIP) enjoying the period of exclusivity in a Chapter 11 case—a governance value even where there is no economic value.

TRUTH 4: RESTRUCTURINGS ARE COSTLY FOR CREDITORS

The creditors of a distressed company are going to be ripped off by investment bankers, lawyers, and managements, whether the reorganization or liquidation process takes place out of court or in Chapter 11 or Chapter 7. Unlike common stock investing for control, when a company is distressed it is likely to pick up all the professional expenses for attorneys, accountants, investment bankers, and appraisers incurred by dominant creditors, whether the company is reorganized in Chapter 11 or out of court or it is liquidated under either Chapter 11 or Chapter 7; see Chapter 4 in this volume.

Academic finance is way off base in attempting to measure the direct and indirect costs for a troubled company for professionals, particularly attorneys and investment bankers—the so-called direct costs of distress. In lead articles, including "Bankruptcy Resolution" by Lawrence A. Weiss (*Journal of Financial Economics* 27, 1990), it has been estimated that in Chapter 11 reorganizations direct costs average 3.1 percent of the book value of debt plus the market value of equity, with book value measured as of the end of the fiscal year before a filing for Chapter 11 relief. Two things are terribly wrong with this approach. First, as a percentage of asset value, asset value has to be measured, not as of the date before filing, but as of the date of confirmation of a POR. Such asset value would be either reorganization value or market prices immediately after confirmation. More important, though, is the failure of academics to realize that these professional fees and expenses are administrative expenses, virtually always paid in cash and always the beneficiary of a super-priority giving them precedence over prepetition debt. Thus, it is most meaningful to examine professional fees as a percentage of the cash in the distressed company at the time of reorganization.

Professional costs are highly burdensome in the reorganization of troubled issuers either in court or out of court. The debtor normally picks up the professional expenses of each creditor constituency, except the U.S. government. Those claiming these costs are not burdensome know not whereof they speak. The expenses are so large that it has become uneconomic to be involved in small Chapter 11 cases unless they are done pursuant to a prepackaged (or equivalent) plan.

In trying to measure the indirect costs of Chapter 11, it is important to add back its four benefits:

1. No requirement to pay interest to unsecured creditors during the pendency of a case, and probably not as part of a POR.
2. Debtor better able to take advantage of benefits under the U.S. tax code if reorganized in Chapter 11 rather than out of court.
3. The automatic stay during the pendency of a case.
4. The availability of postpetition DIP financing, because postpetition lenders obtain super-priority as an administrative expense.

TRUTH 5: CREDITORS HAVE ONLY CONTRACTUAL RIGHTS

A creditor has only contractual rights, not residual rights. Residual rights belong to owners (e.g., a duty of directors for fair dealing in relationships with owners). The law is well settled for solvent companies. The beneficiaries of duties of care and fair dealings by boards of directors and other control persons flow directly to the owners of firms. Lenders to solvent firms are entitled only to those rights that are spelled out in loan agreements and bond indentures, plus several other rights provided by law. Specifically, lenders obtain protection under statutes governing fraudulent conveyance and fraudulent transfers. But the lender to a solvent corporation has no residual rights (e.g., to be the beneficiaries of duties of care and fair dealing by the people running companies). These benefits belong to the business itself and specifically to business owners.

When a corporation enters into a zone of insolvency, most commentators agree that there tends to occur a shift in the duties of boards of directors from protecting the interests of owners to protecting the interests of creditors. This is somewhat vague since there is difficulty in defining exactly what a zone of insolvency is. When actually insolvent, the role of the board of directors shifts from protecting the interests of owners to protecting the interests of creditors.

Two

Restructuring Troubled Issuers

7

Voluntary Exchanges

The contractual right to a money payment, which can't be abridged except with either the individual creditor's consent or relief from a court of competent jurisdiction, has all sorts of ramifications, including:

- The right to a money payment makes it harder for voluntary exchange offers to succeed, since they create the holdout problem; that is, creditors will not exchange their instruments in anticipation of becoming credit enhanced if the exchange succeeds without their participation.
- It gives issuers and managements who wish to avoid acceleration, Chapter 11, or Chapter 7, very strong incentives to continue to pay cash service in accordance with contractual requirements (see GMAC analysis in Chapter 6).
- It gives issuers an incentive to try to market new issues of debt with provisions that do not require cash service in short-term periods, including:
  - Toggle switches (i.e., a contractual provision that gives the debtor the option to pay interest either in cash or by issuing more debt). For example, in May 2008, Momentive Performance Materials Inc., a supplier of specialty materials, disclosed that it planned to make an upcoming interest payment on $300 million of its bonds with additional debt instead of cash. This is an example of a payment-in-kind (PIK) toggle bond.
  - Options to repay principal by issuing common stock (Enron).
  - Options to issue zero coupon bonds, or almost a zero coupon bond (MBIA Insurance 14 percent surplus notes).
- A company cannot prime existing lenders (i.e., have their collateral subordinated to the DIP lender in a voluntary exchange) without the existing lenders' contractual consents, whereas in Chapter 11, the debtor can get postpetition financing through DIP loans and trade financing, both of which can have super-priority. Secured prepetition lenders also

may be primed if the prepetition secured lender has been determined to have adequate protection.

PROBLEMS WITH VOLUNTARY EXCHANGES

Voluntary methods for the recapitalization of troubled companies are attempted prior to a Chapter 11 filing. These voluntary methods usually involve offers to current holders to trade their existing securities or debt instruments for new instruments, usually with a lower principal amount (typically set at a meaningful premium over the current market price) and with less onerous cash service requirements. Exchange offers often seek forbearance on defaulted cash service to creditors, hoping that no creditor group forecloses on collateral, accelerates the debt, or files an involuntary Chapter 11 or Chapter 7 bankruptcy petition. Occasionally, there are offers to buy out creditors for cash with the consideration representing a substantial discount from the face value of the claim but at a premium over the then current market value. For example, the Petro-Lewis Corporation and First City Bancshares transactions involved cash offers to public bondholders.

The biggest problem with the exchange offers is their voluntary aspect. As explained in the previous chapter, no creditor in the United States can ever be forced to give up rights to cash interest or principal payments outside of a Chapter 11 case or a similar state proceeding. The list is large and growing of companies that have experienced difficult and lengthy exchange offers or were totally unsuccessful in effecting recapitalizations through voluntary exchange offers. Exchange offers frequently fail when troubled companies seek exchanges for 80 percent or more of outstanding debt issues. Issuers unable to achieve their objectives of drastically reducing cash service to existing creditors through voluntary exchanges have included, inter alia, Mirant Corporation, Coleco, Petro-Lewis Corporation, Western Union, First City Bancorp, and Public Service Company of New Hampshire.

It is now obvious that, in reality, voluntary exchange offers often do not work. Proponents of exchange offers frequently fail to understand how difficult it is to induce voluntary exchanges when the debt instruments are publicly traded and the market prices of these credit instruments are at a substantial discount from their principal amount. There often are misconceptions by management as to the uses and limitations of Chapter 11, especially involving prepackaged bankruptcy reorganization.

Put simply, when there is a voluntary exchange, creditors know two things: (1) They cannot be forced to give up their contractual rights to money payments, and (2) if they refuse to tender their securities and then become holdouts, the chances are that the market value of the nontendered securities will increase dramatically if other creditors accept the voluntary exchange offer and the troubled company elects to consummate same. This is true because the creditworthiness of the instrument will be improved after the voluntary exchange is completed and the company's debt service requirements are materially lessened. For voluntary exchanges to succeed, they must show the creditor that there will be a meaningful downside for the creditor failing to exchange. Sometimes the downside resides in, in effect, making nonexchanging debt junior to exchanging debt. Sometimes the downside is to announce that Chapter 11 relief will be sought if the voluntary exchange is unsuccessful. In most cases, the threat of Chapter 11 will not scare most creditors. As a result, public bondholders seem to be a different breed of animal than public stockholders when it comes to voluntary exchanges. Offer public stockholders a premium over the market price and they may stampede to exchange. Not so for creditors, especially if the issuer cannot show the creditors meaningful risks if the creditors do not exchange. It is also true that many of the holders of large positions in the debt of troubled companies are secondary market purchasers, not the original purchasers of the debt. Professional vulture investors in these troubled securities are not likely to rush to accept voluntary exchange offers.

Issuers will invariably attempt to coerce creditors in a voluntary exchange by seeking nonmonetary consents or amendments to the indentures or agreements under which the outstanding debt instruments were issued. These amendments or consents usually are structured so that nonexchanging creditors will have their collateral invaded or their seniority reduced if the exchange offer succeeds. Exchange offers were structured this way by the advisers to AES Corporation, Petro-Lewis Corporation, and Public Service Company of New Hampshire.

THE HOLDOUT PROBLEM ILLUSTRATED

Any exchange of securities as part of a plan to aid distressed companies has to be viewed as a credit enhancement of the distressed company. There are two forms of seniority for distressed instruments:

1. Contractual (i.e., security agreements and covenants providing security and seniority).
2. Time to maturity (an earlier maturity date gives that debt instrument de facto seniority in the absence of a money default).

Without showing downside for nonexchanging bondholders, it is almost impossible in a voluntary exchange of public bonds to have most bondholders exchange. This is so because without de facto subordination, a nonexchanging bondholder will be credit enhanced by not exchanging. For example:

- Company XYZ has outstanding $100 million of 6 percent unsecured 10-year debentures selling at 60.
- Exchange offer requiring 90 percent acceptance, issue of $85 million (if 100 percent acceptance) of 7 percent coupon, 12-year bonds that are payment in kind (PIK) for the first five years. Estimated market price of 72 to 73.

Despite the improved market price, the exchange offer seems bound to fail to achieve 90 percent acceptance. Holdouts know that if the exchange offer succeeds, the issuer will be credit enhanced because there is no longer a need to pay cash interest on the 6 percent bonds, and there are no cash payments on the PIKs for five years. The nontendered bonds are likely to sell at around 80, or a yield to maturity of 9.09 percent.

MAKING A VOLUNTARY EXCHANGE WORK

The only way to make a voluntary exchange work is by showing downside to the nonexchanging bondholder. One way to achieve such downside is to amend the indenture of the bond so that the nonexchanging holders will become junior to the new bonds. In our example, the exchanging bondholder will consent as part of the exchange to amend the 6 percent indenture so that the 6 percent bonds become subordinated to the 7 percent new PIK bonds. This is a feasible solution since nonmoney provisions of indentures can be amended by the consent (or vote) of 50 percent or more of the outstanding issue in the case of most, but not all, publicly traded bonds.

The second way to show downside to nonexchanging bondholders is to shorten the maturity of the new 7 percent PIKs so that they are paid off before the 6 percent bond—say, have the 7 percent PIKs mature in nine years and six months. This gives exchanging bondholders de facto priority over the nonexchanging ones.

In today's market, bondholders usually place great premiums on issuers that are going to continue to pay in cash for performing loans. This is understandable for most creditors where asset management is first and foremost a function of liability management. If liabilities have to be serviced in cash (e.g., time deposits at banks or insurance claims at insurance companies), appropriate management seeks out cash-pay assets (i.e., performing loans). For distressed investors who don't need periodic cash return, however, there are great investment opportunities in bonds that will be the equivalent of zero coupon bonds, or almost zero coupon. These exist where, after thorough analysis, the analyst is convinced that if the loan ceases to be a performing credit, upon reorganization the issue will be paid off at its principal amount plus accrued but unpaid interest and most frequently interest on interest.

As was described in Chapter 3, USG Corporation and its subsidiaries filed for Chapter 11 in 2001 to manage USG's litigation costs, not because it needed to either restructure or manage a liquidity crisis. From the beginning, USG was determined to preserve value for its common stock, and to do so it had to obtain the affirmative vote for a plan of reorganization from each class of creditors who would participate in a reorganization by the requisite majorities of two-thirds in amount and one-half in number of those voting. The only impaired class of claims in USG's reorganization plan was the class containing the asbestos personal injury claims. All other classes were reinstated, including the 6 percent unsecured notes, which were paid in cash including postpetition interest and interest on interest. The notes could have been purchased for a zero coupon bond equivalent yield to maturity of 12 percent.

MBIA, Inc. 14 percent surplus notes represent another example of a bond that could become a quasi zero coupon bond but that in all likelihood would be repaid in full, including accrued interest, even in the event that interest payments were to be temporarily suspended. The notes could be purchased in October 2008 for $48.10 with a current yield of 29.1 percent, a yield to call (on 1/15/13) of 39.6 percent, and a yield to maturity (1/15/33) of 29.1 percent.

TAX DISADVANTAGES OF A VOLUNTARY EXCHANGE VERSUS CHAPTER 11 REORGANIZATION

Cancellation of debt (COD) income arises where debt of the corporation is canceled or discharged for less that its adjusted issue price (usually its principal amount plus or less any unamortized premium or discount). The amount of COD generally equals the excess of the adjusted issue price over the consideration paid in the exchange, which could consist of cash (rarely), the market price of newly issued common stock, and the market price (or fair value) of newly issued debt instruments.

A solvent corporation not in bankruptcy involved in a voluntary exchange offer must recognize COD currently as taxable income (subject to offset by any available net operating losses or tax credits). If a corporation is insolvent for tax purposes, but not in bankruptcy, the corporation excludes COD from taxable income up to the amount of the corporation's insolvency. Insolvency is measured by a balance sheet test (i.e., the extent to which the adjusted issue price of its liabilities exceeds the fair market value of its assets, as determined immediately prior to the debt discharge giving rise to the COD). In contrast, a corporation that is in bankruptcy does not include any amount of COD in taxable income.

The solvent corporation involved with a voluntary exchange may have to pay some, or all, of the COD created by the voluntary exchange in cash. The corporation that is insolvent or bankrupt for tax purposes, but not in bankruptcy, excludes COD from taxable income up to the amount of the corporation's insolvency. The insolvent or bankrupt corporation must reduce various tax attributes by the amount of COD excluded from income after calculating its tax for the taxable year. There are two choices for reducing the tax attributes. First, the corporation can opt to reduce the tax attributes in the following order: net operating losses, general business credits, minimum tax credits, capital loss carryover, basis in the corporation's property, passive activity losses, passive activity credits, and foreign tax credits. Alternatively, the corporation can opt to reduce first its basis in its depreciable property.

In general, where the financially troubled corporation exchanges new debt for old debt, if both the old debt and the new debt constitute securities for tax purposes, the exchange will constitute a recapitalization. The exchanging bondholder will not recognize gain or loss. Whether a debt instrument is a security for tax purposes is an inherently factual determination. As a rule, debt instruments with a maturity of five years or more tend to be viewed as securities for tax purposes.

Where readily traded bonds are securities, the exchanging bondholder is likely to have income based on original issue discount (OID). In OID, the bondholder accretes on a monthly basis income based on the difference between purchase price (i.e., market price on the date of issuance) and the principal amount payable at maturity. For example, assume the exchanging bondholder received a new bond in an exchange where the first trading day's price is 60, and the bond matures in 50 months with a scheduled payment at maturity of 100. The 40 discount constitutes OID and is to be included in the taxpayer's income at the rate of 80 cents per month, or $9.60 per year. OID is the most pernicious form of taxation: (1) The taxpayer pays tax at the maximum rate; (2) the taxpayer has no control over when the tax becomes payable (versus, for example, realizing capital gains); and (3) the event that gives rise to the tax OID does not also give rise to the cash with which to pay the tax.

A comprehensive discussion of the income tax aspects involved in restructuring distressed companies, and distressed securities, is beyond the scope of this book.[1]

Most voluntary exchange offers are exempt from registration under the Securities Act of 1933 pursuant to a Section 3(a)(9) exemption. The exemption arises if the corporation offers to exchange its existing securities for new securities (and cash). To obtain a Section 3(a)(9) exemption, the exchange offer cannot be underwritten. However, the corporation can use a dealer-manager, usually an investment bank.

8

A Brief Review of Chapter 11

The U.S. bankruptcy courts are units of the district courts and exercise the bankruptcy jurisdiction that was established by statute and referred to them by their respective district courts. The Bankruptcy Reform Act of 1978 established a bankruptcy court in each judicial district to exercise such bankruptcy jurisdiction. Bankruptcy judges are appointed by the court of appeals, and district courts automatically refer bankruptcy cases and proceedings to the bankruptcy court, which is authorized to decide all referred business. Appeals from judgments, orders, or decrees of a bankruptcy judge are made either to the corresponding district court or a bankruptcy appellate panel.

Codified in 11 United States Code (11 USC), the substantive law of bankruptcy is divided into several different chapters:

Chapter 1	General Provisions and Definitions
Chapter 3	Case Administration
Chapter 5	Creditors, the Debtor, and the Estate
Chapter 7	Liquidation
Chapter 9	Adjustment of Debts of a Municipality
Chapter 11	Reorganization
Chapter 12	Adjustment of Debts of a Family Farmer or Fisherman with Regular Annual Income
Chapter 13	Adjustment of Debts of an Individual with Regular Income
Chapter 15	Ancillary and Other Cross-Border Cases

In this book we are primarily interested in briefly reviewing the substantive law that refers to reorganizations, and to do so we must also review the relevant rules of case administration and those about the relationships among creditors, debtors, and the estate.

LIQUIDATIONS AND REORGANIZATIONS

There are essentially two types of bankruptcies: *liquidations* and *reorganizations*. The liquidating chapter of 11 USC is Chapter 7, albeit there also can be Chapter 11 liquidations. Like the majority of insolvency laws in other countries, in a Chapter 7 case a receiver (the bankruptcy trustee) collects all of the debtor's assets, sells them, and then distributes the proceeds to creditors in accordance with the rule of absolute priority. The bankruptcy trustee is in charge of the administration of the estate as the liquidation proceeds. The expectation from filing for Chapter 7 is a discharge of all debts by the debtor, although bankruptcy discharges only certain debtors from certain debts. These objections to a full discharge are contained in section 727(a) of the bankruptcy code.

The second type of bankruptcy involves *reorganizations*. Reorganizations focus on the rehabilitation of the debtor rather than the liquidation of its assets, and Chapter 11 is the business reorganization chapter of the bankruptcy code. A debtor in Chapter 11 retains control of its assets as debtor in possession (DIP) and continues operating the business while seeking to restructure its debts and pay off creditors in accordance to a plan agreed on by creditors and approved by the bankruptcy court.

STARTING A CASE: VOLUNTARY VERSUS INVOLUNTARY PETITIONS

A Chapter 11 may begin either voluntarily by a debtor (Section 301) or involuntarily by creditors or their indenture trustee (Section 303). The overwhelming majority of Chapter 11 filings are voluntary filings. For the companies that we are concerned about in this book,[1] an involuntary case can be commenced by the filing of a petition by three unsecured creditors with an aggregate amount of claims of not less than $12,300. Certain debtors are protected from involuntary petitions, like insurance companies and banking institutions (Section 109). Involuntary petitions are rarely used, since petitioning creditors may be liable for damages to the company, and courts will generally listen to debtors who can claim that they are working out the problem. An involuntary filing does not immediately put the debtor into bankruptcy but gives it the right to answer and litigate whether or not it should be in bankruptcy. The creditor filing the petition must prove that either:

- "the debtor is generally not paying such debtor's debts as such debts come due unless such debts are the subject of a bona fide dispute as to liability or amount" (Section 303(h)(1)) or

▪ "within 120 days before the date of the filing of the petition, a custodian, other than a trustee, receiver, or agent appointed or authorized to take charge of less than substantially all of the property of the debtor for the purpose of enforcing a lien against such property, was appointed or took possession" (Section 303(h)(2)).

Without such proof, an involuntary petition will not succeed and will pose significant liability risks to its petitioners.

FORUM SHOPPING

Under the venue rules of 28 USC Section 1408, a debtor has four alternative ways of selecting the district of a bankruptcy filing: (1) domicile, (2) residence, (3) location of principal place of business, and (4) location of principal assets. The relative latitude afforded to debtors in choosing the district where they may file their case will obviously be used to their advantage in voluntary filings. Large debtors will tend to seek courts that are sympathetic to their case, are known for being highly competent, and have experience dealing with complex cases. Some districts, like the Southern District of New York and Delaware, tend to be debtor and management friendly and have captured a large proportion of the large Chapter 11 cases. For example, it has become routine in these districts that the debtor will be allowed to pay the prepetition unsecured claims of vendors deemed critical to the reorganization, giving debtors considerable leverage over suppliers and increasing postpetition financing needs. Other districts have not been as accommodating, as was shown in the Kmart case where the district court reversed the critical vendor order, subjecting the 2,300 vendors to having to disgorge the payments they had received as preferential transfers; and upon appeal the Seventh Circuit Court of Appeals affirmed the district court's decision.

PARTIES IN A CHAPTER 11 CASE

The Debtor

As we previously discussed, a debtor in Chapter 11 retains control of its assets and continues to operate the business while seeking to restructure its debts as debtor in possession (DIP) unless a petition of a party in interest is filed for cause (including bad faith, gross mismanagement, or outright fraud) for the replacement of the DIP with either a Chapter 11 bankruptcy trustee or an examiner with powers to conduct an investigation of the debtor's affairs. The bankruptcy trustee is separate and distinct from the U.S. Trustee that is discussed next.

Office of the U.S. Trustee

The office of the U.S. Trustee is responsible for overseeing the bankruptcy case in a supervisory and administrative role. Its primary role is to form an official committee of unsecured creditors or any other committees, to conduct a preliminary meeting of creditors held under Section 341 of the bankruptcy code, to oversee the retention of professionals to be retained by the debtor and any committees, and to oversee any fee hearings of professionals.

Creditors' Committee

After the filing of a Chapter 11 petition, the U.S. Trustee solicits the 20 largest creditors for the formation of an official committee of unsecured creditors, known as the official creditors' committee. The committee is usually composed of members holding claims that are representative of the creditor population, and trade creditors frequently comprise the majority of its membership. The role of the committee is to oversee the DIP reorganization or liquidation for the benefit of unsecured creditors. The committee retains its own counsel and other professionals, which are paid by the estate.

Other Committees

In larger cases, other committees are formed, such as an equity committee, a committee of creditors with particular claims like asbestos claims, and a bondholder committee. According to Section 1102(2) of the bankruptcy code, any party in interest can request that the U.S. Trustee form one or more additional committees.

Secured Creditors

A creditor that has a lien on property owned by the DIP or that has a right of setoff against property of the DIP is known as a secured creditor. Secured creditors are active participants in the reorganization process of a DIP, and their activities include: (1) seeking relief of the automatic stay to foreclose on their prepetition collateral, (2) protecting their prepetition collateral, (3) providing postpetition financing to the debtor, (4) contesting plans of reorganization, and (5) receiving adequate protection payments in instances where an adequate equity cushion exists.

Unsecured Creditors

A creditor having claims that do not have a lien on property owned by the DIP or that do not have the right of setoff against property of the

DIP is known as an unsecured creditor. The official creditors' committee is constituted with holders of unsecured claims.

Professionals

In addition to attorneys and accountants, the debtor and any committee may want to retain additional professionals: financial consultants, real estate consultants, investment bankers, appraisers, turnaround specialists, or any other professional who can assist them in the achievement of their goals. All professionals retained by the debtor or any committee must be approved by the court and are paid with priority as an administrative expense by the debtor and the estate.

ADMINISTRATION OF A CHAPTER 11 CASE

Automatic Stay

The immediate benefit that a debtor gets from filing for Chapter 11 protection is a stay of the acts of creditors to collect from the debtor. This stay is granted automatically upon filing (Section 362). Upon the filing of the petition, an estate is created and the debtor becomes the debtor in possession (DIP). The DIP acts as a fiduciary and has all the duties and powers of a bankruptcy trustee; the DIP is in charge of the business and is accountable for the property of the estate (Section 541) and its operations. The scope of the stay is quite broad and is designed to give the DIP time to prepare and propose a plan of reorganization (POR). Creditors cannot proceed to enforce liens and/or seize property, and the accrual of interest on prepetition debts is stopped postpetition. Section 362(d) provides that a bankruptcy court may grant relief from stay on request of a party in interest. Secured creditors are generally the ones who will seek relief from the stay, which will be granted only either "for cause" (Section 362(d)(1)), which includes the lack of adequate protection, or in situations where the debtor has no equity in certain property or such property is not necessary for an effective reorganization (Section 362(d)(2)).

Adequate Protection

In exchange for giving up the ability to foreclose on their collateral, secured creditors are given what is known as adequate protection. Section 361 is very specific in that it provides *adequate protection of an interest of an entity in property*, not adequate protection of an entity having its claim repaid.

Although the bankruptcy code does not define what adequate protection actually means, it does give examples of the different forms it can take. It can take the form of additional or replacement liens given, cash payment or periodic cash payments, control protections on the use of the collateral, and the allowance of a super-priority administrative claim (Section 507(b)). Secured creditors hold the only class of claims that are likely to continue to receive interest payments during bankruptcy, especially when their collateral is essential to a company's operation.

Asset Sales

When a debtor is in Chapter 11, transactions outside the ordinary course of business can be accomplished only after notice and hearing (Section 363). The court evaluates requests to use or sell property of the estate taking into consideration the issue of adequate protection, but the burden of proof on this issue lies with the DIP. The court will also evaluate whether the request attempts to bypass protections afforded to creditors. Asset sales outside of the ordinary course of business take place through a competitive bidding procedure. The debtor (or the court) appoints a stalking horse bidder from those who have put in preliminary bids, and subsequently a bidding contest ensues where the stalking horse has the following advantages: (1) other bidders are required to pay a premium over the stalking horse bid, say 5 percent to 10 percent; (2) the stalking horse can get a topping fee; and (3) the estate pays the stalking horse's reasonable expenses.

There really is no such thing as a liquidation of assets, whether out of court, in Chapter 11, or in Chapter 7; there is only conversion of assets to other uses and/or other ownership.

Executory Contracts

When a debtor files for Chapter 11, it is likely to have unperformed obligations with third parties, generally known as executory contracts. Although the bankruptcy code does not define what an executory contract is, the definition that most courts have adopted is the Countryman[2] definition:

> *A contract under which the obligation of both the bankrupt and the other party to the contract are so far unperformed that the failure of either to complete the performance would constitute a material breach excusing the performance by the other.*

Those executory contracts that are beneficial to the estate are likely to be assumed and/or assigned, and those that are not will be rejected with court approval (Section 365(a)). The assumption of a contract requires that both parties perform according to its provisions. Clauses that prohibit either the assumption or the assignment of unexpired leases and other executory contracts are not enforceable in bankruptcy. If there has been a default in an executory contract, the DIP may not assume it unless: (1) it cures the default or provides adequate assurance that it will promptly cure; (2) it compensates or provides adequate assurance that it will compensate for damages; and (3) it provides adequate assurance of future performance under such contract (Section 365(b)(1)).

The rejection of a contract frees the DIP from any obligation under its terms but allows the other party to file an unsecured claim for damages for the breach. Nonresidential real estate leases are a special and separate class of executory contract. The deadline for the assumption of nonresidential real property unexpired leases is 210 days. Under the old law, the debtor had 60 days to assume or reject a nonresidential real property unexpired lease, but this was usually extended indefinitely. Damages for the rejection of nonresidential real property are limited to the greater of one year's rent or 15 percent of the remainder of the lease, not to exceed three years' rent. If there is a subsequent rejection of a previously assumed lease, the lessor may claim two years' rent as an administrative claim. Damages in excess of two years' rent are treated as general unsecured claims limited to the greater of one year's rent or 15 percent of the remainder of the lease, not to exceed three years' rent.

Avoidance Powers

The bankruptcy code discourages debtors from favoring selected creditors over others through the transfer of assets or other prepetition actions and also discourages prefiling actions by creditors who may want to seek an advantage over other creditors. These protections are contained in Sections 547 (preferences); 548 (fraudulent conveyances); 544, 545, 547, and 548 (invalid liens); and 546 (limitations on avoiding powers).

Under Section 547(b) a trustee in bankruptcy or a DIP may avoid any transfer of an interest of a debtor in property when such transfer:

- Is to or for the benefit of a creditor.
- Is for or on account of an antecedent debt owed by the debtor before such transfer was made.
- Was made while the debtor was insolvent.
- Is made on or within 90 days before filing for bankruptcy, or between 90 days and one year before filing if the creditor was an insider at the time of the transfer.

▪ Enables such creditor to receive more than the creditor would receive (1) in Chapter 7, (2) had the transfer not been made, and (3) if the creditor received payment of such debt to the extent provided by the bankruptcy provisions.

The exceptions to Section 547(b) are contained in 547(c). The presumptions of 547(b) are: (1) that the debtor has been insolvent on and during the 90 days immediately preceding the date of the filing (Section 547(f)); (2) that the trustee or DIP has the burden of proving the avoidability of a transfer (Section 547(g)); and (3) that the creditor against whom recovery is sought has the burden of proving nonavoidability of a transfer under Section 547(c).

The 2005 BAPCPA amendments greatly expanded the reclamation rights of suppliers of goods by limiting the avoiding powers in such cases. Under Section 546(c), sellers of goods to debtors in the ordinary course of business can reclaim such goods if the debtor has received such goods while insolvent, within 45 days before the petition date, provided that the seller makes a written reclamation demand within 45 days of receipt of the goods by the debtor or 20 days after the petition date if the 45-day period expires after the petition date. If the seller fails to provide such written notice, the seller may still assert an administrative expense claim for the value of any goods received by the debtor within 20 days before the commencement of a case (Section 503(b)(9)).

Transfers that are made by the debtor or for the benefit of the debtor with the actual intent to hinder, delay or defraud creditors are subject to avoidance as fraudulent conveyances. Because establishing direct evidence of an intent to defraud is quite difficult and subject to circumstantial evidence, more emphasis is placed on transfers whose construction appears fraudulent (i.e., where the debtor receives less than a reasonable equivalent value from such transfer and is likely to become insolvent as a result of it). This approach to fraudulent conveyances is the basis for the legal attacks on intercorporate guarantees and leveraged buyouts.

Other types of transfers that are voidable in bankruptcy are those that are not recorded or otherwise perfected (Section 544(a)) and those that are not timely recorded or otherwise perfected (Section 547(e)). In other words, technical imperfections in a creditor's liens can be avoided in bankruptcy.

Claims, Secured and Unsecured Status

The bankruptcy code deals with claims, not creditors. The term *claim* is defined in Section 101(5) as:

1. the right to payment, whether or not such right is reduced to judgment, liquidated, unliquidated, fixed, contingent, matured, disputed, undisputed, legal, equitable, secured, or unsecured; or
2. the right to an equitable remedy for breach of performance if such breach gives rise to a right of payment, whether or not such right to an equitable remedy is reduced to judgment, fixed, contingent, matured, disputed, undisputed, secured, or unsecured.

A creditor's claim secured by a lien on property in which the estate has an interest or that is subject to setoff is a *secured claim* to the extent of the value of the creditor's interest in such property or to the extent of the amount subject to setoff. The right of setoff or offset allows parties that owe each other money to apply their mutual debts against each other (Section 553). For example, a debtor holds a demand deposit at BankCo for $1 million and also has a loan from BankCo for $2 million. BankCo has a secured claim for $1 million. In order to have a proper right to offset, the debts must be mutual, they should have arisen before the commencement of the case, and they must be an allowed claim under Section 502.

A creditor's claim is unsecured if the creditor has not obtained a lien or the value of the property subject to the lien is less than the value of the creditor's claim. For example, if the debtor borrows $1 million from a creditor and pledges as collateral property that at the time of filing is worth only $800,000, then the creditor has a secured claim for $800,000 and an unsecured claim for $200,000.

Allowance of Claims

Although in Chapter 7 a claim or interest is allowed only if the creditor or party in interest files a proof of claim or interest, in Chapter 11 a proof of claim or interest is deemed filed and thus allowed if it appears in the schedules filed by the debtor under Section 521(a)(1), except for claims or interests that are scheduled as disputed, contingent, or unliquidated. There are several grounds for disallowing claims, and these are contained in Section 502(b). One such disallowance is for unmatured interest. Interest on unsecured claims generally stops accruing postpetition, but it is permitted to accrue on allowed secured claims that are secured by property whose value is greater than the amount of such claims.

Subordination Agreements

Filing for Chapter 11 relief means that the debtor is abrogating its contracts with the creditors. The contract terms are contained in an indenture or loan agreement. Almost all contract terms are stayed, or eliminated, upon the filing of Chapter 11, although many are subsequently reinstated (i.e., Section 1110 for aircraft in 60 days, executory contracts that are assigned, wage agreements, etc.).

However, some terms are unaffected by the Chapter 11 filing. Of particular note are subordination agreements between and among creditor groups. These are intercreditor agreements with which the debtor is not involved. Subordination agreements stipulate that consideration otherwise payable to a subordinated creditor is required to be paid to a senior creditor until such party is paid in full. In the case of Home Products International (HPI) presented in Chapter 15 of this book, HPI senior subordinated notes entered into an agreement with HPI bank lenders to subordinate. The subordination provision can be found in the indenture of the notes being subordinated. If HPI defaulted, subsequent payments were then made to all creditors. All payments due to the HPI subordinates would be paid over to the bank lenders until the banks were made whole. The enforceability of contractual subordination agreements is codified in Section 510(a), and it is quite important for the potential distressed investor. Most publicly traded debtors will have multiple layers of debt obligations that will contain provisions subordinating certain of those obligations to others.

Under Section 510(b), sellers or purchasers of equity securities seeking damages or rescission will also be subordinated. Finally, the courts are also given discretion to subordinate any claim to other claims based on the principle of equitable subordination (Section 510(c)).

Financing a Debtor in Chapter 11

The very reason why most debtors must file for Chapter 11 protection is that it has either lost access to capital markets, cannot generate sufficient cash to meet its financial obligations, or both. Even though the automatic stay provides the debtor with some temporary financial relief arising out of not making cash payments to unsecured and undersecured claims, it will often need further financing to pay for the administration expenses of the case and/or to make payments called for by the plan of reorganization. Section 364 provides the statutory basis that allows the debtor to obtain debtor-in-possession (DIP) financing. DIP lenders tend to be the same lenders that have provided prepetition credit. However, the bankruptcy code offers very valuable benefits and inducements to DIP lenders. Among such inducements, DIP lenders will be granted an affirmation or extension of their existing liens, new liens, and super-priority claim status in the event that the value of their collateral is not sufficient to pay those claims and even priming liens; this makes DIP lending a very safe and profitable business.

THE CHAPTER 11 PLAN

Period of Exclusivity

Upon filing for Chapter 11, the debtor has the exclusive right to file a plan of reorganization. It can file this plan at the time of the petition or at any time thereafter within certain limits (Section 1121). Exclusivity gives the DIP very significant advantages over creditors. Perhaps more important is the power that is given to management in terms of corporate governance as part of a plan of reorganization. Managements can extract benefits from exclusivity such as (1) huge compensation, (2) huge entrenchment, and (3) restrictions on newly issued securities.

Statutorily, the debtor has 120 days after the date of the order for relief to file a plan of reorganization and up to 180 days to seek approval of the plan. Under the 2005 BAPCPA amendments, these two periods cannot be extended to more than 18 and 20 months respectively. Whether these changes will shorten the time to either reorganize or sell assets is an open question.

Priorities

A principal purpose of Chapter 11 is to treat all creditors similarly situated the same and not to advantage one creditor over another. Secured creditors receive the first proceeds from their collateral up to the value of their claim. If their claim is larger than the value of their collateral, the amount of the excess is deemed an unsecured claim.

By statute, certain expenses and claims are given priority over other claims (Section 507):

- **Administrative expenses** for corporate Chapter 11 cases are expenses allowed under Section 503(b) and are given first priority in payment under Section 507(a). Moreover, these expenses are paid on a pay-as-you-go basis and in cash. A more detailed review of the magnitude of these expenses is presented in Chapter 4.
- **Wage and pension plan contribution claims** arising within 180 days before the petition date or cessation of debtor business, whichever is first, and only to the extent of $10,000 for each individual or corporation. Under the old law the look-back period was only 90 days and the maximum amount was $4,925.
- **Allowed unsecured claims of governmental units,** only to the extent that such claims are for income, sales, property, withholding, employment, excise taxes, or customs duties.

Other de facto priorities have been granted by certain courts even though they are not explicitly provided for in the bankruptcy code.

One such priority is given to **critical vendor payments**. Except for certain limited statutory exceptions,[3] the bankruptcy code provides for an equitable distribution of the debtor's assets among similarly situated holders of claims. All similarly situated prepetition unsecured claims are impacted the same by the automatic stay, and generally no payments on any such claims are made until the end of the case. Trade creditors extending credit for goods and services to the debtor prepetition would normally have to wait the same as any other unsecured creditor until the end of the case to be paid. Several courts have made exceptions to this implicit rule in what is known as the critical vendor doctrine. Critical vendors are those whose continued deliveries to the debtor are considered vital to the success of the reorganization and who refuse to ship goods or services unless their prepetition debt is paid first. Under Section 547, such payments would be considered voidable preferences. However, several courts have relied on the "necessity of payment" doctrine[4] and the strong-arm section of the bankruptcy code (Section 105a) which allows them to *"issue any order, process, or judgment that is necessary or appropriate to carry out the provisions of this title"* to allow such preferential payments. In some districts, such as New York and Delaware, critical vendor payments have become routine, giving the debtor great leverage with suppliers since the debtor can decide who gets paid, and increasing the postpetition financing needs to make such payments.

The recent Kmart case discussed in Chapter 16 of this volume highlights the risks associated with venue selection with respect to the treatment of critical vendor payments. Shortly after filing for Chapter 11 in Illinois, Kmart Corporation obtained court approval for payment of the prepetition obligations to unspecified critical vendors totaling roughly $300 million. A prepetition creditor of Kmart that did not receive critical vendor status appealed the bankruptcy court decision and obtained a reversal in U.S. district court; in 2004 the Seventh Circuit Court of Appeals affirmed the district court order and upheld the reversal of the bankruptcy court's critical vendor order.

Unsecured claims get paid only after all secured claims, administrative claims, and priority claims are paid in full unless such senior creditors voting as a class elect to take less. The required vote here is the acceptance by two-thirds in amount of the class of claims, and one-half in number of those voting. If there are insufficient funds available to pay unsecured creditors in full, their claims will be paid on a pro rata basis if there is no consent by senior creditors to take less.

Without the affirmative vote of the various classes of creditors, **equity holders** do not receive any distribution until all creditors are paid in full.

This is contained in the "rule of absolute priority" of Section 1129(b)(2)(C). In certain jurisdictions an exception has been made to the absolute priority rule known as the "new value exception" whereby holders of equity interests have been allowed to retain such interests if they have provided "new value" to the debtor. The statutory caveat is that equity holders must allow others to bid for such equity interests or propose a competing reorganization plan.

Disclosure to Security Holders

The idea behind the rehabilitative nature of Chapter 11 is that the debtor restructures its debts and pays off creditors in accordance to a plan agreed on by creditors and approved by the bankruptcy court. The acceptance or rejection of a plan of reorganization cannot be solicited from holders of claims or interests unless a copy or summary of a plan has been provided to such holders together with a written disclosure statement approved by the court as having adequate information (Section 1125). The bankruptcy court reviews the information provided to creditors and shareholders in the disclosure statement to ensure that such information would enable a *hypothetical investor typical of the holders of claims or interests* to make an *informed judgment* about the plan.

Although determining what constitutes adequate information will be very dependent on the complexity of a case, there are certain types of information that are customarily included in disclosure statements, including: the events that led to the filing of the Chapter 11 case, background information about the debtors, debtor's ownership and management, a description and value of assets, the future prospects of the debtor's business, the present condition of the debtor, the general structure of the plan, a summary of treatment of claims and interests under the plan, a summary of certain other provisions of the plan, a liquidation analysis and a going concern analysis, the sources of information used in the preparation of the disclosure statement, accounting methods, and litigation that may affect the plan.

Contents of a Plan

Section 1123 sets out both the mandatory and allowable provisions of a Chapter 11 plan. There are five mandatory provisions:

1. A plan must designate classes of claims and classes of interests. The statutory rules for putting claims or interests in one particular class only require that such class or interest is *substantially similar* to the other claims or interests of such class (Section 1122(a)). The bankruptcy code does not define what substantially similar is, but courts tend to

look at the legal rights of claimants as the discriminating factor. Thus, priority claims under Section 507 are placed in a different class from secured claims, and in turn these are placed in different classes than unsecured claims. The requirement that claims in a class are substantially similar does not preclude a situation where similar claims or interests are put in different classes. As we shall see in the next section, since the plan confirmation process requires that at least one class accepts the plan under the "cram down" rule, the proponent of a plan can virtually guarantee confirmation of its plan by placing claims that will vote for the plan in one separate class, provided these claims are substantially similar.

2. A plan must specify any class of claims or interests that are not impaired under the plan. A class of claims or interests is impaired under a plan unless (1) the legal, equitable, and contractual rights of the holder are left unaltered or (2) the only alteration is a reversal of an acceleration upon default by curing such default and reinstating the original maturity of such claim or interest.

3. A plan must specify the treatment of any class of claims or interests that are impaired under the plan.

4. It must provide the same treatment for each claim or interest of a particular class unless by requisite vote holders agree to a less favorable treatment.

5. It must provide the adequate means for the implementation of the plan. This is the section of the plan where the restructuring transactions are presented in detail. The section will include information about the new financing, if any; how claims will be paid; what the form of consideration will be; timing and delivery of the distributions; and so on.

Acceptance of a Plan

Acceptance of a plan involves determining which classes of claims or interests are eligible to vote, and determining the required majorities needed to establish that a class of claims or interests has accepted the plan. Creditors with allowed claims and shareholders with allowed interests can vote for the plan. However, there are two broad classes of claims or interests who are deemed to have either rejected the plan or accepted the plan and whose votes are not required to be solicited. The first such class or classes are those that do not receive anything under the plan. These classes are deemed to have rejected the plan. The other class or classes are those that are not impaired under the plan. These classes are deemed to have accepted the plan and their votes are not solicited. All other classes of claims and interests will be solicited for their votes.

Section 1126 sets out the rules for plan acceptance. A class of claims accepts a plan if such plan has been accepted by the vote of creditors that hold at least two-thirds in amount and more than half in number of the allowed claims of such class. The two-thirds in amount rule (but not the 50 percent in number) applies for the acceptance of a plan by a class of interests.

Plan Confirmation: Feasibility, Best Interest, and Cram Down

After the votes on the plan are in, the court will hold a confirmation hearing where it will ascertain whether the plan complies with the rules set out in Section 1129 for its confirmation. Of particular importance among the criteria in Section 1129 are: (1) Section 1129(7), also known as the best interests test; (2) the so-called "cram down provision" (1129(b)(1)), which requires that in the event not all impaired classes accept the plan, the court may still confirm it if it does not discriminate unfairly and it is fair and equitable with respect to those nonaccepting classes; and (3) the feasibility test contained in Section 1129(11).

The best interests test applies to impaired classes of claims or interests and requires that in order to confirm a plan each holder either has accepted the plan or will receive or retain under the plan, on account of their claim or interest, property of value as of the effective date of the plan that is not less than the amount that such holder would receive or retain if the debtor were liquidated under Chapter 7. Section 1129(a)(7) gives rise to the requirement that the plan proponent presents a hypothetical liquidation analysis as of the effective date of the plan, which is usually included as an exhibit.

The statutory conditions on how a plan does not discriminate and it is fair and equitable are detailed in Section 1129(b)(2) for secured claims classes, unsecured claims classes, and classes of interests. The requirements for impaired secured claims are that the holders of such claims retain the liens securing those claims to the extent of the allowed amount of such claims *and* that they receive on account of such claims deferred cash payments totaling at least the allowed amount of such claims, of a value as of the effective date of the plan (present value) of at least the value of such holders' interests in the debtor's property. The sum of the cash payments received over the life of the plan will equal their allowed claim amount, and the present value of such payments will be at least equal to the value of those holders' interests in the debtor's property. The introduction of present value in the statute requires that a cram-down interest rate be determined. An example will help in the understanding of the steps involved.

First, the impaired dissenting secured classes are determined. Then, we determine the amount of their secured claim. For example, XYZ

Corporation has a claim of $10 million secured by collateral whose value is $7 million. Then, XYZ Corporation has a secured claim of $7 million and an unsecured claim of $3 million (Section 506(a)). Suppose that the cram-down interest rate is determined to be 8 percent annually. The cram down rule for secured claims requires that: (1) the sum of cash payments over the plan duration totals at least the allowed amount of the secured claim ($7 million) and (2) the present value of such payments, discounted at 8 percent, totals at least the value of the holder's interest in the estate interest in the property, which is $7 million. If the plan contemplates making equal cash payments for five years, at the end of each year the amount of such payments can be found by applying the following formula:

$$Payment = \frac{PV \times i}{1 - \dfrac{1}{(1+i)^n}}$$

$$\$1,753,195.2 = \frac{\$7,000,000 \times 0.08}{1 - \dfrac{1}{1.08^5}}$$

where n is the number of annual payments over the life of the plan, and i is the cram-down interest rate per year.

The sum of annual cash payments during the life of the plan is $8,765,976 ($1,753,195.2 × 5); thus it satisfies both requirements set out by Section 1129(b)(2)(A)(II). Note that the satisfaction of the second condition will automatically ensure the satisfaction of the first one, because the amount of the allowable claim is the same as the holder's interest in the property. There is an instance when this is not the case, and it is when a class of impaired secured claims makes an 1111(b) election, by at least two-thirds in amount and more than half in number of those voting, that their whole claim is a secured claim notwithstanding Section 506(a). In our example, should the secured class make the election, it will no longer have a $7 million secured claim and a $3 million unsecured claim, but a $10 million secured claim. In this case, under the cram down rule, the sum of cash payments must total at least $10 million, and the present value of such cash payments must be at least $7 million. In our previous example such conditions are not met, and thus larger annual payments must be made over the same time period.

With respect to a class of impaired unsecured claims that have rejected the plan, the plan must provide that each holder of such class receive or retain property of value as of the effective date of the plan (present value) on account of their claim or interest equal to the allowed amount of such claim *or* the holder of any claim or interest that is junior to the claims of such class will not receive or retain under the plan any property (Section 1129(b)(2)(B)(i)). Simply put, junior classes to the dissenting class in question must get nothing under the plan if the plan is to be crammed down on a dissenting class that gets paid less than their allowed claim. This is also called the rule of absolute priority. The nondiscriminatory and fair and equitable criteria for classes of interests are very similar to those for unsecured claims.

Recall that these conditions apply only to those impaired classes that have not accepted the plan and will be crammed down by the court. However, the absolute priority rule does not apply when the plan is accepted by all voting classes by the requisite majorities. In other words, if a class of claims so consents, a class below them can get something even though the consenting class has not been paid in full on account of its claims. Nothing in the statute says that distributions in a consensual plan need to comply with the absolute priority rule.

Confirmation of a plan also requires that the debtor will not likely liquidate or will experience the need of further financial reorganization in the future (commonly referred to as Chapter 22s or Chapter 33s). This is known as the feasibility test and it is codified in Section 1129(11).

Expediting Bankruptcies: Prepackaged and Preplanned Chapter 11 Plans

As was discussed in Chapter 4, the expenses involved in a standard Chapter 11 case can cripple the chances of a debtor to reorganize and survive as a going concern. Smaller debtors' only chance of surviving as going concerns through an in-court reorganization is by effecting what is known as a prepackaged or preplanned Chapter 11 plan. A prepackaged plan is an out-of-court proceeding in preparation of a debtor filing for a Chapter 11 petition where the debtor prepares a disclosure document and a plan of reorganization that will be accepted by the necessary classes of creditors and equity interests; it is designed to accelerate the time and eliminate the expense involved in consummating a Chapter 11 plan. The bankruptcy code recognized creditors' committees formed before the commencement of a Chapter 11 case in Section 1102(b)(1) and allows a debtor to file a plan concurrently with the filing of a petition in Section 1121(a). The statutory basis for the solicitation of acceptances of a plan before the commencement of a Chapter 11 case is set out in Section 1126(b), which states that a holder of a claim or interest that has accepted the plan before the commencement of a case is deemed to have accepted the plan if either of the following is true:

- The solicitation of such acceptance or rejection was in compliance with any applicable nonbankruptcy law, rule, or regulation governing the adequacy of disclosure in connection with such solicitation.

- If there is no such law, rule, or regulation, such acceptance or rejection was solicited after disclosure to such holder of adequate information, as defined in Section 1125(a) of the bankruptcy code.

A prepackaged bankruptcy combines the cost benefits of an out-of-court exchange offer and the statutory benefits provided by the bankruptcy code.

9

The Workout Process

PARTIES AND THEIR DIFFERING NEEDS AND DESIRES

A clear understanding of the parties involved in a reorganization, their differing desires and goals, and the different ways in which they can exert leverage over the reorganization process is quite important to those involved in distress investing.

The judge assigned to the Chapter 11 case is of paramount importance to all parties involved. The only limited control the debtor has over this key factor is given by the flexibility afforded by the venue rules of 28 USC §1408 in making the decision of where to file a voluntary petition (forum shopping) and perhaps seeking counsel that has had previous successful experience dealing with a particular judge.

After petitioning the court for Chapter 11 protection, **management** continues to operate the business under court supervision. Managements can be removed only after a claimant or party in interest makes a request to the court and for cause (i.e., gross mismanagement, bad faith, or outright fraud), and can be replaced with a trustee. Alternatively, an examiner can be appointed with powers to conduct an investigation of the debtor's affairs while management remains in place. Management removals are relatively infrequent. The exclusive right to propose a plan of reorganization given to the debtor by the bankruptcy code gives management a substantial amount of leverage over the reorganization process, and management will likely use this power to protect its own interests for control, entrenchment, compensation, and job security.

Banks, or holders of secured claims in general, are important participants in reorganizations. A claim is secured only to the extent of the value of its collateral. If the collateral is less valuable than the amount of the claim, then the secured claimant holds a secured claim to the extent of the value of the collateral and an unsecured claim for any deficiency. Each secured claim is a separate class of its own and will have to be paid before any other claim is paid, including priority and administrative claims, unless the secured claim can be primed. A secured claim can be primed only insofar as the court finds that the claim is adequately protected. To the extent that a secured claim is oversecured, the holder may also collect interest to the extent provided in the credit agreement.

Secured creditors' interests lie in the protection of their collateral, which they will pursue by seeking relief from the automatic stay to foreclose on their prepetition collateral, seeking adequate protection in the form of cash payments and/or replacement liens, contesting plans of reorganization, or even proposing their own plans. The actions taken by secured creditors to protect their collateral are a force to be reckoned with and their major source of leverage in any reorganization. On the downside, if successfully challenged, secured claims can be voided and disallowed on perfection issues (Sections 544(a) and 547(e)) or on collateral avoidance issues. To the extent that the holders of secured claims are adequately protected, they tend not to be overly concerned with whether the debtor will be able to reorganize or will liquidate but have a strong preference for cash as a form of consideration for payment of their claims. Adequately secured claims, at the end of the case, are reinstated as a general rule. Upon reinstatement, the claimant receives the original instrument back along with unpaid interest, and compensation for any damages incurred (usually equal to interest on interest). Classes of claims that are not impaired under the plan of reorganization are deemed to have accepted the plan, and their votes are not solicited. Thus, if reinstated, a secured creditor does not vote on a plan of reorganization.

Trade claims usually are general unsecured claims and as such they will be paid only after all secured, administrative, and priority claims are paid in full. However, trade creditors differ from general unsecured creditors in two respects: reclamation rights and critical vendor status. Those vendors who have sold to the debtor while insolvent have reclamation rights for goods received by the debtor up to 45 days prior to its Chapter 11 filing. These rights allow for the undoing of the transaction and the return of the goods by the debtor. Besides their reclamation rights, trade vendors may threaten not to ship and they get preferential treatment if they are deemed to be a critical vendor by the debtor. As discussed previously, certain jurisdictions tend to approve critical vendor motions almost routinely, granting management considerable leverage in deciding which vendors are critical and in determining which prepetition trade claims will be paid in full and which ones will not.

Unlike secured creditors, trade vendors' interest is to continue to do business with the debtor, and generally it is in their best interest to make a reorganized debtor feasible. They may be also be interested in prolonging cases while repositioning their business with other companies.

General unsecured creditors will be paid only after all secured, administrative, and priority claims are paid in full. All unsecured creditors are extremely sensitive about any and all expenses that reduce the value of the estate and put their claims further underwater, as well as their classification into different classes pursuant to a plan of reorganization. The cram down provisions of the bankruptcy code make it such that a plan of reorganization can be confirmed even when the majority of classes dissent, making unsecured creditors' classification a very sensitive issue. Unsecured creditors of different standing would also prefer to form separate committees with counsel and investment advisers funded by the estate instead of being grouped in a single committee where it may be more difficult to challenge other creditors' positions.

Noncontrol vulture investors do not generally have a continuing relationship with the debtor (or ex-debtor) and care very much about the near-term market prices of the credit instruments they hold. Their primary interest is a market-out, and their driving force will be the internal rate of return on their investment calculated based on outside passive minority investor (OPMI) market prices. The amount they recover relative to their original purchase price and time of purchase will be their major concern.

Control vulture investors have continuing relationships with the debtor and generally hold controlling amounts of the fulcrum security in a reorganization that will allow them to obtain controlling equity interests in the reorganized company. Their primary motivation is to make the reorganized company feasible, and place a heavy weight on business values based on a longer-term business outlook. See the Kmart case in Chapter 16.

Professionals include mainly attorneys and financial advisers. Both the debtor and the official committee of unsecured creditors will hire their own set of professionals, whose fees and expenses will be paid by the estate on a pay-as-you-go basis, in cash, and with administrative expense priority. Whenever other committees are formed pursuant to the U.S. Trustee's approval and they hire their own counsel and financial advisers, those expenses will likely be picked up by the estate also. Professional fees and expenses can represent a major drain on the value of the estate. Although complex reorganizations could not be accomplished without the help of competent professionals, there is no downside risk for them to prolong cases. In fact, there is ample evidence that total professional compensation is proportional to the time a debtor remains in Chapter 11, and financial advisers customarily charge large success fees where success only means the conclusion of the case. See Chapter 4.

TYPES OF CHAPTER 11 CASES

We divide Chapter 11 cases based on the degree of prepetition planning by the debtor and its creditors, and by the types of dispositions of a case other than a conversion to a Chapter 7 liquidation. Filings that are the result of substantial prepetition planning between the debtor and its creditors before filing the Chapter 11 petition are either prenegotiated or prepackaged filings, and we discuss them in some detail in this section. We group all other Chapter 11 filings in what we call conventional filings, as they represent the most frequently encountered type, as shown in Exhibit 9.1. Of the 368 big case Chapter 11 dispositions during the 2000–2007 period, 73 percent were the result of standard filings (not preplanned) and 27 percent were either prenegotiated or prepackaged.

While the majority of the cases were disposed of as confirmed reorganizations, 12.5 percent of the cases were disposed of as confirmed Section 363 asset sales. In the following three sections we examine conventional filings, preplanned filings and Section 363 asset sales in some detail.

EXHIBIT 9.1 Number of Cases That Were Disposed of Either as Reorganizations or as Section 363 Asset Sales and Filed Either as Preplanned or as Nonpreplanned (Conventional) Chapter 11s for the Period 2000–2007

	Disposition			
	Reorganization		Section 363 Asset Sale	
	Degree of Planning Prefiling			
Year	Conventional	Preneg/Prepack	Conventional	Preneg/Prepack
2000	22	10	1	
2001	28	13	7	
2002	48	28	6	
2003	47	18	14	
2004	29	15	11	1
2005	19	8	2	
2006	17	3	2	
2007	13	4	2	
Total	223	99	45	1

Exhibit constructed with data from Lynn M. LoPucki's Bankruptcy Research Database.

Conventional Chapter 11 Reorganizations

A Chapter 11 recapitalization has the distinct advantage over a voluntary recapitalization because of the mandatory nature of the recapitalization. In a Chapter 11, the reorganization is implemented and becomes binding on all claimants pursuant to a bankruptcy court order of confirmation. A court is entitled to confirm a plan of reorganization if two-thirds in amount and a majority in number of holders of each separate class of claimants who voted on the plan (such as holders of secured debt and unsecured debt) elected to approve the plan and two-thirds of the amount voted by interest holders (e.g., preferred and common stockholders) elect to approve the plan. In addition, if some classes of claimants and interest holders approve the plan and other classes reject the plan, the bankruptcy court may confirm the plan over those rejections (known as a cram down) if the court determines that the plan does not discriminate unfairly, that it is fair and equitable to each class, and that the rejecting classes will receive more under the plan of reorganization than they would if the company were liquidated. However, there can be no cram down of a rejecting class if (1) the rejecting class will obtain less than the full value of their claims and (2) a more junior class will receive any value at all under the plan of reorganization.

Companies that become troubled almost always suffer from a cash shortage. Prior to filing for Chapter 11 relief, companies frequently find it impossible to obtain new funding at any price, because the new lender will be a prepetition creditor. After filing for Chapter 11 protection, however, the corporation tends to find it easier to obtain new financing. Lenders now become postpetition creditors and enjoy a priority for repayment compared with prepetition creditors. So-called debtor in possession (DIP) loans that are postpetition borrowings are an attractive area for lenders.

Notwithstanding the merits of a Chapter 11 bankruptcy as a tool to restructure a troubled company, most troubled issuers and investment banks have considerable reluctance to use Chapter 11. The reluctance is premised on factors such as perceived stigma, large administrative expenses, and loss of management control. While the stigma issue may have little basis in fact, the expense and control issues are very real considerations in uncontrolled Chapter 11 bankruptcies.

With respect to the stigma issue, there seems to be little difference for large troubled companies whether reorganization takes place within or without a Chapter 11. Troubled companies are stigmatized (if at all) when they are not able to discharge debts on a timely basis, and that stigma will last only as long as the troubled financial condition exists. Whether or not the recapitalization takes place in Chapter 11 seems to be a detail that is beside the point, because the stigma, if any, already exists. In fact, experience with bankruptcies and exchange offers leads one to believe that the stigma factor is somewhat overblown. Today, people do not perceive Chrysler, Kmart, Texaco, or Pacific Gas & Electric (and numerous smaller recapitalized companies) as being stigmatized. In many cases operations during the pendency of Chapter 11 become less efficient, but this does not seem to be a factor that is all-pervasive.

Ironically, an uncontrolled bankruptcy tends to be a very expensive proposition for the debtor company. The troubled company pays not only the fees and expenses of a whole host of professionals—attorneys, investment bankers, accountants, and sundry experts—that represent the company, but also the fees and expenses of various official creditors' committees, official equity committees, and court-appointed officials such as examiners. In addition, the debtor may be liable for the fees and expenses of others who have made substantial contributions to the reorganization of the company in Chapter 11. This heavy expense factor is offset to some extent by the existence of the automatic stay in bankruptcy that allows the company to forgo cash service on prebankruptcy unsecured claims and certain secured obligations.

There is little doubt that an uncontrolled Chapter 11 case poses large threats to continued control of a business enterprise by its current management and stockholders. The loss of control issue, however, must be viewed in context. Even without seeking Chapter 11 relief, in connection with exchange offers and other voluntary attempts to recapitalize, troubled companies most often are required to cede large blocks of control to creditors and others. Prior to a money default, most troubled companies have to act as supplicants in order to obtain relief from bank lenders, trade suppliers, labor unions, government agencies, and so on. However, once a company has filed for Chapter 11, there can be an additional and material loss of control during the pendency of the Chapter 11:

- The debtor company generally lays bare its business and financial soul.
- The company cannot take any actions outside its ordinary course of business without requisite notice and approval by the bankruptcy court.
- The company must share business and strategic plans with claimants and major parties in interest.
- The company subjects itself to massive reporting, discovery, and testimony under oath.

In an uncontrolled Chapter 11, the odds are that claimants and parties in interest will be organized and knowledgeable, and their opposition to any proposals by the debtor company will be financed by the debtor company.

In an uncontrolled bankruptcy, there is also a risk that a trustee or examiner will be appointed to run, oversee, or investigate the affairs of the company. The trustee risk is remote if there is an absence of fraud or gross malfeasance. In the past two years, examiners have been appointed in two major cases. These examiners had duties that clearly impinged on management's ability to run the business and the reorganization. For practical purposes, though, the appointment of an examiner remains an unlikely event.

A key element giving management a certain amount of control inside of Chapter 11 is that during the first 120 days of the case the debtor is granted the exclusive right to propose a plan of reorganization. During this period of exclusivity, the debtor is allowed an opportunity to negotiate with parties in interest to formulate a plan of reorganization. If a plan or reorganization is formulated, the debtor has an additional 60 days to solicit consents to its plan of reorganization. In the past, bankruptcy courts have routinely extended the periods of exclusivity. Once the exclusive period is terminated, creditors can put forward their own plan that will likely result in a resolution of reorganization issues in a far different fashion than contemplated by management. Examples of this are found in the Texaco, A.H. Robins, and Evans Products cases.

The ultimate loss of management control occurs if it is perceived that the Chapter 11 case is making no progress. Any party in interest may seek to have the Chapter 11 dismissed or else have the case converted to Chapter 7 liquidation. If dismissed, the automatic stay is lifted and creditors are then entitled to move to assert their contractual remedies (i.e., foreclose on collateral and accelerate payments of debt). If the case is converted to a Chapter 7, a trustee is appointed and the company is liquidated. Liquidation proceeds are paid out to parties in interest in accordance with a strict rule of absolute priority under which secured creditors have first priority and common stockholders come last. For large public companies, however, the vast majority of Chapter 11 cases have resulted in plans of reorganization rather than a dismissal or a conversion of the case.

The ability to control the timing of events is a key element of management control. Timing is a difficult thing to predict in a controlled Chapter 11 and impossible in an uncontrolled case. An average time for public companies to remain in Chapter 11 seems to be in a range between 18 months and three years.

Prepackaged/Prenegotiated Reorganizations

A prepackaged plan of reorganization is a plan that has been negotiated, documented, disclosed, and accepted by the requisite creditor majorities as set out in the bankruptcy code before the debtor files a Chapter 11 petition.

In a prenegotiated plan, in contrast, the debtor and the major stakeholders will enter into either a lockup or a plan-support agreement spelling out the relevant terms of the restructuring, and once support is achieved, file for Chapter 11.

Statutorily, prepackaged and prenegotiated plans are made possible by three sections of the bankruptcy code that (1) allow the debtor to file a plan of reorganization concurrently with the filing of a petition (Section 1121(a)); (2) recognize prepetition creditors' committees (Section 1102(b)(1)); and (3) set out the criteria for deeming a plan of reorganization accepted or rejected (Section 1126(b)).

In practice, debtors filing either prepackaged or prenegotiated Chapter 11 plans tend to be either smaller firms, firms with relatively simple capital structures (large or small), or both. For smaller firms, say less than $200 million in assets, this type of filing is their only chance of surviving as going concerns, as the costs of a prolonged contested Chapter 11 would very likely wipe out their estates. An obvious advantage of these plans is the shortened time spent in Chapter 11 with the attendant significant expense savings.

Prepackaged and prenegotiated plans are frequently used to bring about what is effectively an exchange offer of public debt while leaving other classes of creditors unimpaired. Such exchange offers can be accomplished with the two-thirds in amount and one-half in number of creditor votes that are the requisite approval numbers for a Chapter 11 plan. This could not be accomplished out of court since public debt indentures prohibit the change of money provisions without the consent of the individual creditors, creating the typical holdout problem in out-of-court exchange offers. Thus, one of the advantages of a prepackaged or prenegotiated plan is that it eliminates the holdout problem that exists in out-of-court exchange offers if the requisite votes can be obtained.

Another important advantage is that a court-approved disclosure document is not needed in the prefiling solicitation document as long as it complies with applicable nonbankruptcy law. Often, nonbankruptcy law refers to securities laws relating to exchange or tender offers when applicable. If no securities laws are applicable, then the disclosure document will be reviewed by the court at the time of filing.

Asset Sales

Asset sales in a bankruptcy case can be accomplished in a variety of ways. The debtor can file for Chapter 7 liquidation if there is no chance for a successful going-concern reorganization and have the trustee sell all of its assets. If the debtor files for Chapter 11, it can sell some or substantially all of its assets in three different ways. It can propose a liquidating plan of reorganization as allowed by Section 1123(b)(4) and sell all of its assets, it can sell some of its assets as part of a plan of reorganization, or it can effect asset sales pursuant to Section 363. If the debtor plans to sell substantially all of its assets, using Section 363 in a Chapter 11 case instead of a Chapter 7 liquidation has the advantage that management can continue running the operations of the business until the sale of assets is consummated, control the sale process, and perhaps negotiate better terms for the sale. Section 363 sales are also more time-efficient and cost-effective than pursuing such sales as part of a plan of reorganization.

Asset sales that are outside of the ordinary course of business can be effected after notice, a hearing, and competitive bidding, only if *any* of the following conditions are met as set forth in Section 363(f): (1) applicable nonbankruptcy law permits sale of such property free and clear of liens; (2) an entity's lien, encumbrance, or interest consents to such sale; (3) such interest is a lien and the price at which such property is to be sold is greater than the aggregate value of all liens on such property; (4) such interest is not in bona fide dispute; or (5) such entity can be compelled, in a legal or equitable proceeding, to accept a money satisfaction of such interest.

In approving a sale outside of the ordinary course of business, the court will weigh whether the sale is in the best interests of the estate; that is, it has been given adequate marketing, it has been negotiated and proposed in good faith, the buyer is acting in good faith, and so on. To achieve these objectives, courts will require that the sale is pursued through a competitive bidding procedure whereby either the debtor or the court will appoint a stalking horse bidder from those that have put in preliminary bids. As an incentive for stalking horse bidders, sellers give them protections that take several forms: First, if the stalking horse bid is not the winner, it is entitled to a negotiated breakup fee and/or a topping fee (a percentage of the difference between the winning bid and the stalking horse bid). Second, other bidders must submit bids at fixed premiums over the stalking horse initial bid, say 5 percent or 10 percent. These premiums are negotiated between the seller and the initial bidder. The stalking horse is likely to push for larger incremental premiums to discourage other bidders, while the seller would prefer smaller incremental premiums. Finally, the estate will pay for the stalking horse's reasonable expenses.

LEVERAGE FACTORS IN CHAPTER 11

The advantages of a speedy in-court reorganization are evident to all creditors in a case. Creditors would prefer faster and larger recoveries, less deterioration of the debtor's asset values, lower professional fees and expenses reducing the value of the estate, and so on. However, the parties involved in a Chapter 11 reorganization have not only communities of interests but conflicts of interest as well. The amount recovered by a creditor class under a proposed plan may determine the size of the loss of another class, and this creates inherent conflicts of interest between the different parties involved.

Exclusivity: Leverage of Management over Creditors

Section 1121(b) of the bankruptcy code gives the debtor the exclusive right to file a plan of reorganization for 120 days, and 60 extra days to solicit acceptances for the plan. As long as the debtor seems to be working in good faith toward rehabilitating the business, the exclusivity period can be routinely extended up to a maximum of 18 months to file a plan, with an extra two months to seek plan acceptances. Previous to the 2005 BAPCPA, there was no statutory time limit to the period of exclusivity, and the debtor could drag out a case for long periods of time. The debtor's exclusive right to file a plan of reorganization gives management a considerable amount of leverage over the reorganization process. It gives management control over the reorganization process and the drafting of a plan. Managements can extract important advantages in the area of corporate governance as part of a plan of reorganization in the form of: (1) huge compensation, (2) huge entrenchment, (3) charter and bylaws favorable to management, and (4) restrictions on trading newly issued securities. Even with the more stringent requirements for key employee retention plans (KERPs) set out in Section 503(c) of the bankruptcy code, managements have been able to keep control over their compensation by reworking their traditional KERPs into incentive plans instead.

Since exclusivity also gives the debtor and management time, and time is quite costly to unsecured creditors who do not get paid interest on their claims, management and/or equity control groups have the upper hand negotiating with them. Short of seeking the removal of management, which can be expensive and hard to accomplish, there is little unsecured creditors can do other than negotiate on the issues close to management like incentive plans that will encourage management to work toward a quick resolution of the case.

Secured Creditors' Leverage

The first order of business for holders of secured claims after the debtor files for bankruptcy protection is to seek the lifting of the automatic stay with respect to their claims so that either they can have debt service resumed (i.e., the debtor pays interest, principal, and premium as per the loan agreement) or the creditors can proceed to foreclose on their collateral. There are two statutory grounds for lifting the stay with respect to a secured claim that are spelled out in Section 362(d) of the bankruptcy code. The stay can be lifted for cause, including the lack of adequate protection of the interest in the collateral, or if the debtor does not have equity in such collateral *and* the collateral is not necessary to an effective reorganization.

At the center of disputes regarding how much of a claim is a secured claim and/or whether it is adequately protected is the issue of collateral valuation. Section 506(a) of the bankruptcy code states that "such value shall be determined in light of the purpose of the valuation and of the proposed disposition or use of such property, and in conjunction with any hearing on such disposition or use or on a plan affecting such creditor's interest." *Disposition* and *use* are the two key words to take into consideration to determine what the likely valuation methodology of the secured claim collateral will be.[1] If the collateral is needed to generate cash through a sale but does not add to the going-concern value of the debtor, it will likely be valued at its liquidation value. If the property will add to the going concern of the debtor, then it will likely be valued at replacement cost.

The valuation of the collateral is important for several reasons. The obvious one is that it is a determinant of the extent to which a secured claim is actually secured. The value of the collateral in relation to the amount of the claim determines whether the holder of the claim is undersecured, just secured, or oversecured. In the event that the secured claim is undersecured, the holder has a secured claim to the extent of the value of the collateral and an unsecured claim for the deficiency, provided the secured claim holder does not make an 1111(b) election; if the secured claim is oversecured, Section 506(b) assures that the holder of such claim shall be allowed interest on the claim and any reasonable fees, costs, or charges provided for under the credit agreement.

The valuation of the collateral also plays an important role in the determination of adequate protection payments should a petition to lift the stay be denied. The lower the valuation of the collateral, the easier it is in principle to provide adequate protection by the debtor. However, if the adequate protection scheme approved by the court were to prove inadequate after the fact, the secured claim holder will have a priority administrative claim for the deficiency.

Leverage over Secured Creditors

Although rarely used, courts have the discretion to subordinate any claim to other claims based on the principle of equitable subordination (Section

510(c)(1)). Equitable subordination is an intercreditor remedy that effects a reordering of priorities between claims, and courts use it based on the specific facts of a case. Case history shows that equitable subordination is used to punish misconduct of holders of claims that are either insiders or fiduciaries, and courts have been reluctant to use it in other cases. In Enron's Chapter 11 case, the debtor sought to use equitable subordination for certain of Citigroup's claims, arguing that Citigroup, one of its main lenders, had a hand in its collapse, which became apparent in July 2003 when the Securities and Exchange Commission (SEC) announced that it had settled enforcement proceedings against Citigroup in connection with its alleged role in Enron's manipulation of financial statements.

Both the debtor in possession (DIP) and unsecured creditors may also have leverage over secured creditors in the area of invalid liens. Challenges to a secured claim can be made based on technical imperfections on liens. The statutory bases for such challenges are the avoiding powers granted by Sections 544(a) and 547(e) of the bankruptcy code.

The debtor has leverage over the holders of secured claims through the treatment of their collateral in the proposed plan of reorganization and how such treatment will influence the collateral valuation.

Foreclosure sales of property before the debtor files for Chapter 11 protection can be challenged on the basis of the fraudulent conveyance section of the bankruptcy code, Section 548(a)(1)(B), provided the debtor was insolvent at the time such foreclosure took place and within two years of the petition date. The 2005 BAPCPA extended the look-back period from one year to two years. However, in fraudulent conveyance and fraudulent transfer matters, debtors are free to use the Universal Fraudulent Transfer Code adopted by 38 states. This code tracks Section 548(a)(1)(B) except for statutes of limitations, which in many states are six years rather than the two years in the bankruptcy code. Perhaps the statute of limitations should be capped?

Leverage over Unsecured Creditors

The debtor has considerable leverage over trade creditors in jurisdictions where critical vendor payment motions are regularly approved by the court. Critical vendor payments pose a serious threat to general unsecured creditors, especially those trade creditors not deemed critical and other general unsecured creditors. These payments constitute preferential transfers that take away value from other similarly situated creditors. Although the Kmart decision may have provided some pause to the approval of such motions in some jurisdictions, it may have only accentuated the need for the debtor to forum shop.

Intercorporate guarantees, especially upstream guarantees where an operating subsidiary (where all the valuable assets usually reside) provides guarantees to parent company creditors, can also be challenged on the basis of the fraudulent conveyance section of the bankruptcy code.

Corporate structure plays an important role in providing structural priorities to the claims of creditors of different entities in such structures. For example, trade claims at an operating subsidiary will have priority in payment over parent company unsecured claims in the absence of subsidiary guarantees of parent company debt. This vertical priority, known as structural subordination, as well as other horizontal (subsidiary-subsidiary) priorities can be eliminated if a party in interest to the case convinces the court to substantively consolidate the two entities. Substantive consolidation is an equitable remedy created by the court to pool the assets and liabilities of two or more entities, and to use the pooled assets to satisfy the claims of creditors of all the consolidated entities. By substantively consolidating two or more entities, the court eliminates intercompany claims, as well as guaranty claims against any consolidated entity that guaranteed the obligations of another consolidated entity. Courts are usually reluctant to require substantive consolidation unless it can be shown that the businesses were always operated as one entity with, for example, the same board of directors and no keeping of separate books and records.

Three

The Investment Process

10
How to Analyze: Valuation

The importance of corporate valuation in the context of distress investing cannot be overemphasized. Whether a company will be reorganized out of court or in a Chapter 11 proceeding, the workout potential of a specific credit instrument will depend on corporate values, among other things. Most credit analyses revolve around trying to predict whether a money default will occur in the future. Distress investing starts with the assumption that a money default will occur, and evaluates the workout potential of different credit instruments in the corporate capital structure, taking into consideration the rules governing Chapter 11. This is so because the actual rules governing a Chapter 11 reorganization will heavily influence any reorganization that takes place, whether in court or out of court. For example, the use of the rule of absolute priority, combined with a reasonable valuation, will help the distress investor estimate how deeply in-the-money or out-of-the-money a particular credit instrument may be, and thus its potential workout value. The period of exclusivity during which only the debtor can propose a plan of reorganization may provide a benchmark time to workout.

The analysis that goes into the valuation of a company in financial distress is very similar to the analysis of a leveraged buyout (LBO) or a management buyout (MBO). Several factors complicate the valuation process, however. Unlike someone valuing an LBO company, distress investors seldom have the chance to undertake a thorough due diligence investigation. Rather, they have to rely exclusively on the public record. Moreover, companies in financial distress tend to be weaker and not as well managed as LBO targets. What were formerly viewed as valuable assets become less valuable in the hands of a debtor that files for Chapter 11. These factors introduce substantially higher valuation risks that will be reflected in the difference between the true economic value of the estate and that used to value the postreorganization company.

Traditional valuation approaches give much weight to the view that firms are strict going concerns. Accordingly, most valuations focus only on the ability of firms to generate cash flows or earnings from operations in the future. We view companies as having elements of both going concern and resource conversion. Thus, our approach to valuing companies is less a matter of general principle and more a matter of understanding the business and valuing both the going concern as well as its resource conversion attributes.

STRICT GOING CONCERN VALUATION

Cash Flow- or Earnings-Based Valuation

The reader should be aware that almost all estimates of future cash flows and future earnings are notorious for their unreliability. Thus, for any reasonable Chapter 11 plan of reorganization to meet a feasibility standard, the capitalization of a company upon reorganization should be conservative. Forecasts, while essential for valuation, are famously unreliable in the real world.

We define a going concern as a business operation devoted to the same day-to-day operations it has always conducted, within the same industries in which it has operated, managed and controlled as it has always been managed and controlled and financed pretty much as it has always been controlled and financed. Based on this definition, it is easy to see that strict going concerns generate wealth only by generating either free cash flows or earnings from operations. For us, corporate earnings are defined as creating wealth while consuming cash. Earnings are what occurs for most successful companies over the intermediate and longer term; corporate earnings cannot have going-concern value unless combined with access to capital markets to make up for cash shortfalls. Strict going concerns tend to be a rarity.

Corporations also generate wealth by converting assets to other uses (divestitures, mergers, and acquisitions) or to other ownership and control (LBOs, MBOs, and IPOs), and by financing asset acquisitions, refinancing liabilities, or both. We refer to these activities as resource conversion activities. A casual inspection of the resource conversion activities of the component companies of the Dow Jones Industrial Average for the past five years drives the point home that strict going concerns are rare. (See Exhibit 10.1.)

Although pure going concerns tend to be rare, much of the academic and professional literature implicitly assumes that firms are strict going concerns when discussing firm valuation.

This view seems also embedded in the bankruptcy code. Whether an estate is to be reorganized or liquidated is pursuant to Section 1129(a)

EXHIBIT 10.1 Resource Conversion Activity for the Companies in the Dow Jones Industrial Average, 2001–2006

Name	Total	Acquisitions	Spin-Offs
3M Co.	32	32	0
Alcoa Inc.	28	28	0
Altria Group Inc.	12	12	0
American Express Co.	22	15	7
American International Group Inc.	38	38	0
AT&T Inc.	14	14	0
Boeing Co.	9	9	0
Caterpillar Inc.	16	16	0
Citigroup Inc.	96	90	6
Coca-Cola Co.	24	24	0
E.I. Du Pont de Nemours & Co.	22	22	0
Exxon Mobil Corp.	9	9	0
General Electric Co.	277	277	0
General Motors Corp.	39	39	0
Hewlett-Packard Co.	32	32	0
Home Depot Inc.	31	31	0
Honeywell International Inc.	25	25	0
Intel Corp.	15	15	0
International Business Machines Corp.	71	71	0
Johnson & Johnson	36	36	0
JPMorgan Chase & Co.	98	97	1
McDonald's Corp.	8	2	6
Merck & Co. Inc.	11	6	5
Microsoft Corp.	47	47	0
Pfizer Inc.	23	23	0
Procter & Gamble Co.	19	17	2
United Technologies Corp.	46	46	0
Verizon Communications Inc.	43	37	6
Wal-Mart Stores Inc.	13	13	0
Walt Disney Co.	21	19	2

or (b) (i.e., the rules for the confirmation of a plan of reorganization). Section 1129(a)(7) creates a "best interest of creditors" test requiring that all dissenting members of a class—even those belonging to a class that accepts the plan—receive at least as much under the plan as they would have received in a Chapter 7 liquidation. In other words, for a plan of reorganization to be approved, creditors have to be better off if the business remains a going concern than if it is liquidated under Chapter 7, albeit valuation in a plan of reorganization can sometimes, but not frequently, reflect resource conversion opportunities. Reflecting a going concern test, the exhibits to a plan of reorganization will always have pro forma financial statements projecting results for three to five years for the going concern, as well as a Chapter 7 liquidation analysis. A going concern analysis and valuation of the debtor is a crucial part to most Chapter 11 plans.

The earnings proxy most commonly used is adjusted generally accepted accounting principles (GAAP) EBITDA. EBITDA stands for earnings before interest, taxes, depreciation, and amortization. Exhibit 10.2 shows a sample calculation of EBITDA. EBITDA calculation involves adjusting net income to arrive at an estimate of earnings from operations. The first adjustment is to add back interest expenses. This adjustment removes the capital structure effect on the generation of earnings from operations. The second adjustment is to add back taxes paid. Since the tax liability also depends on the company's capital structure, this adjustment further removes this effect from the estimation of earnings. Finally, depreciation and amortization expenses are added back, because they are noncash expenses.

For GAAP EBITDA to represent the most likely future earnings from operations, the number usually needs to be adjusted further. The distress investor is interested in estimating earnings likely to continue in the future, and all adjustments to EBITDA need to reflect this goal. Since the calculation of EBITDA starts with net income, the analyst needs to find out whether nonrecurrent and/or nonoperating income and expenses went into its calculation. If so, net income needs to be adjusted to be reflective of only income and expenses from continuing operations. A few of the likely adjustments are discussed next.

EXHIBIT 10.2 Sample EBITDA Calculation

Income Statement		EBITDA Calculation	
Sales	$500.00	Net Income (Loss)	$26.00
Cost of Goods Sold	$375.00	Interest Expense	$15.00
Gross Margin	$125.00	Taxes	$14.00
Sales, General, & Admin.	$ 40.00	Depreciation & Amortization	$30.00
Depreciation & Amortization	$ 30.00	EBITDA	$85.00
Interest Expense	$ 15.00		
Pretax Income (Loss)	$ 40.00		
Taxes	$ 14.00		
Net Income (Loss)	$ 26.00		

Depreciation and Capital Expenditures   In the calculation of EBITDA shown in Exhibit 10.2, net income sometimes needs to be adjusted by depreciation because depreciation sometimes represents a noncash expense. Depreciation as a noncash expense is common in the valuation of income-producing real estate. For going concerns involved in manufacturing or distribution, most depreciation becomes a cash expense in the analysis of the going concern. This is the general rationale for making the adjustment to estimate earnings from operations. Depreciation expenses also reflect historical capital investment decisions, and the choices that managements made regarding the depreciation method used to calculate those expenses. Adding back depreciation expenses to net income removes the effect of these factors. However, since GAAP gives management choices on how to depreciate assets, the amount of book depreciation may be quite different from the required capital expenditures needed to maintain those assets. In cases when depreciation is lower than the required capital expenses, unadjusted EBITDA will overestimate earnings; and the reverse will be true when depreciation expenses are larger than the required capital expenses. Exhibit 10.3 shows three technology companies that represent examples of each of these situations. Most of their depreciation charges were the equivalent of a cash expense.

For illustration purposes, we chose the annual median capital expenditure (capex) reported in the past five years as a proxy for the required amount. In the Intel Corporation case, the median five-year reported capex matches depreciation expenses closely. For Texas Instruments, capex is larger than depreciation expenses, and in the case of Micron Technology, capex is considerably lower than depreciation expenses. In the case of Intel it is justifiable to use earnings before interest and taxes (EBIT) as the proxy for earnings from operations, but EBIT would overestimate operating earnings for Texas Instruments and underestimate them for Micron Technology. Of course, estimating the needed capital expenditures is easier said than done and requires a thorough understanding of the business. Also, one must be

EXHIBIT 10.3 Median Annual Capital Expenditures versus
Depreciation Expenses, 2006

Company	Five-Year Median Annual Capex ($Millions)	Depreciation Expenses ($Millions)
Texas Instruments	$1,260	$1,052
Intel Corporation	$4,703	$4,654
Micron Technology	$1,081	$1,718

aware that reported capital expenses on the statement of cash flows might be quite different from the amount actually required by the business. This can be especially important for companies in distress since it is very likely that these companies preserved liquidity by postponing the necessary capital expenditures, and the investor may get a very distorted picture of its earnings experience if only reported capex is considered in the analysis. In analyzing technology companies, earnings will be far more important than cash flows. In estimating earnings for, say, the next five years, the analyst will also have to estimate how cash shortfalls will be financed.

In sum, a more accurate measure of a company's earnings going forward will be EBITDA minus the necessary capital expenditures to maintain the capital stock. This last amount may be considerably different from the one reported on the financial statements of a company in financial distress.

Restructuring Charges When companies restructure by closing production facilities, laying off workers, or selling unprofitable businesses, they take a one-time charge that bundles together the costs of this restructuring. GAAP requires that estimated current and future costs associated with the restructuring be charged against income in the year in which the decision to restructure is made even though the actual expenditures will take place over time. A liability reserve is created, and the actual expenses are charged against this reserve. The analyst should remember that (1) not all of these charges are cash charges, (2) these expenses are actually incurred over time even though they are charged all at once, and (3) judgment should be used to determine which of these charges are truly one-time charges and will affect operating earnings in the future. Under GAAP, information about these activities should be part of the footnotes to the financial statements, and footnotes should include:

- A description of the exit or disposal activity and the expected completion date.
- The place in the income statement or statement of activities where exit or disposal costs are presented.
- For each major cost attributable to the exit activity, the total cost expected, the amount incurred in the current year, and the cumulative amount to date.
- Reconciliation of the beginning and ending liability balances, presenting the changes during the year associated to costs incurred and charged to expense, costs paid or otherwise settled, and any adjustments of the liability along with the reasons for doing so.

EXHIBIT 10.4 Statement of Operations: Special and Restructuring Charges—Home Products International, Inc. ($ in Thousands Except EPS)

	53 Weeks Ended 12/29/96		52 Weeks Ended 12/24/95	
Net Sales	$297,048	100.0%	$294,297	100.0%
Costs of Goods Sold	$235,144	79.2%	$209,641	71.2%
Special Charges, Net	$ 1,920	0.6%	$ 8,589	2.9%
Gross Profit	$ 59,984	20.2%	$ 76,067	25.8%
Operating Expenses	$ 44,732	15.1%	$ 45,845	15.6%
Restructuring and Other Charges	$ 10,482	3.5%	$ 5,966	2.0%
Asset Impairment Charges	$ 53,348	18.0%	$ —	0.0%
Other Nonrecurring Charges	$ —	0.0%	$ 445	0.2%
Operating Profit (Loss)	$ (48,578)	−16.4%	$ 23,811	8.1%
Interest Expense	$ 22,363	7.5%	$ 20,271	6.9%
Other Income (Expense)	$ (467)	−0.2%	$ 542	0.2%
Earnings (Loss) before Income Taxes	$ (71,408)	−24.0%	$ 4,082	1.4%
Income Tax Expense	$ 103	0.0%	$ 2,072	0.7%
Net Earnings (Loss)	$ (71,511)	−24.1%	$ 2,010	0.7%
Net Earnings (Loss) per Common Share (Basic)	$ (9.77)		$ 0.27	
Net Earnings (Loss) per Common Share (Diluted)	$ (9.77)		$ 0.27	

Exhibit 10.4 presents the statement of operations for Home Products International, Inc. for fiscal year 1996, where we can find special and restructuring charges of $1.92 million and $10.482 million, respectively.

Included as part of Note 2 to the financial statements are Exhibit 10.5, which itemizes the expected total restructuring costs charged to both the cost of goods sold and operating expenses, and Exhibit 10.6 which summarizes the charges for the year, the amounts utilized for such year and the reserve balance.

Armed with this information, the analyst must decide which adjustments to make to EBITDA and net income.

Asset Impairment Charges An impairment exists when the carrying amount of a long-lived asset exceeds its fair value and is nonrecoverable. Impairments may arise from significant decreases in the market price of a long-lived asset, a change in how the company uses an asset, or changes in the business climate that could affect the asset value. Fair value is the amount

EXHIBIT 10.5 Summary of Cash and Noncash Charges—Home Products International, Inc., 2000

	Expected Cash Charge	Noncash Charge	Totals
Cost of Goods Sold			
Special Charges:			
Inventory Dispositions	—	$ 2,912	$ 2,912
Obsolete and Duplicate Molds	—	$ 221	$ 221
SKU Reduction and Inventory Adjustments Related to 1999 Special Charges	—	$ (1,213)	$ (1,213)
Total Charge to Cost of Goods Sold	—	$ 1,920	$ 1,920
Operating Expenses			
Restructuring and Other Charges:			
Plant and Facilities Asset Disposition and Lease Termination Costs	$3,950	$ 2,086	$ 6,036
Elimination of Obsolete Molds	—	$ 2,585	$ 2,585
Employee-Related Costs	$ 884	—	$ 884
Other Costs	$ 477	$ 500	$ 977
Subtotal	$5,311	$ 5,171	$10,482
Asset Impairment Charges:			
Goodwill Impairment	—	$44,404	$44,404
Impairment of Equipment and Molds	—	$ 8,944	$ 8,944
Subtotal	—	$53,348	$53,348
Total Charge to Operating Expenses	$5,311	$58,519	$63,830
Total Net Charges	$5,311	$60,439	$65,750

EXHIBIT 10.6 Utilization of Reserves Established for Year 2000 Charges—Home Products International, Inc.

	2000 Charge	Amounts Utilized in 2000	Reserve Balance at 12/30/2000
Inventory	$ 2,912	$ (612)	$2,300
Molds	$ 2,806	$ (2,806)	—
Plant and Facilities	$ 6,036	$ (726)	$5,310
Employee Costs	$ 884	$ (21)	$ 863
Other	$ 977	$ (130)	$ 847
Goodwill Impairment	$44,404	$(44,404)	—
Impairment of Molds	$ 8,944	$ (8,944)	—
Total	$66,963	$(57,643)	$9,320
1999 Special Charges	$ (1,213)		
	$65,750		

an asset could be bought or sold for in a current transaction between willing parties. Although quoted prices in active markets are the best evidence of fair values, theses prices are not always available. In such cases, fair-value estimates or use valuation techniques such as the expected or the traditional present value method are used. GAAP requires that a description of the impaired asset and the facts and circumstances leading to the impairment be disclosed in the notes to the financial statements. The technique used to calculate fair value must also be footnoted together with the business segment associated with the impaired asset.

The 2000 charges and asset impairment charges are summarized in Exhibit 10.5.

The 2000 charges and asset impairment charges include a $1,213 reversal of SKU reduction and inventory adjustments relating to the 1999 special charges. The total 2000 charges and asset impairment charges were $66,963 after excluding the impact of the $1,213 1999 special charges reversal.

The 2000 utilization of the reserves established in connection with the 2000 charges and asset impairment charges was as shown in Exhibit 10.6.

The amounts utilized during 2000 totaled $57,643, of which $57,492 was noncash costs.

Companies in distress will likely have a history of asset impairment charges and corresponding asset write-downs. Although these charges do not represent cash outlays and should be added back to the adjusted EBITDA or net income calculation, they will likely contribute to the generation of net operating losses (NOLs) that may become deferred tax assets for a reorganized company.

Interest and Rent Expenses The purpose of adding back interest expenses to net income when calculating EBITDA is to remove the effect of how the firm is financed from the estimation of earnings from operations or net income. This allows the analyst to compare firms with different amounts of debt in their capital structures.

Operating lease payments are fixed obligations that are included in the income statement as expenses. When comparing two firms, one that owns and one that leases, the one that owns will very likely appear to have a larger unadjusted EBITDA. To make both companies' EBITDAs comparable, the analyst should add back the lease expense to net income. The resulting adjusted EBITDA is known as EBITDAR. (See Exhibit 10.7.)

This adjustment has liabilities and assets implications as well. The capitalized operating lease expenses are equivalent to a long-term obligation that increases the amount of long-term debt on the balance sheet. However, since unexpired commercial leases can be either assumed or rejected by the debtor

EXHIBIT 10.7 Calculation of EBITDAR for Starbucks Corporation and Darden Restaurants, Inc.

	Starbucks	Darden Restaurants
Exchange	NASDAQ	NYSE
Ticker	SBUX	DRI
Source of Financial Data	10-K, Dec. 14, 2006	10-K, July 19, 2007
EBITDAR Calculation ($ in 000s)		
Net Income	$ 564,259	$ 201,400
Interest Adjustment	$ 8,400	$ 40,100
Tax Adjustment	$ 324,770	$ 153,700
Depreciation & Amortization Adjustment	$ 387,211	$ 200,400
EBITDA	$1,284,640	$ 595,600
Net Revenue	$6,583,098	$5,567,100
EBITDA as % of Net Revenue	19.51%	10.70%
Lease Expense	$ 498,809	$ 75,900
EBITDAR	$1,783,449	$ 671,500
EBITDAR as % of Net Revenue	27.09%	12.06%

in Chapter 11, the actual size of this liability for a company in financial distress will be dependent on the specifics of the Chapter 11 reorganization process. Most important, should the debtor carry below-market-rate leases, these can become a significant asset for the reorganized company. We discuss this matter later in this chapter.

What Is the Valuation Multiple?

The valuation multiple is simply a present value factor. Multiples can be interpreted as the present value of a one-dollar annuity. The reciprocal of this number is also called the capitalization rate. When one multiplies adjusted EBITDA by a multiple, the resulting number can be interpreted as the present value of the series of adjusted EBITDA flows in the future; this quantity is commonly known as the *fixed multiple enterprise value* (FMEV) to differentiate it from the market *enterprise value* (EV), defined in the next section.

The size of the multiple is a function of a discount rate, an assumed constant growth rate for the EBITDA flows over time, and a length of time over which this present value is calculated. Exhibit 10.8 shows the calculation of different multiples, given different assumptions for the discount rate and growth rate per period when we assume 25 periods as the time horizon.

EXHIBIT 10.8 Multiples Calculated under Different Growth and Discount Rate Assumptions

Discount Rate	Growth Rates				
	0.0%	2.0%	4.0%	6.0%	8.0%
10%	9.1×	10.6×	12.6×	15.1×	18.4×
15%	6.5×	7.3×	8.4×	9.7×	11.3×
20%	4.9×	5.5×	6.1×	6.8×	7.7×
25%	4.0×	4.3×	4.7×	5.2×	5.7×
30%	3.3×	3.6×	3.8×	4.1×	4.5×
35%	2.9×	3.0×	3.2×	3.4×	3.7×

The formula used to calculate the multiples in Exhibit 10.8 is:

$$\text{Multiple} = \sum_{i=1}^{25} \frac{(1+g)^i}{(1+r)^i}$$

where g is the annual rate of growth and r is the discount rate. This way of calculating multiples is consistent with the discounted cash flow (DCF) practice of discounting estimated cash flows for a short time period and then adding the perpetuity present value of the nongrowing cash flows thereon. Using more than 25 periods in the calculation of the multiples has negligible effects on their size when we deal with the low-growth assumptions that a distress investor would typically use.

The EBITDA multiple method to valuing a strict going concern is a close substitute to the more time-consuming DCF methodology. Only when future cash flows are influenced by non-going-concern factors like acquisitions, major recapitalizations, and so on are the two methods not good substitutes for each other. The advantage of DCF in these situations is that the specifics of nonrecurring and/or nonoperating one-time events can be easily included in the valuation process.

How to Choose a Valuation Multiple?

The goal in selecting a multiple is to arrive at a valuation figure that is realistic enough for the case at hand. Should the company under consideration file for Chapter 11 and be reorganized, it is likely that the financial adviser doing its valuation will use, among other things, a comparable company analysis. Since this type of analysis is likely to play a role in the final determination of the value of the reorganized company value and affect the potential recoveries of the creditors participating in the reorganization, a distress investor needs to know what the likely outcome of such valuation would be.

The comparable company methodology consists of estimating the value of a company based on the implied valuations of similar companies. This type of analysis can be performed using comparable companies that are publicly held and/or using values based on prices paid in announced mergers and acquisitions involving companies similar to the one at hand. We refer to the first type of analysis as the comparable public company analysis, and to the second type as the comparable acquisition analysis or deal-based valuation. These implied valuations are summarized in the comparable firms' enterprise value to EBITDA multiples. The *enterprise value* (EV) of a firm is defined as the market value of its equity plus the market (or book) value of its debt, minority interests, and preferred stock, minus excess cash. This value is the outside passive minority investor (OPMI) market indication of the going-concern value of the company's assets. When this number is divided by adjusted EBITDA, we obtain a comparable firm valuation multiple. If the comparable companies are publicly held we call the multiple the *public comparable multiple*, and if the comparable companies are recent acquisitions we call the multiple the *comparable deal multiple* or *comparable acquisition multiple*.

A key practical factor to this valuation approach is the selection of companies with business and operational characteristics relatively similar to those of the company at hand. Criteria for selecting comparable companies include but are not limited to:

- Similar lines of business.
- Similar growth prospects.
- Comparable size and scale of operations.
- Similar business risks.

The use of Standard Industrial Classification (SIC) codes, North American Industry Classification System (NAICS) codes, or Global Industry Classification System (GICS) codes can help find companies in the same industry and sector. However, the selection of truly comparable companies requires substantial amounts of judgment, can be difficult, and is subject to limitations like the lack of availability of meaningful market-based information.

To illustrate the process of comparable company analysis, we have chosen to show the going-concern valuation of Home Products International, Inc. as an investment adviser performed it during its prepackaged Chapter 11 reorganization in early 2007. This is a case of a comparable public company analysis. Exhibit 10.9 shows the list of comparable companies, together with their EV/EBITDA multiples.

EXHIBIT 10.9 Public Comparable Company Analysis—Home Products International, Inc. (Forward Analysis, $ in Millions)

Company	Annual Revenue	EBITDA Margin	Market Cap	Net Debt[b]	Total Enterprise Value	LTM[a] TEV Multiples Revenue	EBITDA	2007 TEV Multiples Revenue	EBITDA
Home Products International, Inc.[c]	$ 210	5.00%							
Newell Rubbermaid Inc.	$6,771	13.90%	$8,455	$2,171	$10,625	1.6×	11.3×	1.6×	10.7×
Tupperware Brands Corporation	$1,619	12.30%	$1,395	$ 601	$ 1,996	1.2×	10.0×	1.1×	7.6×
Myers Industries Inc.	$ 943	10.80%	$ 580	$ 202	$ 781	0.8×	7.6×	0.9×	7.6×
National Presto Industries Inc.	$ 260	15.80%	$ 428	$ (122)	$ 306	1.2×	7.5×	N/A	N/A
Craftmade International Inc.	$ 115	13.40%	$ 93	$ 21	$ 114	1.0×	7.4×	1.0×	7.6×
					Mean	1.2×	8.8×	1.2×	8.4×
					Median	1.2×	7.6×	1.1×	7.6×

Capital IQ was the source of the comparables data, and Reuters Estimates was the source for the forward estimates.

[a]Last 12 months.

[b]Net debt calculated as the sum of total debt, preferred stock, and minority interests, less cash.

[c]Home Products International, Inc. 2007 forecast.

Since the enterprise value of a troubled company is always open to question, comparable multiples will only serve as upper bounds for valuation. The actual multiples used to value the troubled debtor will generally be lower than those of their comparable peers. In the case of Home Products International, Inc. valuation, the chosen EV multiple was 4.63×, which was considerably lower than the multiples that public markets were giving its healthy peers.

RESOURCE CONVERSION VALUATION

Separate and Salable Assets

As we said before, we approach the valuation of companies in distress taking into consideration both their pure going concern and their resource conversion attributes. GAAP requires that companies report financial results by business segments in their annual reports, but segmental information is not required for unconsolidated subsidiaries or investees. This information may be provided in the body of financial statements, in separate schedules, or in the footnotes. Company operating segments are based on the company's organizational structure, revenue sources, and the nature of its activities.

The segregation of company EBITDA into segment EBITDAs can lead to spotting underperforming segments that weigh down on consolidated adjusted EBITDA. A detailed analysis of segment performance may help to:

- Identify underperforming segments.
- Improve the appraisal of the adjusted EBITDA number on a consolidated basis.
- Identify assets that could be sold and not affect (or might even improve) the adjusted EBITDA generation ability of the company.

An example of this last point can be illustrated by a retailer that owns its properties and identifies locations with very poor performance. In this case, selling the losing properties will provide cash and improve consolidated cash flow generation by removing units that weighed down on historical consolidated EBITDA. For example, one year after emerging from Chapter 11, Kmart Holdings reached agreements with Home Depot U.S.A., Inc. to sell four properties for about $59 million.

Chapter 11 and the Assignment of Leases

If the company in distress is a tenant under an unexpired commercial lease, it will have to either assume or reject the lease after filing for Chapter 11. The debtor in possession has 210 days to make this decision, and although many leases contain restrictions or outright prohibitions on the debtor's ability to assign the lease, many of these provisions will be unenforceable in Chapter 11. This can allow a debtor to assume and assign a lease to a third party over the lessor's objection, and since third parties will often pay substantial sums to take over leases with rent obligations below current market rates, these below-market leases can be valuable assets for debtors. This is an example of where the rules of Chapter 11 play a very important role in uncovering valuable assets. As an example of such value, in June 2004, Kmart Holdings reached agreements with Home Depot U.S.A., Inc. and Sears Roebuck & Company to assign up to 72 properties for cash in excess of $800 million.

Net Operating Losses

Companies that file for Chapter 11 protection are likely to have several years of net operating losses (NOLs). The value of these NOLs is that, with certain limitations, the Internal Revenue Code (IRC) will allow companies to use the losses and apply them against future profits, thus sheltering future profits from taxation. Generally, NOLs can be carried back for two years and to the extent not used may be carried forward for 20 years. Needless to say, the size of this asset can be substantial. The catch is that the IRC significantly limits the ability of a company to preserve its NOL upon a change in ownership, and unfortunately, the vast majority of Chapter 11 reorganizations result in a change in ownership under Section 382 of the IRC. The tax attributes that remain under the change of ownership are subject to an annual limitation on their future use. However, under certain circumstances, a debtor can undergo a change in ownership in Chapter 11 and emerge without any Section 382 limitation on its NOLs. To qualify for this election, the following conditions must be met:

- Shareholders and creditors of the company must end up owning at least 50 percent of the reorganized debtor's stock by vote and value.
- Shareholders and creditors must receive their 50 percent stock ownership in discharge of their interest in and claims against the debtor.
- Stock received by creditors can be counted toward the 50 percent test only if it is received in satisfaction of debt that (1) had been held by the creditor for at least 18 months on the date of the bankruptcy filing ("old and cold") or (2) arose in the ordinary course of the debtor's business and is held by the person who at all times held the beneficial interest in that indebtedness.

If the company's business enterprise is not continued at all times during the two-year period beginning upon the confirmation of the plan of reorganization, or if a second change in ownership occurs within two years, the company will forfeit the benefit from rule 382(1)(5). As the reader can guess, these rules place a heavy burden on the debtor to monitor the identity of its creditors and shareholders since a significant amount of stock or claims transfers can jeopardize the debtor's valuable tax attributes. As an example, in a recent case, United Airlines Corporation was successful in preventing its employee stock ownership plan (ESOP) from selling its majority stockholdings, and so was able to preserve NOLs estimated to exceed $20 billion.

The preservation of valuable tax attributes by companies that file for Chapter 11 is an important consideration in the valuation of such companies. The value of the NOLs is heavily dependent on how successful the debtor is in preserving this tax attribute, and this may not be perfectly known at the time a distress investor is considering making a purchase. The lower bound for the value of the debtor's NOLs will be given by the IRC annual limitations on the NOL's future use after a change of ownership under Section 382. Under FASB 109, the present value of future expected cash savings from the use of NOLs is carried on a company's balance sheet as a "deferred tax asset." As the cash savings from the NOL are realized in the future, the accounting treatment is to credit the deferred tax asset and charge the company income with an income tax expense.

LIQUIDATION VALUATIONS

Finding the liquidation values of the assets of a company in distress is a needed step in assessing the likely workout potential of a credit instrument. Although not readily obvious, the analysis of a party's hypothetical position and degree of negotiating leverage in a Chapter 11 reorganization will depend on the same party's position in a hypothetical Chapter 7 liquidation. Chapter 11 reorganization negotiations depend on what would happen to each party if the case were converted to a Chapter 7. Under the rules of Chapter 11 for the confirmation of a reorganization plan, a *best interests* test needs to be performed. The best interests test requires a finding that the amount that each creditor will receive under the plan of reorganization has a present value of at least as much as the total amount to be obtained by selling each asset in a Chapter 7 liquidation. Exhibit 10.10 presents the results of the liquidation analysis performed for the prepackaged Chapter 11 reorganization of Home Products International in early 2007.

EXHIBIT 10.10 Home Products International, Inc. Liquidation Analysis ($000 Omitted)

Account	Chapter 7 Liquidation Scenario		
	Adjusted Book Balance 1/10/07	Estimated Recovery	Liquidation Value
Cash	$ —		
Accounts Receivable	$ 38,446	60%	$ 23,068
Trade	$ 72	0%	$ —
Miscellaneous Receivables	$ 220	100%	$ 220
Insurance Claims			$ —
Inventory			$ —
Raw Material	$ 4,873	41%	$ 2,002
Inventory in Transit	$ 1,172	41%	$ 481
Work in Progress	$ 1,365	41%	$ 561
Finished Goods	$ 16,974	41%	$ 6,973
Prepaids	$ 2,258	0%	$ —
Property, Plant & Equipment—Net Book Value			
Land and Buildings	$ 7,390	100%	$ 7,390
Machinery and Equipment	$ 5,645	75%	$ 4,230
Dies/Patterns	$ 3,109	20%	$ 622
All Other	$ 7,274	2%	$ 145
Goodwill	$ 71,419	0%	$ —
Other Assets	$ 757	0%	$ —
Mexican Assets	$ 778	10%	$ 78
Total Assets	$161,752		$ 45,769
Less: Estimated Liquidation Costs			$ (4,100)
Real Estate Holding Cost			$ (2,000)
Net Available			$ 39,669
Less: Secured Debt			$ (35,064)
Net Available after Secured Debt			$ 4,605
Less: Priority Tax Claims			$ (1,094)
Net Available after Secured Debt and Priority Tax Claims			$ 3,511
Less: Secured Employee Claims			$ (937)
Net Available for Unsecured Claims			$ 2,574
Less: Unsecured Note Holders			$(116,050)
All Others			$ (59,202)
Net Available (Deficiency)			$(172,678)

Recovery by Class	% Distribution
Secured Debt (Class 2)	100%
Priority Tax Claims	100%
Secured Employee Claims (Class 1)	100%
Unsecured Note Holders (Class 5) and All Other (Class 4)	15%

11

Due Diligence for Distressed Issues

Due diligence means reasonable care under the circumstances. By its very nature, research when involved with distressed securities is a document-intensive activity and a legal-intensive activity. One of the reasons why the authors are attracted to distress investing is that, so much more than other types of investing, it involves understanding contractual and legal rights rather than making macroeconomic forecasts. The purpose of this chapter is to impart to the reader information and understanding about the principal documents he or she will make use of before making investment decisions in the distress area.

Before reviewing documents, it is important for the reader to do reverse engineering—that is, understand the factors that motivate the vast majority of people who prepare disclosure documents. These people are corporate attorneys, public accountants, and bankruptcy attorneys. Prepetition, it is corporate attorneys who prepare the various documents filed with the Securities and Exchange Commission (SEC), all of which are readily available online at no cost.

Principal filed documents by troubled corporations include Form 10-K, the annual report; Form 10-Q, the quarterly report; Form 8-K, Material Events and Changes; proxy statements for annual meetings of shareholders; prospectuses, issued when debt instruments are initially sold publicly; and offering circulars, which, while not SEC filings, track prospectuses for new issues of debt instruments that are marketed under the Regulation 144A exemption from a 1933 Securities Exchange Act registration.

The narrative sections of these documents are prepared by corporate attorneys, and the audited financial statements, as well as the footnotes thereto, are, when audited, the province of public accountants. Public accountants provide audits only annually but frequently sign off on the equivalent of "cold comfort" quarterly reviews for corporate clients. Attorneys preparing the narrative for the Form 10-K and Form 10-Q for troubled issuers tend strongly to have a negative bias. They are going to try to state things negatively and not leave out things that might conceivably be material. Particularly important areas for these disclosures in Form 10-K include the following:

- Item 1A—Risk Factors.
- Item 3—Legal Proceedings.
- Item 7—Management Discussions and Analysis of Financial Condition and Results of Operations (MDA).

Of course, in a particular situation any of the other narrative disclosures in Form 10-K can be important. As per the SEC's general instructions, the other narrative parts of Form 10-K for companies that also solicit proxies for the election of directors encompass the following:

- Item 1—Business.
- Item 1B—Unresolved Staff Comments.
- Item 2—Properties.
- Item 4—Submission of Matters to a Vote of Security Holders.
- Item 5—Market for Registrant's Common Equity, Related Stockholder Matters, and Issuer's Purchase of Equity Securities.
- Item 7A—Quantitative and Qualitative Disclosure about Market Risk.
- Item 9—Changes in and Disagreements with Accountants on Accounting and Financial Disclosure.
- Item 9A—Controls and Procedures.

The public accountants, like corporate attorneys, in preparing audited financial statements have every incentive to be as complete as possible, most often with a conservative bias even though auditors insist that the managements of companies have the primary responsibility for the preparation of financial statements. A careful reading of financial statement footnotes can provide a royal road map for a due diligence investigation. The footnotes will refer to important documents to be examined (e.g., pension plans, repurchase agreements, derivative contracts, schedule of investments, description of long-term indebtedness, and credits).

A principal shortcoming of Form 10-K audited financial statements from the point of view of the distress investor is the lack of requirements that a consolidating (as distinct from consolidated) financial statement be provided. However, it is usual that enough information is provided so that the distress investor can ascertain fairly well a parent company's financial position as a stand-alone entity, and also ascertain the financials for guarantor subsidiaries.

Bankruptcy attorneys know that they practice law in an area marked by confrontation. An attorney retained by a debtor knows that skilled professionals are going to be retained by creditors, either out of court or in Chapter 11. These professionals retained by creditors are going to be paid by the debtor whether the creditor is a bank lender, an ad hoc committee of creditors formed prior to a Chapter 11 filing, or an official committee of unsecured creditors appointed by the U.S. Trustee when a company enters Chapter 11 proceedings. Given this environment, creditor professionals tend to press any matter that might favor their clients, even if slightly colorable. Thus the tendency is for documents filed with the bankruptcy courts to be comprehensive and accurate.

Documents of importance for the distress investor in Chapter 11 include the following:

- Initial filing papers are governed by local rules but generally include a relatively comprehensive affidavit signed by a senior officer describing the reasons why the debtor is seeking relief under Chapter 11. Also filed are some financials and a listing of the 20 largest unsecured creditors of record and the five largest secured creditors of record. These listings of creditors do not contain the names of beneficial owners unless such beneficial owners are also holders of record. (A beneficial owner is the true owner of the security bearing all the risks and rewards of ownership. Holders of record are just that, as recorded on the company's books. For publicly traded bonds, the indenture trustee is almost always the holder of record, while the economic interests in those bonds are held by the beneficial owners.)
- Monthly cash reports.
- Court docket: a listing of all filings with the bankruptcy court.
- Any event outside of the ordinary course of business requires notice and hearing.
- Listing of professional fee applications.
- Petition to the court for relief from the automatic stay.
- Listing of preferred creditors, critical vendors, and reclamation credits.
- Debtor in possession (DIP) financing proposals.
- Plans of reorganization.

In most jurisdictions, documents filed with the bankruptcy court are available through electronic means. Public access to the Southern District of New York's case information is provided through a service of the U.S. Judiciary called Public Access to Court Electronic Records (PACER). Unlike Edgar, the SEC's electronic filing system, there is a fee for using PACER: 8 cents per page up to a maximum of $16 per document when the document is over 200 pages long. One may obtain an account at the PACER Service Center (https://pacer.login.uscourts.gov).

As part of due diligence, the distress investor will seek to know which exhibits are part of public filings, many of which he or she would like to examine. Form 10-K contains a list of exhibits, all of which are available from Edgar and include the following:

- Charter and bylaws.
- Bond indentures.
- Loan agreements for obligations that have an initial maturity of over 270 days, albeit a troubled company might be well advised to list all loan agreements.
- Employment agreements.
- Stock incentive and option plans.
- Pension agreements.
- Real estate leases.

While SEC filings and bankruptcy court filings are sine qua nons for distress investors undertaking research, they are hardly the only documents that will be relied on. Other documents include direct company communications with securities holders, filings with other regulatory authorities, trading information, and industry sources of information.

Important direct company communications include the following:

- Annual reports to stockholders. The chief executive officer's letters tend to be extremely important because they can be freewheeling and opinionated, not restricted by the legalese required for the narrative section of Form 10-K. For the distress investor, both opinions of insiders as well as hard facts tend to be important.
- Quarterly reports to stockholders.
- Investor conference calls.

When interested in holding company securities where the operating subsidiaries are in highly regulated industries, the filings with regulatory agencies by the operating subsidiaries tend to be important. Industries where this is so include:

- Insurance (regulated only by states, not the federal government).
- Depository institutions.
- Railroads.
- Electric and gas utilities.
- Airlines.

As an aside, it ought to be noted that there tends to be an onerous structural subordination for holding company debt instruments where the holding company's sole or principal assets are the common stocks of highly regulated, highly leveraged subsidiaries that do not guarantee holding company debt. In this instance there are only four sources of cash with which the holding company can service its debt. The cash has to come from subsidiaries, which pay to the holding company home office charges; payments pursuant to intracompany tax treaties; and dividends paid by subsidiaries. Alternatively, the parent could raise cash by selling subsidiary common stock. As a practical matter, the principal source of cash to the holding company will be dividends. Most regulators have authority to prevent, or limit, the amount of dividends the regulated subsidiary can pay. These types of parent company debt, where there are no subsidiary guarantees, tend to be dicey investments.

The distress investor wants to know the trading environment:

- What is the bid and asked for the securities in which the investor is interested?
- What supply may be available?
- Who are the principal beneficial owners of the bonds in which the distress investor is interested?

The Bloomberg Financial Services are a first-rate source for this type of information.

Many of the claims a distress investor might be interested in buying are instruments that are not publicly traded (e.g., bank loans and trade receivables). Bond desks at leading broker-dealers are a good place to get supplementary information about these nonpublic instruments. Industry publications can be important sources of information about distressed companies. For example, if the distress investor is thinking about establishing creditor positions in General Motors or Ford, a subscription to *Automotive News* might be helpful. Also helpful might be the public filings of competitors.

If one wants general, up-to-date information about the majority of distressed companies that have publicly traded securities, the *Daily Bankruptcy Review* is a good source for this information.

In general, one can't give a laundry list of factors to look out for in a distressed situation. The items of importance exist on a case-by-case basis, and they tend to be different from situation to situation. It is important to worry about the following factors in most cases:

- Structural subordination (discussed earlier in the holding company regulated subsidiaries example).
- Substantive consolidation (relatively rare).
- Events of default for companies with performing loans.
- Amending indentures.
- Negative pledges.
- Equitable and ratable clauses.

The documents just described provide sufficient sources of information for most distress investors in most situations. Occasionally, an investor will seek to go further. Private investigators (e.g., Bishop's Reports, a private company that conducts investigations which can either be confidential or publicly disclosed) can be hired, and attempts can be made to obtain a company's income tax returns, something that the vast majority of the time is unavailable for the distress investor acquiring publicly traded securities.

12

Distress Investing Risks

The word *risk* is perhaps the most misused word in finance. Market commentators and academics alike tend to use the word to refer to market risk—that is, market price fluctuations in outside passive minority investor (OPMI) markets. In deep value investing, we do not use the word unless it is preceded by an appropriate adjective. The word *risk* conveys the idea that there is uncertainty around the realization of a particular outcome, and, depending on what this outcome is, there are all sorts of risks, not merely market risk, including:

- **Investment risk:** degree of uncertainty about whether there will be a permanent impairment of capital in a business.
- **Credit risk:** degree of uncertainty about whether there will be a money default for a credit instrument.
- **Operational risk:** degree of uncertainty about whether the firm will experience an operating loss due to the failed implementation of a strategy.
- **Credit rating risk:** degree of uncertainty about whether a particular credit instrument or issuer of credit instruments will be downgraded.
- **Inflation risk:** degree of uncertainty about whether inflation will reduce real incomes in the future.
- **Market risk:** degree of uncertainty about future market prices, mostly in OPMI markets.
- **Reorganization risks:** questions about how a troubled issuer will recapitalize and what considerations, if any, are to be received by each class of creditor and party in interest.

In this chapter we discuss some of the risks that are relevant to the analysis of distressed situations. We do so from the perspective of a purchaser of claims once the company has filed for Chapter 11 protection.

We divide distress investing risks into four categories; (1) risks associated with the alteration of priority of payments in bankruptcy, (2) risks associated with the valuation of either the collateral in which a creditor has an interest or the company as a going concern, (3) reorganization risks, and (4) other risks.

RISKS ASSOCIATED WITH THE ALTERATION OF PRIORITIES

Equitable Subordination Risk

Section 510(c) of the bankruptcy code gives courts the extraordinary power to subordinate a claim on equitable grounds. Although equitable subordination is an extreme remedy, used rarely and, if used, employed as a remedy for the wrongful conduct of insiders, it poses a tangible risk that impacts the decisions of creditors and/or claim purchasers. A claim may be subordinated only to the extent necessary to offset the harm caused by the claimant to the debtor and its creditors. Its practical significance is that it will put the subject claim at the end of the line of creditor claimants for payment, significantly altering its potential recoveries. In extreme cases, secured claims have been subordinated to general unsecured claims.

There are three basic requirements for equitable subordination as laid out in the Mobile Steel case:[1]

1. A creditor must have engaged in inequitable conduct.
2. That conduct injured other creditors or conferred an unfair advantage to the acting creditor.
3. The subordination of the acting creditor's claim is not otherwise inconsistent with the bankruptcy code.

This remedy will be typically used when a control person influences the debtor to the disadvantage of other creditors or defrauds other creditors, or when a fiduciary misuses his or her position to disadvantage other creditors. What makes equitable subordination a very rare occurrence against noninsiders is that the level of proof against them is quite high due to the presumption that noninsiders have no influence or control over the debtor and thus deal with the debtor in a fair, arm's-length fashion. To add to this difficulty, the proponent of equitable subordination bears the entire burden of proving that inequitable misconduct existed. Although difficult, a category of creditors that have been subject to equitable subordination are lenders who, through contractual provisions, may exert control over debtors. Lenders who have controlled the debtor for the benefit of the lender and to the detriment of other creditors have had their claims equitably subordinated to other creditors. A further twist to this type of risk for the claims' buyer stems from a recent decision in *Enron Corp. v. Springfield Associates, L.L.C.*,[2] that raises the bar on the additional due diligence needed to assess equitable subordination or disallowance risks. Reversing the original bankruptcy judge ruling on equitable subordination, the district court for the Southern District of New York ruled that the doctrine of equitable subordination could not be applied to claims held by a transferee to the same extent it would be applied to the claims if they were still held by the transferor on the basis of alleged acts or omissions on the part of the transferor. Since equitable subordination is a personal disability that does not inhere in the claim, the determination of whether it can be applied to a transferee depends on the nature of the transfer. A personal disability that has attached to a creditor that transfers its claims will travel to the transferee if the claim is assigned, but will not travel to the transferee if the claim is sold.

In view of these recent developments, four issues that merit attention for an investor contemplating purchasing a claim are:

1. Whether there is a pending equitable subordination proceeding on the original claim holder.
2. Whether a purchase will be effected through an assignment or a sale.
3. Whether the original claim holder is an insider, fiduciary, or control entity.
4. Timing of loan agreement amendments and/or indications that lenders are exerting control over the debtor.

Substantive Consolidation Risk

Substantive consolidation is the legal doctrine that pools the assets and liabilities of separate legal entities as if they were merged into a single survivor entity. In effect, substantive consolidation has the potential effect of changing the value of creditor claims through the invalidation of any priority that a claim may have due to corporate structure and thus affect the potential recoveries of certain creditors. In the context of a Chapter 11 reorganization, a surrogate of substantive consolidations is what is known as deemed consolidation, where for the purposes of voting, distributions, or cram down, claims are estimated as if the distinct entities were consolidated even though the reorganized entity that emerges from bankruptcy is not consolidated and may preserve its prepetition corporate structure. For an investor in distressed credits, deemed consolidation has the same effect as substantive consolidation. An example where deemed consolidation was used was in the Chapter 11 bankruptcy of Kmart Corporation that is the subject of a separate chapter in this book (Chapter 16).

Because of the likely alteration in claims' priorities, when addressing the issue of substantive consolidation, the courts initially developed checklist approaches that included factors that focused on whether consolidation would lead to both a more efficient administration of the estate (i.e., difficulty in segregating subsidiaries' assets and liabilities, administrative benefits of consolidation, and how easily the assets and business functions can be combined) and whether the parent and subsidiaries operated as a single enterprise prepetition (i.e., intercorporate loan guarantees or other intercorporate financing, intercorporate transfer of assets, whether creditors relied on the credit capacity of a particular subsidiary or the whole group, etc.). These factors can be useful in due diligence investigations.

These checklists notwithstanding, the principles underlying the remedy of substantive consolidation include the following: (1) unless there are compelling circumstances, courts are required to respect separateness; (2) the harm that substantive consolidation addresses is nearly always that caused by debtors who disregard separateness; (3) mere benefit to the administration of the case does not justify substantive consolidation; (4) substantive consolidation is extreme and imprecise, and should be used rarely and as a remedy of last resort after considering and rejecting other remedies; and (5) substantive consolidation may not be used offensively (i.e., having a primary purpose of tactically disadvantaging a group of creditors in the plan process or altering creditors' rights).

Today, courts use either a three-part test created by the D.C. Circuit in *In re Autotrain Corp.*,[3] a two-part test proposed by the Second Circuit in *In re Augie/Restivo Baking Co.*,[4] or a modified version of the *Augie/Restivo Baking Co.* test that narrows down the circumstances that call for substantive consolidation prepetition or postpetition.[5]

In the three-part test, the proponent of substantive consolidation must prove *both* a substantial identity between the entities to be consolidated *and* that consolidation is needed to avoid harm or realize some benefit. If the proponent does so, then an objecting creditor must show that it actually relied on the separate credit of an entity *and* that it will be prejudiced by the consolidation. Even if objecting creditors are successful in showing this to the court, the court may still consolidate if the benefits of consolidation heavily outweigh the harm.

In the two-part test proposed by the Second Circuit, the proponent of substantive consolidation must prove *either* that all creditors dealt with the separate legal entities as a single economic unit and did not rely on their separate identity *or* that the affairs of the debtor are so entangled that consolidation will benefit all creditors.

Finally, the modified *Augie/Restivo Baking Co.* two-part test that resulted from the Third Circuit[6] held that a proponent of substantive consolidation must prove *either* that, prepetition, the entities disregarded separateness so significantly that creditors relied on the breakdown of entity borders and treated them as one legal entity *or* that, postpetition, the debtor's assets and liabilities are so scrambled that separating them is prohibitive and hurts all creditors.

These tests should serve as guidelines when reading credit agreements and/or indentures to spot the potential for substantive consolidation.

Intercorporate Credit Support and Fraudulent Conveyance Risk

Providing intercorporate credit support to creditors is a relatively common business practice that can enhance the borrowing capacity of a corporate group and provide greater credit support to the creditors involved. The most common type of credit support is that a corporate group member becomes a guarantor of the debts of another. Credit support may come in other forms other than a guarantee, including becoming a co-borrower, a pledgor, or in any other capacity in which a group member becomes indebted to the lender or provides liens or security interests in its properties. In bankruptcy, the granting of credit support by a corporate member to another may be subject to scrutiny and possibly avoidance as a fraudulent transfer.

An example will help highlight the potential problem. Suppose that an operating subsidiary of a corporate group, "Sub," agrees to guarantee a loan that is extended to the corporate group parent, "Parent." The guarantee is secured by a lien on all of Sub's assets. Sub will not receive any of the proceeds of the loan for its own use, but the lender requires the guarantee because it needs the pledged Sub assets as collateral to justify making the loan. If Sub neither receives any of the proceeds nor gets either any direct or indirect benefits from the loan, then the obligation incurred and transfer made by Sub may be avoided on grounds that it is a fraudulent transfer. Even though the parties might not have had any fraudulent intent, this transfer could be deemed a constructive fraudulent transfer as defined in Section 548(a)(1) of the bankruptcy code.[7] Section 548(a)(1) states:

> *The trustee may avoid any transfer ... of an interest of the debtor in property, or any obligation ... incurred by the debtor, that was made or incurred on or within two years before the date of the filing of the petition, if the debtor voluntarily or involuntarily ...*

> *(B) (i) received less than a reasonably equivalent value in exchange for such transfer or obligation;* and

   (ii) (I) *was insolvent on the date of such transfer was made or such obligation was incurred, or became insolvent as a result of such transfer or obligation;*

   (II) *was engaged in business or a transaction, or was about to engage in business or a transaction, for which any property remaining with the debtor was unreasonably small capital [the undercapitalization test];*

   (III) *intended to incur, or believed that the debtor would incur, debts that would be beyond the debtor's ability to pay as such debts matured; or*

   (IV) *made such transfer to or for the benefit of an insider, or incurred such obligation to or for the benefit of an insider, under an employment contract and not in the ordinary course of business.*

For a transfer to be constructively fraudulent, it must satisfy *both* components of the test set forth in Section 548(a)(1)(B)—(i) and any of the components of (ii)—and only a bankruptcy trustee acting on behalf of a creditor or a creditor itself can seek to avoid a transaction on grounds of constructive fraudulent conveyance, most likely to happen in the context of a bankruptcy proceeding involving the debtor. If reasonably equivalent value was given to the debtor, then it does not matter if any of the other financial conditions existed at the time. By the same token, if none of the financial conditions in (ii) existed at the time or happened as a result of the transfer, then it does not matter whether reasonably equivalent value was given.

One can count on intercorporate guarantees being challenged as constructively fraudulent transfers during a Chapter 11 case. This is especially so for upstream guarantees (subsidiary guarantees of the obligations of its parent), and cross-stream guarantees (affiliate guarantees of the obligations of other affiliates). What may make it more difficult for avoidance actions to succeed even in these cases is that *reasonably equivalent value* is not defined in the bankruptcy code; in addition, case history shows that it does not necessarily imply that the value received must be equal to the value given, or that the form of consideration of the value received be the same as that given. Indirect and intangible economic benefits can be a source of reasonable equivalent value.

A risk related to the presence of intercorporate guarantees is that of substantive consolidation. Since lenders may require that all the members of a corporate group provide some kind of credit support in the form of either actual or disguised guarantees, and most guarantees are likely to be challenged as constructive fraudulent transfers in Chapter 11, the threshold for meeting the criteria for substantive consolidation in those cases may be lowered, and substantial litigation is likely to ensue. The Kmart Corporation Chapter 11 is an example where substantial challenges to the enforceability of intercompany guarantees led to a settlement where the estates were deemed consolidated for purposes of distribution.

Critical Vendor Payments Risk

It has become common practice to seek bankruptcy court approval to pay prepetition debt to vendors deemed critical to the reorganization of the debtor. A common rationalization for these payments is that they preserve the going-concern value of the debtor's business in the belief that vendors not paid for prior deliveries will refuse to make new ones, and as a result the firm will not be able to carry on, injuring all creditors. Although this may be accurate in a few very specific instances, it does not represent reality. Vendors in general have an interest to continue shipping to the debtor and to make the debtor feasible. As an example, Fleming Companies, Inc. was the largest single critical vendor to Kmart and was contractually obligated to sell to Kmart. In fact, Kmart's purchases from Fleming accounted for more than 50 percent of Fleming's revenues. It is hard to believe that Fleming would have stopped shipments to Kmart unless its prepetition claims were paid in full postpetition. In fact, Fleming was forced into Chapter 11 when Kmart stopped purchasing from it. Reality notwithstanding, these motions continue to be granted routinely and give the debtor considerable discretion over what payments are to be made to which vendors. What these orders have in common is that they require that the vendor continue to provide goods and services to the debtor under normal terms.

In most cases, critical vendor payments are simply preferences that circumvent priority of payment rules to the detriment of unsecured creditors, who have to wait in line until they get paid pursuant to an approved plan of reorganization (POR) or liquidation. The practical difficulty for the distress investor is the prepetition estimation of which trade claims are likely to be deemed critical and receive full payment postpetition and which ones will not. Since critical vendor payments are frequently authorized by the courts during the first-day motion hearings immediately after the debtor's filing, the potential trade claims buyer must realize that uncertainty about recoveries on these claims may be substantially reduced at this time.

Another important consequence of critical vendor payments is that, depending on the financial condition of the company at the time of filing, these payments may increase its postpetition financing needs. In the Kmart Chapter 11 case, the critical vendor order resulted in payments to 2,330 suppliers for an approximate sum of $300 million. Financing for such payments came from a new debtor in possession (DIP) facility, and DIP lenders received super-priority status for their claims along with liens on all of Kmart's post-petition assets and revenues.

The potential impact of critical vendor payments on the recoveries of other unsecured claims will depend on the specifics of a particular situation.

Defects in the Perfection of Security Interests Risk

Security interests that are unenforceable against the debtor prepetition are also unenforceable against the Chapter 11 estate postpetition. In plain English, what this means is that the secured status of an alleged secured claim will invariably be challenged during a Chapter 11 case in a number of ways, including through avoidance actions under Sections 544(a) and 547, or through claims' objections under Section 502. Although it is beyond the scope of this book to thoroughly discuss the issues related to the perfection of security interests, a brief description of how a claim becomes legally secured will help the investor understand a few of the issues involved.

For a security interest in the collateral of a debtor to be legally enforceable against the debtor, there must be a security agreement. Without a security agreement, a security interest cannot attach to the underlying property; that is, the creditor does not have any rights in the debtor's collateral. Although attachment of a security interest is necessary to give a secured creditor rights in the collateral against the debtor, an extra step is needed if the creditor seeks to enforce these rights against third parties who may assert interests in the same collateral, as well as other creditors or a bankruptcy trustee. This next step is known as the perfection of the security interest. The most common method of perfecting a security interest is by filing a Uniform Commercial Code (UCC) financing statement, which is simply a notice that indicates that the secured party who has filed it may have a security interest in the collateral described.

Recent changes to Article 9 of the UCC were done to simplify the perfection of security interests and the search functions used by third parties to obtain notice of perfected interests in a debtor's property, with the intent of making it easier for third parties to search for the correct debtor names. A creditor is deemed secured if the financing statement can be found through a search of its name, and third parties are under no obligation to conduct exhaustive searches. Small errors in the name of a debtor may make it difficult if not impossible to find out whether a financing statement involving a debtor has been filed. Debtors, creditors committees, and trustees in bankruptcy have successfully challenged secured claims' security interests on the basis of errors in financing statements that were deemed misleading.[8]

Such challenges under either Section 502 or 544 will render an allegedly secured claim into an unsecured one.

RISKS ASSOCIATED WITH COLLATERAL OR ENTERPRISE VALUATION

The reliance of the reorganization process on valuation is extensive. For secured creditors, valuation plays an important role in issues of adequate protection (Section 361), including relief from the automatic stay (Section 362); use, sale, or lease of property and what constitutes cash collateral (Section 363); and obtaining credit and the granting of priming liens to DIP lenders (Section 364). It is also quite important in the process of claims' allowance as secured versus unsecured (Section 506) and as recourse or nonrecourse (Section 1111(b)), and in the analysis of solvency issues that is an integral part of the determination of preferential transfers (Section 547), fraudulent transfers (Sections 548 and 544), and the reclamation of vendor goods (Section 546).

At a later stage in a reorganization, valuation plays a central role in testing the feasibility of a proposed plan of reorganization (Section 1129(a)(11)), calculating the recovery of various creditor classes, meeting the fair and equitable standards required of a cram down of creditors (Section 1129(b)(2)), and making sure that the best interests of creditors test is met through the performance of a liquidation analysis (Section 1129(a)(7)). A few of these risks will be discussed later in this chapter.

Collateral Valuation Risks

Section 506(a) of the bankruptcy code provides guidance about the principles to be used in the valuation of the collateral securing a claim:

> *Such value shall be determined in light of the purpose of the valuation and of the proposed disposition or use of such property, and in conjunction with any hearing on such disposition or use or on a plan affecting such creditor's interest.*

The key to the preceding paragraph are the words *disposition or use*. If the debtor, pursuant to a plan of reorganization, will keep the collateral for its use, then the valuation of the collateral for the purpose of claim determination should follow the replacement value standard; that is, its value should be the cost the debtor would incur to obtain a like asset for the same proposed use. If, however, the debtor will dispose of the collateral, the standard of valuation should be disposition value.

The preceding discussion provides clarity about the nature of the valuation standard to be used only in specific cases, but what is really at stake is the actual valuation amount of the collateral for purposes of determining the amount of a secured claim (i.e., whether a secured creditor is oversecured or undersecured and whether it has both a secured claim to the extent of the collateral value and an unsecured claim for the deficiency.

Bankruptcy valuation disputes will invariably involve a high proposed valuation by one party versus a low proposed valuation by the other, and each party will provide ample evidence to support its position. A low valuation of the collateral will make adequate protection payments more affordable to the debtor but may introduce the risk that the secured creditor may obtain the power to block a plan of reorganization on account of its unsecured claim. The nature of collateral valuation disputes is very case specific, and in the end, the court will adjudicate an outcome to the dispute. One thing is certain: The outcome of valuation disputes is highly unpredictable, and it will be very case specific.

Deterioration of the Value of the Collateral Risk

The questions of adequate protection and the lifting of the automatic stay seem to be the most commonly litigated questions in bankruptcy. The granting of adequate protection to a secured creditor is not automatic, and it will be granted only after bringing a proceeding to lift the automatic stay. Why would secured creditors do this? To either enforce their rights to foreclose on the collateral securing the claim (stay is lifted), or to assure that the value of their interests in the collateral will not diminish over time. Generally but not exclusively, there are three reasons why collateral value may deteriorate over the pendency of a bankruptcy case: (1) the debtor will continue to use the collateral and thus consume it or wear it out, (2) the collateral value will decline due to deteriorating economic conditions, and/or (3) the debtor will be unable to properly maintain or protect its value.

The burden of proof that a secured creditor's interest in property is adequately protected is with the debtor. If the debtor cannot prove that the creditor's interest is protected, the stay will be lifted or the debtor will have to provide the creditor with adequate protection to continue to use the collateral. Adequate protection may come in many different forms, such as cash payments, additional liens on other unencumbered property, and other protection that will result in the secured party realizing the indubitable equivalent of the value of its interest in the collateral. But what would happen if economic or industry conditions worsen much more than expected and it turns out that protection payments prove to be inadequate? In such a case, Section 507(b) of the bankruptcy code provides for the granting of administrative expense priority for the losses. This is an example where the deterioration of collateral value will very likely impact the amount of recoveries expected by unsecured creditors.

Enterprise Valuation Risks

The determination of enterprise value is key to the allocation of creditor classes' recoveries as well as the performance of several bankruptcy-mandated tests that are needed to assess whether a plan of reorganization can be confirmed. As a general rule, the most junior classes (holders of equity in the prepetition debtor, junior subordinated, and junior creditors) will push for a larger valuation of the enterprise seeking to participate in the reorganization and stay in-the-money. The existence of control equity holders (management, large institutional holders) will make this push more contentious since they will likely exercise their power to control the reorganization process and/or delay the confirmation of a plan. The most senior classes are likely to prefer a lower valuation that in all likelihood will make the debtor more feasible and will facilitate the implementation of the plan.

The interplay between the valuation of the enterprise and the availability of internal and/or exit financing will be important in coming up with the form of consideration that the debtor will use to satisfy allowed claims under the plan of reorganization and in shaping the resulting capital structure. The form of consideration of creditor recoveries is not only important to creditors, but also an important determinant of the feasibility of the debtor postreorganization. Certain creditors have a strong preference for cash over any other form of consideration (banks), and the feasibility of the debtor is a less important consideration; others, like trade creditors, want to continue shipping to the reorganized debtor and may favor feasibility over cash or cash pay instruments. The airline industry is full of examples of companies that have filed for Chapter 11 and emerged from bankruptcy with unfeasible capital structures due to their creditors' need for cash pay instruments, only to have to file for Chapter 11 again shortly thereafter. As a general rule, the more senior securities (or cash) that are issued in a reorganization pursuant to a plan of reorganization, the less feasible the plan will tend to be. The more ownership interests that are issued, without contractual or legal requirements for cash pay, the more feasible the plan will be. The one exception to this feasibility rule occurs when issuing cash pay instruments rather than ownership interests results in the debtor having better future access to capital markets than otherwise would be the case. The form of consideration of recoveries pursuant to a reorganization plan plays an important role in the feasibility of the reorganized debtor going forward. We discuss these issues in more detail in Chapters 13 and 17.

REORGANIZATION RISKS

Before a plan of reorganization (POR) is proposed, creditors and parties in interest tend to face very material reorganization risks; they don't know, but have to estimate, how their class will fare in a reorganization.

For creditors unlikely to be reinstated, the reorganization risks can be mitigated to some extent insofar as the creditor or party in interest is a participant in the reorganization negotiations. These elements of control over the reorganization process tend to gravitate to creditors who own or otherwise control large amounts of obligations in a particular class, creditors who are members of the official committee of creditors, as well as managements and control shareholders, especially during the time when there exists a period of exclusivity.

OTHER RISKS

Classification and Cram-Down Risks

A critical part in the development of a plan of reorganization is the classification of claims and interests into classes. The statutory basis for such classification is Section 1122 of the bankruptcy code, which also provides some guidance as to which claims should belong to a class when it states that "a plan may place a claim or interest in a particular class only if such claim or interest is substantially similar to the other claims or interests of such class." Although claims or interests in a particular class must be substantially similar, Section 1122 does not preclude a plan proponent from classifying similar claims or interests in different classes, and the debtor can use this flexibility for strategic purposes, the most important being achieving plan approval. How a plan proponent will use this flexibility is impossible to predict because it is very case specific, and the extent to which it is used will greatly depend on the complexity of the debtor's capital structure, the ownership structure of the different claims, and many other factors. These difficulties notwithstanding, it is instructive to understand how the statutory rules for plan approval give rise to leverage factors that may benefit certain parties.

If a class of claims or interests is not impaired under the reorganization plan (i.e., their legal, equitable, and contractual rights are left unaltered), that class is deemed to accept the plan, and votes from its members are not solicited. Only impaired classes will vote on the plan, and in order to achieve a consensual approval, each impaired class must approve the plan by at least one-half in number and two-thirds in amount of the allowed claims or interests *actually voting* on the plan. This last distinction is important because the requisite majorities are calculated based on the class members that actually vote, not necessarily all the members of the class. These requisite majorities create the situation where a large holder in the class, holding slightly more than one-third in amount of the claims, holds what in effect is a blocking position. The holder(s) of a blocking position can prevent the consensual approval of a reorganization plan and in doing so have considerable leverage over the benefits that they can extract from the negotiation process. However, these benefits may be constrained by the threat of a cram-down plan.

The statutory provisions of Section 1129(b) make it possible to confirm a plan of reorganization over the objection of one or many classes of claims and interests. Under Section 1129(b), plans that are accepted by less than all classes can be confirmed if: (1) at least one impaired class of claims has voted for the plan, (2) the plan does not discriminate unfairly, and (3) the plan is fair and equitable with respect to the objecting classes. The tests for determining whether the plan is fair and equitable with respect to an objecting class have been discussed in Chapter 9. Suffice it to say that the level of judicial oversight in the confirmation of a plan over the objection of dissenting classes is much higher than that over the confirmation of a consensual plan, and out-of-the-money claims and interests tend to fare worse in cram-down plans since the fair and equitable tests involve the implementation of the absolute priority rule.

Uncontrolled Professional Costs and Time to Reorganization Risks

It should be quite apparent by now that every issue that can be litigated in bankruptcy is likely to be litigated, and the completion of a case requires the retention of competent professionals—attorneys, investment bankers, accountants, and consultants. The risk posed to unsecured creditors is that since expenses for professionals constitute an administrative expense, paid with super-priority, as-you-go, and in cash, they can end up representing a substantial value drain on the estate and materially affect unsecured creditors' recoveries and/or the debtor's feasibility as a going concern.

It is pretty well documented that the amount of professional costs in large Chapter 11 cases is largely a function of how long a company remains in bankruptcy before either reorganizing or liquidating, and how many professional firms are retained by the different parties to the case.[9] This is because professionals are mainly paid on a time basis (hourly or monthly). The size of the debtor is also directly related to the amount of professional fees and expenses. Many have associated size with the complexity of a case; others have rationalized size as an opportunity to bill. Whatever the reason, larger debtors tend to incur much larger professional fees and expenses independently of the time they remain in Chapter 11 or how many professionals they hire.

The risk of uncontrolled professional fees and expenses is quite relevant in all cases, large and small, since these costs come out of the hide of those classes of creditors that are not adequately secured. In small cases, these costs can render a debtor impossible to reorganize; that is, they will materially reduce or prevent any creditor recoveries and make the debtor unfeasible. In larger cases, fees and expenses may not materially affect the feasibility of the debtor but can increase its financing needs that will likely come in the form of DIP financing with super-priority that further reduces unsecured and undersecured creditors' recoveries. Either way, time is of the essence; time is the enemy of unsecured creditors, and the sooner a reorganization is accomplished, the larger their potential recoveries. As a practical matter in small cases—see Home Products International—the reorganization had better take place within the period of exclusivity, or no values will likely be left for unsecured creditors. Therefore, in these small cases, prepackaged PORs, or their functional equivalent, are essential if any values are to be preserved for prepetition unsecured creditors.

13

Form of Consideration versus Amount of Consideration

For those of our readers who are, or want to be, involved in planning and negotiating plans of reorganization (PORs), it is important to be conscious of the fact that different beneficiaries (i.e., those who participate and those who are reinstated) have differing desires in terms of the form of consideration they would like to receive.

Banks and insurance companies tend to have a strong desire that the consideration to be received be cash or well-covenanted, cash-pay senior credit instruments. There are two reasons for this: regulatory and economic. For regulatory purposes, depository institutions and insurance companies have to have good assets in order to meet regulatory requirements to be adequately capitalized. Cash and investment-grade credit instruments are good assets. Most other securities and loan holdings are not good assets. In economic terms, asset management is first and foremost a function of liability management. Banks and insurance companies usually have at least 90 percent of their assets offset by cash-consuming liabilities such as deposits for banks and policyholders' claims for insurance companies. Thus as an offset, these institutions require cash and cash-pay assets to meet their obligations. Contrast this, say, with mutual funds. Mutual funds are almost always debt free. Mutual funds' assets, therefore, can, if fund management so decides, to be wholly invested in non-dividend-paying common stocks.

Like most banks, most trade creditors want to have a continuing relationship with the debtor postreorganization. The trade creditor wants to keep shipping, the landlord wants to keep renting, and the employees want to keep working. Thus, these constituencies have a big stake in having the reorganized debtor be feasible. As a result they frequently are willing to compromise their claim for cash and cash-pay senior instruments in order to contribute to a feasible POR.

Public, noncontrol bondholders, of course, have no continuing relationship with the debtor postreorganization. In most cases these bondholders seek a market-out at maximum prices. Market value is what counts. This constituency is usually willing to accept a package of securities consisting of new credit instruments, preferred stocks, and equities, especially common stocks.

Under 2008–2009 economic conditions, there probably will be many more corporate changes of control brought about by restructuring troubled companies than their will be changes of control through the purchase of common stocks in the open market, in private transactions, via tender offers, or through the use of corporate proxy machinery to solicit the votes of common shareholders. Thus, there is that important constituency of prepetition creditors whose objective is to obtain control of companies that have to reorganize under Chapter 11. Recent examples of creditors who upon reorganization obtained control of companies include Eddie Lampert acquiring control of Kmart; Third Avenue acquiring control of Home Products International; Equity Group Inc., a Sam Zell–controlled entity, acquiring control of ACL, Inc.; and Mission Insurance Group (renamed Covanta Energy), acquired by Danielson Holding Company. Like others with a continuing interest in the company postreorganization, this constituency gives a high priority to feasibility.

In reorganizations where there is to be a change of control, it is a mixed bag as to whether old operating management is to be changed. In the cases of Kmart and Home Products International, management changes were desirable. In the cases of Nabors Industries and Covanta Energy, the incumbent operating managements were first-rate and, indeed, essential elements to the success of the companies postreorganization.

For those who receive equity in reorganization, whether passive investors or control entities, the reorganization value determined in the POR is the beginning, not the ending. For passive investors, subsequent market prices are key, whereas for control investors the primary goal usually is to create corporate value on a long-term basis. Also, it is sometimes hard to postulate which constituencies strive for large reorganization value and which seek more modest reorganization values. Junior securities holders—subordinate, preferreds, and common stocks—always strive for the largest possible reorganization value. This permits these junior classes to participate in reorganization and receive something of value (maybe increasing value). Since reorganization value is determined primarily by capitalizing forecasted cash flows, banks and insurance companies frequently encourage large reorganization values because doing so permits them to receive instruments obligated to pay out more cash flow as interest and principal than would otherwise to be the case. However, the larger the reorganization value, the less the feasibility for the corporations—simply because the corporation postreorganization is burdened with more cash payments to creditors than it would be otherwise. Theoretically, large reorganization value can contribute to feasibility insofar as it gives a reorganized company better access to capital markets. However, improved access to capital markets, whether credit markets or equity markets, because of enlarged reorganization value is probably a rarity.

Four

Cases and Implications for Public Policy

14

Brief Case Studies of Distressed Securities, 2008–2009

For analytic purposes, investing in distress instruments really means dealing with four separate and somewhat distinct businesses:

1. **Performing loans likely to remain performing loans.** Even if a performing loan subsequently becomes a nonperforming loan, certain values will be preserved in a reorganization or liquidation, either out of court or in Chapter 11 or Chapter 7.
2. **Small reorganization cases,** either via voluntary exchanges or in Chapter 11 or Chapter 7. Unlike large reorganization cases, reorganization has to take place relatively promptly if any values are to be preserved for prepetition, unsecured creditors.
3. **Large reorganization cases,** either voluntary exchanges or in Chapter 11 or Chapter 7. Cash generation during a reorganization proceeding tends to be positive, given that cash generation from operations and from not paying cash service on prepetition unsecured debt and undersecured debt (to the amount of undersecurity) exceeds payments for administrative expenses during the pendency of the reorganization, especially payments to lawyers and investment bankers. A key consideration for prepetition creditors is whether, upon reorganization, the prepetition credits will receive not only a return of all contracted-for principal payments but also payments for interest forgone and interest on interest. If postpetition interest is not paid, the returns to distress investors decline far more markedly during a long case, compared with situations where postpetition interest is part of the consideration paid.
4. **Making capital infusions into troubled companies** in the forms of senior loans, preferred stocks, hybrid securities, common stocks, or warrants.

PERFORMING LOANS LIKELY TO
REMAIN PERFORMING LOANS

Historically, most performing loans remain performing loans. Even in 2008–2009, in portfolios of residential subprime mortgages, the direst prognostications are that 30 percent to 40 percent of such mortgage loans either are in default or will default. In other words, 60 percent to 70 percent of this subprime junk seems bound to remain performing loans. The percentage of corporate credits likely to not default ought to be considerably better than is the case for residential subprime mortgages. Moody's Investors Service in the November 2008 edition of "Moody's Global Leverage Finance" predicts that "the global speculative grade issuer defaults will climb to 4.3 percent by the end of 2008 and rise sharply to 10.4 percent a year from now. Corporate default rates in this cycle will likely match or exceed the peak levels reached in the previous two US recessions of 1990–91 and 2000–01." Under 2008–2009 conditions many of these performing loans provide yields to maturity of 25 percent to 54 percent. Those high yield issues, which were being acquired by Third Avenue Value Fund in mid-November 2008, are shown in Exhibit 14.1.

Both MBIA and General Motors Acceptance Corporation (GMAC) are effectively in a runoff mode. MBIA, a bond insurer, is currently rated BBB by principal rating agencies, the lowest investment-grade rating. Thus the

EXHIBIT 14.1 Performing Loan Investments by Third Avenue Value Fund, 2008—2009

Issue	Recent Price Percent of Principal	Current Yield	Yield to Maturity
Forest City Enterprises $3^5/_8$% Senior Notes Due 10/15/2011	52.40	6.9%	28.9%
MBIA Insurance 14% Surplus Notes Due 2033	57.05	24.5%	34.0%*
General Motors Acceptance Corp. $7^3/_4$% Due 1/19/2010	59.00	13.1%	62.0%

*Yield to call. Yield to maturity would be approximately 24.6%, assuming a 14% interest rate after 1/15/2013. Actual rate will be 3-month LIBOR plus 11.56%.

company has very limited ability to write new business. Since it lost its AAA rating, MBIA has only been able to reinsure municipal bonds policies guaranteed by the Financial Guaranty Insurance Company (FGIC), a more deeply troubled bond insurer. GMAC has lost most of its access to capital markets and accordingly was in the process of shrinking its asset base at the end of 2008. Our analysis bottoms on the belief that MBIA surplus notes and GMAC senior unsecured notes will remain performing loans insofar as the cash generated from runoffs exceeds by a comfortable margin losses to be realized from insurance claims against MBIA and realized losses on the GMAC receivables and auto lease portfolios.

It would probably take a rather deep depression for Forest City Enterprises to fail to realize enough cash flows from its extensive real estate holdings to be able to service its parent company senior unsecured indebtedness.

At Third Avenue, fund management has concluded that the probabilities that each of the three issuers would remain performing loans until maturity (or prior call) are about as shown in Exhibit 14.2.

The control stockholder of GMAC, Cerberus Capital Partners, L.P., announced in October 2008 that an effort would be made to recapitalize and reorganize GMAC by voluntary exchanges of debt and by having GMAC become a bank holding company. In terms of the $7^3/_4$s and other short-term GMAC senior unsecured debt, it is hard to see how any voluntary exchange can succeed, given the short period of time to maturity—14 months—when measured against the fact that in the United States no one can take away a creditor's right to a contracted-for money payment unless that individual creditor so consents, or the debtor obtains court relief, usually in Chapter 11 or Chapter 7.

If the $7^3/_4$s become a nonperforming loan, the GMAC senior unsecured debt undoubtedly would participate in a GMAC Chapter 11 reorganization. It seems a fair guess that in such reorganization, the senior unsecureds would receive much, if not almost all, of the new GMAC common stock to be outstanding. At that point GMAC would likely become a well-financed

EXHIBIT 14.2 Estimated Probabilities That Loans Will Remain Performing

Issue	Probability Range That Loan Will Remain Performing
Forest City $3^5/_8$%	90%–95%
MBIA Surplus Notes	90%–95%
GMAC $7^3/_4$%	70%–80%

finance company or a well-capitalized bank holding company. It is hard to estimate what amount of reorganization value might be attributable to the $7^3/_4$s. There seems to be a reasonable probability that such reorganization value could exceed the October 2008 price of 59 for the $7^3/_4$s, especially if a reorganized GMAC obtains favorable tax attributes through the creation of net operating loss (NOL) carryforwards, an iffy proposition. Any such analysis has a high speculative component.

The MBIA surplus notes are, in economic fact, really a weakly covenanted preferred stock issued by MBIA, Inc.'s principal insurance subsidiary, MBIA Insurance Corporation. If the subsidiary misses a January 15 or July 15 interest payment, interest arrearages accrue rather than having an event of default occur. The surplus notes are expressly subordinated to all insurance claims. Further, the subsidiary cannot pay interest unless the New York State superintendent of insurance approves such payments. Finally, there is no legal barrier to the subsidiary paying dividends on its common stock, all of which is owned by the parent, MBIA, Inc., while the surplus notes accumulate interest arrearages. Despite these covenant weaknesses, the subsidiary enjoys unusual financial strength in terms of both periodic cash flows and claims-paying ability. For the subsidiary to be in financial trouble, it appears that claims to be paid would have to be three or four times larger than the large amount of claims paid and claims reserved for in MBIA's 2008 financial statements. In the normal course of events, the surplus notes will continue to be a performing loan, which will be called at 100 plus accrued interest on the first call date that does not require MBIA to pay a call premium, January 15, 2013.

In the event that the MBIA insurance subsidiary has to be rehabilitated by the New York State Department of Insurance, which would be the rough equivalent of a Chapter 11 reorganization for a New York–domiciled insurance company, the holders of surplus notes might become the common stockholders of a well-capitalized insurance holding company with, perhaps, favorable tax attributes. This is what occurred for Third Avenue Value Fund when as a holder of unsecured notes it led the 1991 Chapter 11 reorganization of Mission Insurance Group. Subsequently in 2004 Mission acquired Covanta Energy Corporation in a Chapter 11 reorganization. Mission changed its name to Covanta and is today a highly successful company engaged mostly in the conversion of waste to energy.

Analysis frequently does not follow a straight line. Normally, it is better in terms of seniority to be a creditor rather than a preferred stockholder. This seems not so in the case of the MBIA surplus notes. As a creditor, a note holder would have the right to seek acceleration of payments in the event of default. This right, where the creditor is subordinate to the claims of senior creditors, is frequently in reality a right to commit suicide, since as a practical matter all payments would end up with the senior creditors. For the surplus notes, the right to accumulate arrearages seems a much more valuable right than would be the right to seek payment remedies after an event of default has been declared.

The Forest City $3^5/_8$s are holding company indebtedness. The operations of the myriad subsidiaries constitute the construction of high-quality office buildings, shopping centers, and residential properties that are owned and are financed with long-term, fixed-rate, nonrecourse mortgage loans. These high-quality properties are located in the United States. While parent company financials are not published, it appears that there is ample cash thrown off from operating subsidiaries to comfortably service parent company obligations and parent company overhead.

In the event of a reorganization, the $3^5/_8$s would probably fare rather well, especially if, as part of the reorganization, the $3^5/_8$s received Forest City common stock. Forest City is one of the country's premier investment builders, developing various properties in major cities. The odds seem good that its excellent long-term growth record will persist.

An important thing for the well-financed distress investor to remember is that if the investor is right about the performing loan remaining a performing loan, the investor doesn't have to worry about market prices. Time alone will guarantee price appreciation roughly equal to a modest discount from yield to maturity or yield to an event. Yield to maturity or yield to an event (such as a call) is an unrealistic calculation in that it assumes that the interest payments, which are made at six-month intervals, are reinvested at the same rate as the initial yield to maturity. Of course, no one can predict the future well enough to know what an actual reinvestment rate will be. The only credit investments where the investor knows what the reinvestment rate will be with certainty are zero coupon bonds.

Exhibit 14.3 demonstrates price appreciation over time for performing loans. Assume there is a ten-year, 6 percent bullet loan (i.e., no principal amortization) selling at 25 percent yield to maturity. Assume further that the yield to maturity remains at 25 percent. The prices at the end of each year for the ten-year period would be as shown in the exhibit.

Finally, the distress investor again should note the appropriate variable to look at in estimating returns to be earned. Insofar as a performing loan is to remain a performing loan, the key measures are yield to maturity, yield to an event (like call or improved credit rating), and current yield. Insofar as a loan is to be nonperforming and therefore will participate in a reorganization or a liquidation, the key variable is dollar price paid compared to an estimated workout price in an estimated period of time.

One caveat for U.S. taxpayers: Because of income tax rules about market discount, it is likely that most or all of the price appreciation to be realized on the loan acquired at a discount, would be taxable as ordinary income at ordinary tax rates.

EXHIBIT 14.3 Loan Price Appreciation
for a 25 Percent Yield to Maturity,
6 Percent, Ten-Year Bullet Loan

End of Year	Price as Percent of Principal Amount
1	32.16
2	34.20
3	36.75
4	39.94
5	48.90
6	55.13
7	62.91
8	72.64
9	84.80
10	100.00

SMALL CASES

When a company might become distressed even before it enters a zone of insolvency, expenses for the company to pay for attorneys, investment bankers, accountants, and appraisers tend to balloon. As explained in Chapter 4, the company is expected to bear expenses incurred not only by its own professionals, but also by professionals retained by one or more creditor groups, and sometimes even common stock committees. This burgeoning expense item exists whether the company seeks to reorganize out of court via voluntary exchanges or seeks court relief under Chapter 11 or Chapter 7.

In a Chapter 11 reorganization, the expenses of professionals are borne by the estate. As administrative expenses, they constitute a super-priority, are payable in cash, and are payable on a regular periodic basis with only minor holdbacks. In Chapter 11, the estate is no longer required to pay cash service for interest, principal, and premium, if any, on unsecured indebtedness and on undersecured indebtedness to the amount of undersecurity. Sometimes interest and principal payments on adequately secured indebtedness are postponed during the pendency of a Chapter 11 case, provided there is a more than adequate equity cushion, and the secured creditors receive a value that is the "indubitable equivalent" of what the creditor is entitled to as an adequately secured creditor. The authors define small cases as those where the cash outflows from operating losses and from paying administrative expenses are likely to exceed the cash savings from not making cash payments on unsecured and undersecured credits to the amount of undersecurity. Where this cash-negative situation exists, it is important that a reorganization be completed promptly if any values are to be preserved for prepetition, unsecured, or undersecured creditors.

In small cases, speed in reorganization is of the essence. In the case of the prepackaged Chapter 11 reorganization of Home Products International, only 90 days elapsed from the filing for Chapter 11 relief to the consummation of the plan of reorganization (POR). The reorganization of Haynes International did not take much longer.

Third Avenue's modus operandi in cases that would potentially become small cases had been to acquire performing loans that seemed to have reasonable prospects of remaining performing loans at yields to maturity of 15 percent or better. After the 2008 financial meltdown, however, the required yield to maturity jumped from 15 percent to 25 percent. As a performing loan, Third Avenue tries to acquire, or otherwise control, at least 50 percent of the particular issue. This seeking of a 50 percent position revolves around the fact that in the indentures for almost all publicly traded bonds, any nonmoney provision in the indenture can be modified or abrogated by the consent of 50 percent of the outstanding issue. (For money provisions, each bondholder has to consent to a change affecting his, her, or its bonds; see Chapter 6.) Third Avenue does not want changes to be made to indentures without its consent. Furthermore, to approve most changes, Third Avenue will require a fee to be paid to the consenting bondholders.

If the loan remains a performing loan, the company will never hear from Third Avenue or probably from any other bondholder. If there is a money default, however, for companies that appear to have sound operations but are poorly financed, Third Avenue will propose a POR in which Third Avenue and others with whom it will associate will become the dominant stockholders. This was the case in the Chapter 11 reorganizations of Nabors Industries, Mission Insurance Group, Haynes International, American Commercial Lines, LLC (ACL), and Home Products International.

These reorganizations are always prepackaged or prearranged, since speed is of the essence. In order to avoid protracted Chapter 11 cases, senior creditors and trade creditors are reinstated; that is, these creditors are paid cash for past nonpayments, and their debt instruments continue in existence under the old terms and conditions. The typical prepackaged or prenegotiated deal ends up about as follows:[1]

- Obtain new exit financing from banks on normal commercial terms.
- Reinstate or repay old banks, except most will provide the exit financing.
- Reinstate trade creditors.
- Reinstate leases and other executory contracts.
- Issue 90 percent to 95 percent of common stock to former bondholders.

- Issue 5 percent to 10 percent of common stock to former junior (i.e., subordinated) creditors, former preferred stock and/or former common stock holders.
- If there is meritorious litigation pending, set up and finance a litigation trust and give the common stock a small participation in lawsuit recoveries, if any.
- Issue options on 6 percent to 12 percent of the common stock outstanding to management. The exercise price for the options will be reorganization value per share.

LARGE CASES

Large cases such as Kmart, USG, Public Service Company of New Hampshire, and Pacific Gas & Electric can be protracted without wiping out the interests of unsecured creditors. Here cash savings from the nonpayment of cash to unsecureds, and to undersecureds to the amount of undersecurity, exceed administrative expenses. However, the longer the reorganization takes, the smaller the return to the distress investor.

Particular damage from long delays is visited upon creditors who will not receive postpetition interest and interest on interest. Unsecured creditors of USG and Public Service Company of New Hampshire received such payments. (Pacific Gas & Electric was a fast track case.) One drawback to protracted cases is that companies might become grossly mismanaged. This occurs on a case-by-case basis. In the authors' opinion, USG was always superbly managed; but Kmart was mostly mismanaged while in Chapter 11, in part because professionals, especially bankruptcy attorneys, were more influential than they should have been in what as a going concern was a merchandising operation.

One ought to note a truism about large cases. There is a common statement about gigantic companies such as General Motors, Citicorp, and AIG being "too big to fail." Not so! Rather, the more productive view is to think of these companies as "too big not to be reorganized."

CAPITAL INFUSIONS INTO TROUBLED COMPANIES

This is a wonderful business in 2008–2009. Those making capital infusions can almost write their own tickets. And it is much more productive for troubled companies to have investors, private or governmental, buy new securities directly from the company rather than from existing shareholders.

In 2008, Third Avenue made direct capital infusions into MBIA by, in effect, acquiring a unit of common stock and the insurance subsidiary's surplus notes. Third Avenue in a separate transaction also acquired a new issue of Ambac common stock.

Others have made capital infusions. A few examples are as follows:

- JPMorgan Chase acquired Bear Stearns by issuing common stock and delivering to Bear Stearns creditworthiness.
- Bank of America also delivered creditworthiness to Merrill Lynch, Countrywide, and Washington Mutual in what appears to have been bargain purchases.
- Wells Fargo acquired Wachovia Bank at a huge discount from net asset values.
- The federal government acquired controlling interests in Fannie Mae, Freddie Mac, and AIG by receiving in exchange for cash infusions units of preferred stock and warrants to acquire majority interests in the troubled companies.
- Berkshire Hathaway, in return for cash infusions, received units of preferred stock and common stock issued by Goldman Sachs and General Electric.
- The U.S. government is investing $700 billion into troubled financial institutions through the Troubled Asset Relief Program (TARP), presumably by purchasing units consisting of perpetual preferred stocks and warrants to buy common stock. The perpetual preferred stocks pay dividends of 5 percent (9 percent after five years), are callable, are transferable, and have limited voting rights. The perpetual preferreds, in other words, are plain-vanilla. The warrants to purchase common stock permit the owner(s) of the warrants to purchase a number of common shares with an aggregate price equal to 15 percent of the amount of investment in the perpetual preferred stock. The warrants are exercisable at a price equal to the average trading price for the 20-day period prior to the initial issue of the perpetual preferred stock.

All of these capital infusions with equity components result in highly dilutive results for existing stockholders unless such infusions are made pursuant to rights offerings to existing shareholders. Rights offerings are relatively rare. Where undertaken, existing shareholders are given transferable rights permitting them to subscribe to the new issue on a pro-rata basis, usually with an oversubscription privilege. Rights offerings are normally open for a 21-day period. Existing stockholders do benefit from capital infusions even when they are subject to massive dilution, which is the usual case where there is no rights offering, because the companies in which they have invested are credit-enhanced, usually very materially credit-enhanced.

Many of these credit-enhanced companies (e.g., MBIA and Ambac) remain troubled to some extent, but the average distress investor may be able to benefit by becoming a common stockholder at a bargain price. For example, at the time of this writing, one can acquire MBIA common stock, traded on the New York Stock Exchange, at a price equal to less than 20 percent of adjusted book value. Assuming a return to normal times, MBIA might be able to earn, after tax, around 10 percent per annum on adjusted book value. Adjusted book value was $40 per share at September 30, 2008; the MBIA share price on November 14, 2008, was $5.00.

15

A Small Case: Home Products International

In late 1998, Equity Group Investments, LLC (EGI), controlled by Sam Zell, and the Third Avenue Value Fund (TAVF), managed by Martin J. Whitman, were independently considering buying control of Home Products International, Inc. (HPI). The largest shareholder of HPI was Chase Venture Capital Associates, L.P.,[1] which owned 17.6 percent of the shares of common stock outstanding. Chase Venture Capital Associates' asking price for its shares was $20 per share.

EGI was interested in buying control of HPI by purchasing its common stock, but it was estopped from purchasing any HPI securities, whether debt or equity, because it had signed a confidentiality agreement. TAVF was happy buying a majority of HPI's $9^5/_8$ percent senior subordinated notes at an attractive yield to maturity of around 21 percent, and contemplated taking control only if the notes became nonperforming. From November 1998 to November 1999, EGI, through Samstock, LLC, bought 664,000 shares of HPI common and thus accumulated approximately 9.1 percent of the 7,314,702 shares outstanding at an average price of $8.85 per share. Although they were not purchased directly by Samstock, LLC, EGI beneficially owned 150,000 extra shares of HPI common.[2] As of December 31, 1999, Sam Zell controlled 11.2 percent of the common stock of HPI.

By June 2000, second-quarter results showed a deterioration of operating results due to a decrease in sales and an increase in raw materials costs. In September, HPI negotiated a second amendment to the revolving credit agreement "to better suit current business needs." As part of the agreement, the associated line of credit was reduced to $85 million, certain financial covenants were adjusted, and the interest rate charged to the company was increased. Standard & Poor's (S&P) downgraded HPI from BB–/Stable to BB–/Watch Negative. Starting in November 2000, TAVF started buying the HPI $9^5/_8$ percent senior subordinated notes at a yield to maturity of

21 percent and a current yield of 16.8 percent. TAVF bought more than 50 percent of the principal amount and commented to its shareholders that in the event of either a change of control or a reorganization of the company, TAVF seemed to be very favorably situated. The idea was simple: if the notes continued to perform, the company would never hear from TAVF; if not, TAVF would take control of the company in a prepackaged Chapter 11 proceeding.

In November 2004, HPI entered into a definite acquisition agreement with Storage Acquisition Company, LLC (SAC), whereby SAC would acquire all of the outstanding shares of HPI's common stock. SAC was a company formed with the sole purpose of acquiring HPI, and Sam Zell controlled it. A former director of HPI was a member of SAC. This avoided a change-of-control event. Immediately after its purchase, the company went dark and no longer had to file reports with the Securities and Exchange Commission (SEC). To further reduce costs, the company amended the indenture of the $9^5/_8$ percent senior subordinated notes in January 2006. In November 2006, the company missed an interest payment on the notes and entered into negotiations with Storage Acquisition Company (the majority shareholder) and TAVF (the majority note holder) to effect a financial reorganization. HPI filed a prepackaged Chapter 11 shortly thereafter. The Third Avenue Value Fund ended up with the majority of the common stock in the reorganized company.

THE EARLY YEARS

Home Products International was founded in 1952 in Chicago, Illinois, as Selfix, Inc., a privately held company. The original product line included plastic bathroom hooks using suction cups. In 1962, Meyer and Norma Ragir acquired control of Selfix and gradually expanded the product line, establishing Selfix as a key vendor to major discount retailers. In 1987 Selfix acquired Shutters, Inc., a manufacturer of exterior shutters, and in 1988 Selfix became a public company after the completion of its initial public offering (IPO) and the listing of its common stock on NASDAQ. By 1992 the company had net sales of $35 million.

In 1994 the board of directors of Selfix hired James R. Tennant as chairman and CEO and James Winslow as CFO to restructure the company's operations and improve its profitability. See Exhibit 15.1 for results from operations from 1992 to 1995. The company incurred operating losses of approximately $4.5 million in 1994 and $4.1 million in 1995, resulting partly from the costs of this restructuring, including inventory and fixed-asset write-downs, severance pay and plant closing costs. The restructuring was completed in 1995.

EXHIBIT 15.1 Operating Results for Selfix, Inc., for the Period 1992–1995 (In Thousands, Except Share Data)

Statement of Operations Data	Fiscal Year			
	1992	1993	1994	1995
Net Sales	$35,209	$39,711	$40,985	$41,039
Cost of Goods Sold	$22,297	$22,504	$25,587	$25,678
Gross Profit	$12,912	$17,207	$15,398	$15,361
Operating Expenses	$13,501	$14,214	$18,185	$17,385
Restructuring Charge	—	—	$ 1,701	$ 2,051
Operating Profit (Loss)	$ (589)	$ 2,993	$ (4,488)	$ (4,075)
Interest Expense	$ (1,038)	$ (1,066)	$ (999)	$ (896)
Other Income (Expense), Net	$ 192	$ 126	$ (295)	$ 688
Earnings (Loss) before Income Taxes	$ (1,435)	$ 2,053	$ (5,782)	$ (4,283)
Income Tax (Expense) Benefit	$ 654	$ (574)	$ (221)	$ 273
Earnings (Loss) before Cumulative Effect of a Change in Accounting for Income Taxes	$ (781)	$ 1,479	$ (6,003)	$ (4,010)
Cumulative Effect of a Change in Accounting for Income Taxes	—	$ 36	—	—
Net Earnings (Loss)	$ (781)	$ 1,515	$ (6,003)	$ (4,010)
Net Earnings (Loss) per Common and Common Equivalent Share	(0.23)	0.43	(0.70)	(1.11)
Number of Weighted Average Common and Common Equivalent Shares Outstanding	3,448,267	3,511,100	3,538,758	3,616,924

GROWTH BY ACQUISITIONS

Starting in 1996, Mr. Tennant led an intensive program of acquisitions. To prepare for such a strategy, in February 1997, Selfix adopted the holding company form of organizational structure and changed its name to Home Products International, Inc. (HPI). By virtue of the reorganization, Selfix, Inc. became a wholly owned subsidiary of Home Products International, Inc.

Effective January 1, 1997, HPI acquired Tamor Corporation, a leading supplier of closet organizers and storage containers founded in 1947. Tamor was one of the top three suppliers of home storage and organization products in the United States and operated as a stand-alone subsidiary in Leominster, Massachusetts. The purchase price was $42.6 million, of which approximately $27.8 million was paid in cash, $2.4 million in common stock, and $12.4 million in the assumption of short- and long-term debt.

In 1996 Tamor had $75.7 million in sales, and earnings before interest and taxes (EBIT) of $7.3 million, while for the same period HPI had $38.2 million in net sales and EBIT of $1.4 million. HPI targeted 1997 sales of $130 million with the acquisition. The source of the funds for the acquisition included cash from the company, as well as a portion of the proceeds of a new $60 million credit facility (the February 27, 1997, facility) and a new $7 million note purchase agreement.[3] In June the company completed a public offering of two million new shares. The net proceeds in the amount of $18.3 million were used to repay debt and accrued interest. In July an additional 280,000 shares were sold pursuant to an underwriter's overallotment provision, a so-called green shoe where underwriters receive a call to acquire up to an additional 15 percent of the common stock raised in a registered offering. Net proceeds of $2.6 million were used to repay debt and accrued interest.

Effective December 30, 1997, HPI acquired all of the outstanding common stock of Seymour Sales Corporation and its wholly owned subsidiary Seymour Housewares Corporation, a privately held company and a leading designer, manufacturer, and marketer of consumer laundry care products, ironing boards, ironing board covers, and pads.[4] Seymour was acquired for a total purchase price of $100.7 million, consisting of $16.4 million in cash, $14.3 million in common stock (1,320,700 shares), and the assumption of $70 million of debt. The necessary funds for the purchase were obtained from a credit agreement entered into on December 30, 1997 (the December 30, 1997, facility[5]) whereby HPI replaced and augmented the previous facilities with $110 million in term loans and a $20 million revolver. The company also executed a $10 million senior subordinated note.[6] Seymour had net sales of $93 million and operating profit of $2.6 million. At the end of the first quarter of 1998, HPI had total long-term obligations (including current maturities of long-term debt) of $126.7 million and unused availability under the revolving line of credit of $11.8 million.[7]

In March 1998 the company announced the issue of a $125 million senior subordinated note to pay down debt and pursue more acquisitions. Concurrently with the offering, the company entered into a revolving credit agreement in the maximum principal amount of $100 million that replaced the company's prior $20 million revolver (the May 14, 1998, facility[8]). In August, HPI purchased certain assets (inventory and molds) from Tenex Corporation's product storage line for $16.4 million in an all-cash transaction, and in September HPI amended and restated the revolver to include, among other things, a $50 million term loan (the September 8, 1998, amended and restated credit agreement). The term loan along with $28 million of available funds from the revolver were used to complete the acquisition of certain assets and the assumption of certain liabilities comprising the businesses of

EXHIBIT 15.2 Measures of Liquidity, Leverage, and Credit Support for Home Products International, Inc. for the Period 1995–1998 ($ in Millions)

	1995	1996	1997	1998
Net Sales	$41,039	$38,200	$129,324	$252,429
Gross Margins	37.4%	39.8%	31.3%	33.0%
Operating Cash Flows	$ 2,575	$ 1,823	$ 878	$ 20,693
Long-Term Debt	$ 7,914	$ 7,650	$ 34,550	$223,085
Interest Expense	$ 896	$ 707	$ 5,152	$ 15,568
EBITDA	$ 1,313	$ 3,579	$ 18,435	$ 45,381
Long-Term Debt/EBITDA	6.0	2.1	1.9	4.9
Interest Coverage	1.5	5.1	3.6	1.3
Sales to Top 3 Customers	24%	27%	41%	39%

Anchor Hocking Plastics, a leading supplier of food storage containers, and Plastics, Inc., a leading supplier of disposable plastic serving ware, for $78 million in an all-cash transaction from Newell Company.[9] Availability under the revolver as of December 1998 was $51.9 million. As of the end of 1998, several troublesome trends were developing. Although the company had increased sales to $250 million, it had done so by incurring increasing amounts of debt. The concentration of sales to the top three discount retailers had increased from 24 percent to about 40 percent, and the ratio of cash flows provided by operations to interest payments had decreased substantially. (See Exhibit 15.2.)

In May 1999 HPI acquired certain assets (mainly inventory and molds) from Austin Products, Inc. The acquisition was completed for $6 million in cash and the acquired product line brought in $8.5 million in sales. Although the price of resin remained at depressed levels compared to previous years, the company was forced to pass on those savings due to increased competitive pressures.

A loss of sales of $5.8 million resulted from Caldor's Chapter 7 bankruptcy liquidation and the divestiture of Shutters. (Caldor was a discount retailer which purchased goods from HPI.) Management embarked on yet another restructuring program to reduce operating costs. The company recorded a pretax restructuring charge of $15 million. By August, Samstock, LLC had filed a Schedule 13D with the SEC disclosing that it had accumulated more than 5 percent of the common stock of HPI. This was a sign that the company might be for sale. By the end of 1999 the combination of margin erosion and a large amount of interest expenses was clearly a drag on GAAP performance. (See Exhibit 15.3.)

EXHIBIT 15.3 Operating Results for Home Products International, Inc. for the Period 1995–1999 (In Thousands, Except Share Data)

Statement of Operations Data	Fiscal Year				
	1995	1996	1997	1998	1999
Net Sales	$41,039	$38,200	$129,324	$252,429	$294,001
Cost of Goods Sold	$25,678	$22,992	$ 88,888	$169,213	$195,301
Special Charges	—	—	—	—	$ 8,589
Gross Profit	$15,361	$15,208	$ 40,436	$ 83,216	$ 90,111
Operating Expenses	$17,385	$13,843	$ 27,688	$ 52,566	$ 59,889
Restructuring and Other Expenses	—	—	—	—	$ 5,966
Other Nonrecurring Expense	—	—	—	—	$ 445
Restructuring Charge	$ 2,051	—	—	—	—
Operating Profit (Loss)	$ (4,075)	$ 1,365	$ 12,748	$ 30,650	$ 23,811
Interest Expense	$ (896)	$ (707)	$ (5,152)	$ (15,568)	$ (20,271)
Other Income (Expense), Net	$ 688	$ 148	$ 70	$ 269	$ 542
Earnings (Loss) before Income Taxes and Extraordinary Charge	$ (4,283)	$ 806	$ 7,666	$ 15,351	$ 4,082
Income Tax (Expense) Benefit	$ 273	$—	$ (346)	$ (6,601)	$ (2,072)
Earnings (Loss) before Extraordinary Charge	$ (4,010)	$ 806	$ 7,320	$ 8,750	$ 2,010
Net Earnings (Loss) before Extraordinary Charge per Common Share—Basic	(1.11)	0.21	1.35	1.11	0.27
Net Earnings (Loss) before Extraordinary Charge per Common Share—Diluted	(1.11)	0.21	1.29	1.07	0.26

RETAIL INDUSTRY WOES

Although net sales increased slightly in 2000 aided by the 1999 acquisition and strong growth in the serving ware line of products, net sales were negatively affected by reduced selling prices and decreased placement with the existing customer base. There was a $2.9 million decrease in sales to Bradlees, and sales were further reduced in anticipation of Bradlees' likely bankruptcy filing. Sales were also affected by the previous-year restructuring plan. In September 2000, the company negotiated a second amendment to the May 18, 1998, credit agreement. The amended and restated agreement reduced the revolver to $85 million, relaxed leverage and interest coverage covenants, eliminated the minimum EBITDA requirement, and significantly increased the interest rates on the facility.[10] HPI was also downgraded by S&P. The Third Avenue Value Fund (TAVF) started buying the $9^5/_8$ percent senior subordinated notes at a 21 percent yield to maturity and a current yield of 16.8 percent. In his letter to shareholders, Martin J. Whitman commented that in the event of either a change of control or a reorganization of the company, TAVF seemed to be very favorably situated. The idea was simple: if the notes continued to perform, the company would never hear from TAVF; if not, TAVF probably could take control of the company in a prepackaged Chapter 11 proceeding.[11] By the time TAVF issued its second-quarter report for 2001, it already owned 50 percent of the notes' principal outstanding, giving it control over a class of claims should the company file for Chapter 11 or try to reorganize out of court by seeking shareholders' consents to certain indenture amendments. Having control of this potential class gave TAVF effective control over a potential reorganization either out of court or in Chapter 11. In December 2000, the company started another restructuring that included the closing of the Tamor manufacturing facility in Leomister, Massachusetts. The company took a charge of $12.4 million for the closing and was also required to take an asset impairment charge of $53.3 million ($44.4 million to reduce the carrying value of goodwill and $8.9 million to reduce the carrying value of equipment and product molds of its plastic storage business). During 2000, the company experienced margin erosion due to both increases in the price of resin and competitive pressures that led to product price reductions. Gross profits dropped to only 20 percent of sales compared to 30 percent of sales in 1999.

The first quarter of 2001 saw more restructuring charges, increased interest rate expenses, and decreased sales as a result of Bradlees and other clients filing for Chapter 11 bankruptcy protection. The company estimated that it had lost $10 million in sales due to these bankruptcies. By the end of the first quarter, the availability of funds from the revolver was only $28.3 million and the company was highly leveraged, with total debt of approximately three times its net tangible assets or $222 million. On June 7, HPI entered into a definitive agreement to sell its commercial serving ware unit, Plastics, Inc., to A&E Products Group LP, an affiliate of Tyco International, for $71 million in cash. The net sale proceeds of $69.5 million were used to retire the company's term debt and a portion of its revolving credit borrowings. During 2001 and 2000, Plastics, Inc. contributed net sales of $19.7 million and $39.5 million respectively and operating profits of $3.7 million and $7.8 million. On October 31, the company entered into a four-year asset-based $50 million loan and security agreement with Fleet Capital Corporation as its sole lender. The loan agreement replaced the revolver and was secured by all of the company's assets, and borrowings were limited to the lesser of $50 million or a specified percentage of the collateralized asset base. By year-end HPI had reduced long-term obligations from $222 million to $130 million and interest expenses from $22 million to $18 million, with further reductions in 2002 to $13 million. In addition, annual interest payments on the $125 million of $9\frac{5}{8}$ percent senior subordinated debentures amounted to $12 million.

In 2002, company sales suffered from the Chapter 11 filing of Kmart, Bradlees, and Ames, and the divestiture of Plastics, Inc. The lost sales from the serving ware line were partially offset by an increase in sales to the big three (Wal-Mart, Kmart, and Target). For the first time, 74 percent of the company sales were accounted for by the big three, compared to between 40 to 50 percent in the past. The results of rising resin costs and less negotiating power with the big three started showing in the company's operating results. Margins deteriorated further. (See Exhibit 15.4.) By the first quarter of 2003, the company reported that the announced closing of 326 Kmart stores after it emerged from Chapter 11 would materially reduce sales. Kmart was the company's largest customer, with $74 million net sales in 2002. The value of net sales for 2003 decreased by 6 percent compared to 2002, while the cost of goods increased by 4 percent. Gross margins were further reduced to 15 percent of sales.

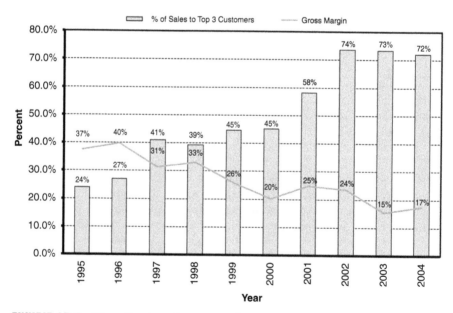

EXHIBIT 15.4   Home Products International, Inc. Gross Margins versus Sales to Top Three Customers, 1995–2004

THE FIGHT FOR CONTROL

In February 2004 the company received a proposal letter from JRT Acquisition, Inc. (an entity controlled by James R. Tennant, chairman and CEO of HPI) to buy all the company's common stock for $1.50 per share. In June, the company issued a press release and filed a DEF14A with the SEC announcing that it had entered into an agreement and plan of merger pursuant to which JRT Acquisition, an entity formed by James R. Tennant, would merge with and into the company. The company believed that the senior subordinated bondholders would not have the right to require a repurchase of their notes pursuant to the change-of-control provisions in the indenture since Mr. Tennant would beneficially own a majority of the voting power of the voting stock of the new company.

On June 10, a complaint was filed in Cook County, Illinois, against the board of directors by a stockholder. The complaint included a request for a declaration that the action be maintained as a class action and sought, among other relief, injunctive relief enjoining the company from consummating the transactions set forth in the merger agreement and rescinding the transactions already entered into pursuant to the merger agreement. The complaint alleged, among other things, that the consideration to be paid under the merger agreement was inadequate and that the company's board of directors had breached their fiduciary duties of loyalty, due care, independence, good faith, and fair dealing by entering into the merger agreement.

The company called for a special meeting of shareholders to approve and adopt the merger agreement in July. A special committee consisting solely of independent, disinterested directors of Home Products was formed by the board of directors to analyze, consider, and negotiate the terms of the merger and to make a recommendation to the entire board of directors as to whether to adopt the merger agreement. On September 23, Triyar Capital, LLC; Joe Gantz; and Equity Group Investments, LLC (EGI) submitted a written proposal to acquire 100 percent of the outstanding common stock of Home Products International, Inc. Pursuant to the terms of the proposal, a company to be formed by these three investors (Storage Acquisition Company, LLC) would acquire all of the outstanding common stock of HPI for $1.75 per share in cash without interest through a merger with the company. Mr. Gantz was a former member of the board of directors of both HPI and EGI, and was also a stockholder of HPI. EGI stated that it was willing to roll over its existing shares of common stock and would vote against approval and adoption of the agreement and plan of merger, dated June 24, by and between the company and JRT Acquisition, Inc. On October 14, JRT raised the offer to $1.80 per share and on October 15, the three investors submitted a proposal letter to purchase all of the outstanding common stock through a tender offer subject to a minimum offer of 70 percent of all the outstanding shares for $2.25 per share. On November 12, the company entered into a definite agreement pursuant to which the acquirer was to commence the tender offer to acquire all of the outstanding shares of the company's common stock. By the end of the year the purchase was consummated (the purchaser owned 93 percent of shares), a management restructuring took place, and the company filed to terminate registration, delisted its common stock from the NASDAQ exchange (went dark), and stated that it was unlikely that its shares would be traded on the over-the-counter bulletin board. At the same time the company amended and restated the previous loan and security agreement with Fleet Capital (the October 31, 2001, loan and security agreement) to increase the revolver loan commitment to $60 million (from $50 million) and amended some of its covenants.

Although gross profits improved slightly over 2003, operating expenses increased by $9 million mainly due to legal and investment banking fees and officers' and directors' severance related to the shareholder transaction. Earnings before taxes continued to be negative, and first-quarter results in 2005 did not improve. The high concentration of sales to the big three retailers continued to erode product pricing. During the first 13 weeks of fiscal 2005, the average cost of plastic resin had increased approximately 48 percent and average steel prices had increased approximately 59 percent compared to the average costs in the first 13 weeks of 2004. The increase in steel and plastic resin costs added approximately $5.9 million to cost of goods sold. Cost of goods climbed to 88 percent of sales, but by the third quarter of 2005 cost of goods was brought back to 85.4 percent on sales that were 11 percent lower than same quarter of 2004. In December 2005, the company amended the amended and restated loan and security agreement of December 14, 2004. The changes effected by the amended loan agreement included (1) the elimination of the financial covenant pertaining to a minimum cash interest coverage ratio, (2) a reduction of applicable interest rates by 50 basis points, (3) an increase in the minimum excess availability requirement from $5 million to $10 million (decreasing back down to $5 million with 12 months), and (4) the addition of a termination fee payable to the agent equal to 0.25 percent on the $60 million secured line of credit in the event that the company terminates the amended loan agreement before November 14, 2008.

AMENDMENT OF INDENTURE AND EVENT OF DEFAULT

In the pursuit of more cost reductions, on January 24, 2006, the company amended the senior subordinated notes indenture with the consent of the majority note holder (TAVF). The company paid a one-time consent fee of 25 basis points multiplied by the amount of principal due under the note held by each such consenting holder, and the amendment allowed the company to avoid having to file financial reports regularly with the SEC under the terms of the indenture.[12]

Pursuant to the indenture, a $5,600,000 interest payment came due on November 15, 2006, that the company was unable to pay due to a lack of available cash. The company had until December 15, 2006, to cure the default. As of December 8, 2006, the company owed lenders $37,821,000 on the revolving line and $2,825,000 in outstanding letters of credit. Unused availability on the line of credit was $6,100,000, which was insufficient to pay the interest due on the notes and pay for the company's operating needs. Management realized that they were unable to cure the payment default by December 15 and that the result would be that the indenture trustee could at any time accelerate the date the notes were due and payable. As of the end of October 2006, the company had losses of $31 million on sales of $178 million. During the same period of 2005, the company had losses of $10 million on net sales of $188 million. Cognizant of their inability to repay, the company and its majority shareholder—Storage Acquisition Company (SAC)—contacted the majority holder of the notes, TAVF, to begin negotiations for a financial restructuring. Third Avenue Management, LLC, the management entity for TAVF, engaged in discussions with other note holders and formed an ad hoc committee to continue negotiations with the company and SAC to facilitate the company's reorganization. The result of these negotiations was the decision to file a prepackaged Chapter 11 bankruptcy.

Several significant factors led to the deteriorating performance that ultimately led to the filing of Chapter 11. The price of resin steadily increased in 2006, aggregating to a 9-cent increase in cost, which translated into a $12 million cost increase on a yearly basis. The company was unable to pass on the cost increases to customers, and its vendors tightened their credit terms and reduced their credit lines in response to the company's deteriorating performance.

THE DECISION: PREPACKAGED CHAPTER 11

The company realized that it needed to reorganize to become a feasible going concern. HPI and its majority shareholder, Storage Acquisition Company, LLC (SAC) entered into negotiations with TAVF (the majority note holder) to effect a prepackaged bankruptcy plan. In a prepackaged Chapter 11 plan, a reorganization plan is negotiated and voted on by creditors and stockholders before the company actually files for bankruptcy protection.

This shortens and simplifies the process, saving the company money and frequently generating larger recoveries for creditors, as there is less spent in legal and other professional fees. The statutory bases for a prepackaged plan include Section 1121, which allows a debtor to file a plan of reorganization at the time it files a petition; Section 1126(b), which allows for the solicitation of acceptances for the plan prior to filing; and Section 1102, which recognizes prepetition creditors' committees.

TREATMENT OF IMPAIRED CLASSES UNDER THE PLAN

By early December 2006, after extensive negotiations, the debtor reached an agreement in principle with SAC and the ad hoc committee of note holders on the terms and conditions of a financial restructuring. The parties negotiated a restructuring term sheet that provided for a debt-for-equity swap whereby the notes would be extinguished and note holders would receive 95 percent of the company's new common stock (provided the note holders and the HPI interests voted for the plan), and the company's interest holders would receive 5 percent of HPI's new common stock. Under the proposed plan of reorganization there were seven classes of claims, as listed in Exhibit 15.5. Only two of the seven classes were impaired: one unsecured creditor class (Class 5, note holder claims—the senior subordinated note holders) and one class of interests (Class 6, HPI interests, comprised of the HPI shareholders). All other classes were not impaired and were deemed to accept the plan. Each holder of an allowed Class 5 claim would receive its pro rata share of 95 percent of the new HPI stock, and each holder of an allowed Class 6 HPI interest would receive its pro rata share of 5 percent of the new HPI stock issued and outstanding on the effective date when HPI came out of bankruptcy.

EXHIBIT 15.5 Classification of Claims under Proposed Plan of Reorganization for Home Products International, Inc.

Class	Claim	Treatment
Class 1	Priority Nontax Claims	Unimpaired
Class 2	Prepetition Secured Lender Claims	Unimpaired
Class 3	Miscellaneous Secured Claims	Unimpaired
Class 4	General Unsecured Claims	Unimpaired
Class 5	Note Holder Claims	Impaired
Class 6	Interests in HPI	Impaired
Class 7	Interests in HPI-NA	Unimpaired

FINANCIAL MEANS FOR IMPLEMENTATION OF THE PLAN

The implementation of the plan was made possible through exit financing provided by an exit facility, and the issue of new convertible notes (the new convertible notes election option). As of the effective date, to the extent necessary, the reorganized HPI–North America (HPI-NA) as borrower and the exit lenders executed and delivered the exit credit agreement for the exit facility to (1) refinance amounts outstanding under the DIP credit agreement, (2) make other payments required to be made on the effective date, and (3) provide additional borrowing capacity to the reorganized debtors following the effective date. As of the effective date, the principal amount of the exit facility financing was $15 million.

Further financing was provided by the issuance of $25 million of new second-lien convertible notes by the reorganized HPI. These notes were guaranteed by the reorganized HPI–North America, secured by a second priority security interest in all of the collateral securing the senior exit facility, and convertible at any time. The notes had a time to maturity of ten years unless they were otherwise converted, repurchased, or redeemed earlier, and offered a 6 percent per annum payable-in-kind (PIK) coupon that accrued on a semiannual basis. Pursuant to the plan, Class 5 claims and Class 6 interests had the right but not the obligation to purchase the new notes issued under the new convertible notes facility on a pro rata share of their claims. TAVF served as the backstop purchaser of 85 percent of the notes and SAC backstopped the purchase of 15 percent for a 2 percent fee of their respective backstop commitments. The funds raised would be used to fund transactions and distributions contemplated by the plan and for postbankruptcy business operations of the company.

GOING-CONCERN AND LIQUIDATION VALUATIONS

An enterprise value (EV) estimation was conducted to assist the holders of claims and interests in the evaluation of their recoveries under the plan of reorganization. This valuation, together with a hypothetical liquidation analysis, was also used to demonstrate that the plan satisfied the best interests test under Section 1129(a)(7) of the bankruptcy code. As discussed in Chapter 10, the going concern valuation involves the estimation of EV based on historical financial and operational information for the debtor and information about the market value of companies deemed generally comparable to its operating business. The publicly traded comparable companies selected for the analysis are shown in Exhibit 15.6.

EXHIBIT 15.6 Publicly Traded Comparable Companies Selected for the Enterprise Value Analysis

Company Name	Ticker
Newell Rubbermaid Inc.	NWL
Tupperware Brands Corporation	TUP
Myers Industries, Inc.	MYE
National Presto Industries, Inc.	NPK
Craftmade International, Inc.	CRFT

Exhibit 15.7 contains the calculations of EBITDA, EV, and last 12 months (LTM) and forecasted 2007 EV multiples of EBITDA for the comparable companies. Based on this analysis, it was estimated that the EV of the debtor could be approximated using a range of EBITDA multiples of 4.5x to 4.75x and an EBITDA forecast of $10,476,000 for 2007. The range of multiples used was lower than the comparable companies to reflect a lower revenue base and EBITDA, as well as factors such as depressed operating performance, the concentration of the debtor's customers, and uncertainty regarding tariffs, which resulted in lower near-term projected growth and profit margins than those that had been historically realized by

EXHIBIT 15.7 Valuation Multiple Calculation for Comparable Companies ($ in Millions)

Company	EBITDA	EV	LTM EV EBITDA Multiples	2007F EV EBITDA Multiples
Home Products International	$ 11			
Newell Rubbermaid Inc.	$941	$10,625	11.3×	10.7×
Tupperware Brands Corp.	$199	$ 1,996	10.0×	7.6×
Myers Industries, Inc.	$102	$ 781	7.6×	7.6×
National Presto Industries, Inc.	$ 41	$ 306	7.5×	N/A
Craftmade International, Inc.	$ 15	$ 114	7.4×	7.6×
Average			8.8×	8.4×
Median			7.6×	7.6×

EXHIBIT 15.8 Hypothetical Liquidation Analysis—Home Products International, Inc.

Account	Chapter 7 Liquidation Scenario		
	Adjusted Book Balance 1/10/07	Estimated Recovery	Liquidation Value
Cash	$ —		
Accounts Receivable	$ 38,446	60%	$ 23,068
Trade	$ 72	0%	$ —
Miscellaneous Receivables	$ 220	100%	$ 220
Insurance Claims			$ —
Inventory			$ —
Raw Material	$ 4,873	41%	$ 2,002
Inventory in Transit	$ 1,172	41%	$ 481
Work in Progress	$ 1,365	41%	$ 561
Finished Goods	$ 16,974	41%	$ 6,973
Prepaids	$ 2,258	0%	$ —
Property, Plant & Equipment—Net Book Value			
Land and Buildings	$ 7,390	100%	$ 7,390
Machinery and Equipment	$ 5,645	75%	$ 4,230
Dies/Patterns	$ 3,109	20%	$ 622
All Other	$ 7,274	2%	$ 145
Goodwill	$ 71,419	0%	$ —
Other Assets	$ 757	0%	$ —
Mexican Assets	$ 778	10%	$ 78
Total Assets	**$161,752**		**$ 45,769**
Less: Estimated Liquidation Costs			$ (4,100)
Real Estate Holding Cost			$ (2,000)
Net Available			$ 39,669
Less: Secured Debt			$ (35,064)
Net Available after Secured Debt			$ 4,605
Less: Priority Tax Claims			$ (1,094)
Net Available after Secured Debt and Priority Tax Claims			$ 3,511
Less: Secured Employee Claims			$ (937)
Net Available for Unsecured Claims			$ 2,574
Less: Unsecured Note Holders			$(116,050)
All Others			$ (59,202)
Net Available (Deficiency)			$(172,678)

Recovery by Class	% Distribution
Secured Debt (Class 2)	100%
Priority Tax Claims	100%
Secured Employee Claims (Class 1)	100%
Unsecured Note Holders (Class 5) and All Other (Class 4)	15%

the comparable companies. The midpoint EV for the debtor was estimated to be $48,454,000.

Under the plan, the projected debt at exit would be $44 million, consisting of $15 million from the exit credit facility, $25 million provided by the new convertible notes, and $4 million in capital leases; the value of the new equity would be $4,454,000 ($48,454,000 − $44,000,000), and interest holders would get 5 percent of the new equity in the reorganized company.

Under the hypothetical liquidation analysis presented in Exhibit 15.8, the net amount available for unsecured claims would have been $2,574,000 (a 1.5 percent recovery) and interest holders would have received nothing. Clearly, the plan satisfied the best interests test with respect to Section 1129(a)(7) of the bankruptcy code.

16

A Large Reorganization Case: Kmart Corporation

On January 22, 2002, Kmart Corporation and 37 affiliated entities filed petitions for relief under Chapter 11 of the bankruptcy code in the United States Bankruptcy Court for the Northern District of Illinois. The filing was the result of a liquidity crisis brought about by unsuccessful sales and marketing initiatives, the erosion of supplier confidence, and the recession that had already hit other general merchandise companies like Bradlees and Ames, which had already filed for Chapter 11 in 2000 and 2001, respectively.

The protection given by a Chapter 11 filing would allow Kmart to eliminate unprofitable stores and leases, improve store operations and inventory management, and restructure its balance sheet. The Kmart Chapter 11 case is particularly interesting because its analysis helps one understand the interplay between the important constituents in the reorganization of a retailer and many of the issues that are specific to a Chapter 11 reorganization. The issues in the Kmart Chapter 11 case include:

- Use of Section 365 of the bankruptcy code to either reject, assume, or assign unexpired leases and executory contracts.
- Critical vendor motions.
- Key employee retention plans (KERPs).
- Fraudulent transfers.
- Challenges to subsidiary guarantees.
- Substantive consolidation; deemed consolidation for distribution purposes.
- Number of Chapter 11 committees and out-of-control professional costs.
- Control of a reorganization afforded by holding blocking positions.
- Buying claims in Chapter 11.
- Debtor in possession (DIP) financing.

LANDLORDS AND UNEXPIRED LEASES

For a retailer to exist, it needs to operate stores. At the time of filing, Kmart operated 2,114 stores under the Big Kmart or Kmart Supercenter formats in all 50 states in the United States, as well as Puerto Rico, the U.S. Virgin Islands, and Guam. These stores were generally one-floor, freestanding buildings that ranged in size from 40,000 to 190,000 square feet. Of the 2,114 stores, Kmart owned 133 and leased 1,981 from unrelated third parties (the landlords). The leases on these buildings were generally long-term (25 years) and contained valuable five-year renewable options that could extend the life of a lease for up to 50 years. Many of them carried below-market rents.[1]

One important part of Kmart's reorganization was the elimination of unprofitable stores and the corresponding restructuring of the lease portfolio that resulted from these closings. Operating under Chapter 11 protection gave Kmart considerable flexibility in pursuing this restructuring. The source of this flexibility is Section 365 of the bankruptcy code, which enables debtors to assume, assign, or reject executory contracts and unexpired leases. The provisions of Section 365 also give debtors considerable leverage negotiating voluntary modifications or changes to leases with landlords.

From the debtor's point of view, the decision to either assume, assign, or reject a lease will depend on whether the store will be closed as part of a plan or reorganization and whether the leasehold is valuable. When a lessee is paying below-market rents for a store that can be easily re-leased at market rates, the leasehold can have substantial value. Large retailers like Kmart are usually the anchor tenants in shopping centers; they attract traffic to other stores and usually get large discounts on their contractual rents. If a debtor decides to keep a store, it benefits from a heavily discounted rent. If it decides to close the store, it can also benefit from the assignment of the lease to a third party at higher market rates. Exhibit 16.1 summarizes the possible decisions faced by a debtor generally, and Kmart specifically, as a function of these two factors.

EXHIBIT 16.1 Debtor's Decision to Assume, Assign, or Reject an Unexpired Lease

	Keep Store	Close Store
Good lease	Assume	Assign
Bad lease	Negotiate	Reject

EXHIBIT 16.2   Types of Lessor Claims against Estate, Depending on Debtor's
Decision to Assume or Reject an Unexpired Lease*

Claim	Assume	Reject
Unsecured Claim for:	—	Prepetition defaults and breach from rejection
Administrative Expense Priority Claim for:	All lease obligations pre- or postpetition	Postpetition obligations, if any

*If a debtor assigns a lease, the lessor has no claim against the estate.

What the debtor will decide in Chapter 11 will determine the type of
claim that a lessor has against the estate. Exhibit 16.2 shows the different
types of claims that landlords (lessors) will have, depending on the debtor's
decisions to either assume or reject a lease.[2]

The threat of rejecting bad leases also gives the debtor considerable
negotiating leverage over lessors to voluntarily modify or change the terms
of the leases if they want to keep operating profitable stores. In these cases,
landlords would prefer to make concessions and continue to rent rather than
getting a bad store back and holding a general unsecured claim against the
estate. In the case of good leases that the debtor will likely assign, landlords
are not without leverage of their own. The bankruptcy code does not allow
for the terms of leases to be unilaterally changed by the debtor, and potential
assignees that need to make modifications to the stores may be deterred from
entering into leases that the debtor wants to assign but that landlords will
not change.

This ability granted by Section 365 to force lessors to accept lease assignments provides debtors with an option to raise cash, temporarily relieves
them from their financial lease obligations, and helps them realize the potential value of leases from stores that it plans to close. Debtors can sell
property designation rights. A designation rights sale involves the transfer-
ring of the debtor's right to decide which leases to assume, to whom they
will be assigned, and under what terms such assignments will be made to a
third party for a price. In a designation rights sale, the purchaser will pay
cash to the debtor, assume the responsibility to market the leases to potential assignees, and bear the carrying costs of the leases until they are either
assumed or rejected (i.e., the designation period).

These designation rights sales were used in the Kmart Chapter 11
case. For example, the debtor entered into designation rights agreements
with Kimco Realty Corporation, Schottenstein Stores Cororation, and Klaff

Realty, LP to sell the designation rights with respect to 56 leaseholds for closed stores. The purchasers agreed to pay $46 million for such rights, all of which was paid to the estate on December 31, 2002.

Landlords view these designation rights sales and the ability of the debtor to assign leases as infringing on their rights to control their property and the process of tenant selection. Before the 2005 Bankruptcy Abuse Prevention and Consumer Protection Act (BAPCPA), the debtor had 60 days to assume or reject a nonresidential real property lease, but this was usually extended indefinitely, as it was during the Kmart Chapter 11 case. Under the new law, the debtor has 210 days to either assume or reject unexpired leases, and this gives lessors more leverage in preventing designation rights sales. In addition, lessors can now oppose debtors' requests for the 90-day extension for assumption afforded by Section 365(d)(4)(B). If a lease is rejected, the lessor is entitled to receive as an unsecured creditor an amount equal to the greater of one year's rent or 15 percent of the unpaid rent on the unexpired lease, not to exceed three years' rent. In the case of Kmart and the vast majority of other real estate locations, the payments on rejected leases were three years' rent. This claim becomes an unsecured claim in Chapter 11.

VENDORS AND CRITICAL VENDOR MOTIONS

A second component to a retailer is merchandise. Without anything to sell in those stores, a retailer has no business. This brings us to Kmart vendors. Any unpaid amounts on account of any merchandise sold to Kmart prepetition constituted a prepetition claim against the estate. Some of these claims were reclamation claims, and a larger number were general unsecured claims. While Section 546(c) deals with the rights of sellers to recover goods sold to the debtor while insolvent, there is no provision in the bankruptcy code for the preferential treatment of critical vendor claims, which are general unsecured claims. However, it has become routine for courts to approve first-day motions seeking the payment of prepetition claims of vendors that are deemed critical to the successful reorganization of the debtor. A common rationalization for the approval of these payments is that they preserve the going-concern value of the debtor in the belief that vendors not paid for prior deliveries will stop shipping. This generalization is utterly unrealistic. Vendor interests and motivations during a reorganization will depend on many things, including the degree of dependency of their overall business on the debtor, their ability to reposition their business throughout the pendency of the case, the amount of time that it will take them to reposition their business with other companies, and so on. For example, one vendor deemed critical to the Kmart reorganization was Fleming Companies, Inc. Kmart

EXHIBIT 16.3 Main Components to the Kmart Critical Vendor
Order Payments

Company	Critical Vendor Payment
Fleming Companies, Inc.	$76 million
Handleman Company	$49 million
Egg and Dairy Vendors	$5.2 million
Advertisers	$133.4 million
Foreign Vendors	$16.8 million
Letters of Credit to Pay Foreign Vendors	$6 million
Liquor Vendors	$2 million
Total	$288.4 million

From Kmart disclosure statement.

represented more than 50 percent of Fleming's business. On this fact alone
it is hard to rationalize that Fleming would not have shipped to Kmart if not
paid immediately for its previous deliveries.

Critical vendor payments that were authorized in the Kmart case are presented in Exhibit 16.3. As shown in Exhibit 16.3, vendors deemed critical to
the reorganization were paid nearly $300 million up front even though their
claims were unsecured. In effect, these critical vendor motions granted these
unsecured creditors preferential treatment over other unsecured creditors
who would have to both accept a smaller consideration and wait to get paid
until a plan of reorganization was confirmed. In essence these payments came
out of the hide of other unsecured creditors and unnecessarily increased the
need for postpetition financing. Financing for such payments in the Kmart
case came from a new DIP facility, and DIP lenders received super-priority
status for their claims along with liens on all of Kmart's postpetition assets
and revenues.

In the Kmart case, it turned out that the first-day order to pay critical
vendors was overturned on appeal, and critical vendors were ordered to
return those payments near the end of the case.

Under BAPCPA, vendors now have reclamation rights in Chapter 11 by
having the debtor return goods. The seller now enjoys a reclamation period
for goods received up to 45 days prior to the Chapter 11 filing, with an
additional 20 days after the filing date if the 45-day period expires after the
commencement of the debtor's case. If the seller fails to provide notice of
its reclamation claim, the seller may still assert an administrative claim for
the value of the goods received by the debtor within 20 days prior to the
commencement of the case.

MANAGEMENT AND KERPs PRE-2005 BAPCPA

Management is an important constituent in the reorganization process. As discussed in previous chapters of this book, the bankruptcy code gives the company, usually the management, the exclusive right to propose a plan of reorganization for what used to be an almost indefinite period of time. Under the 2005 BAPCPA, this period of exclusivity has been limited to 20 months. The period of exclusivity gives managements a considerable amount of power that will generally be used to protect their own interests for control, entrenchment, compensation, and job security.

An example of such power in the Kmart case was reflected in the size and scope of the company's first-day motion for the establishment of a key employee retention plan (KERP). Exhibit 16.4 shows the contents of the KERP plan as adapted from the original motion filed with the bankruptcy court. Included in Exhibit 16.4 is a summary of the KERP plan for WorldCom,

EXHIBIT 16.4   Kmart KERP Plan Filed on January 22, 2002

Tier	Position	Max # of Persons Participating	Annual Salaries	Performance Plan	Maximum Stay/ Emergence Bonus
I	CEO	1	$ 1,500,000	$ 1,875,000	$ 2,250,000
II	EVPs	5	$ 2,415,000	$ 1,449,000	$ 2,898,000
III	SVPs/SDVPs/VPs	40	$ 11,178,100	$ 5,030,145	$ 8,383,575
	Subtotal	46	$ 15,093,100	$ 8,354,145	$ 13,531,575
IV	VPs/RVPs/DVPs	133	$ 23,644,500	$ 8,275,575	$ 13,004,475
V	DVPs/Dir./DMs	776	$ 81,414,237	$22,388,915	$ 32,565,695
VI	Corp. Mgrs/Rx DMs	1,959	$134,745,683	$20,211,852	$ 33,686,421
VII	Corp./DC Sal.	1,668	$ 76,532,913	$38,266,456	$ 7,653,291
	Subtotal	4,536	$316,337,333	$89,142,798	$ 86,909,882
VIII	Store Mgrs	1,991	$133,266,487	*	$ 53,306,595
IX	Pharm./Rx Mgrs	3,132	$255,386,993	*	$ 38,308,049
	Subtotal	5,123	$388,653,480	—	$ 91,614,644
	Total	9,705	$720,083,913	**$97,496,943**	**$192,056,101**
WorldCom, Inc.		395		$25,000,000	

*Field Incentive Plan. Information adapted from the original KERP plan motion filed by Kmart.

Inc., which had revenues comparable to Kmart. As is evident from the data presented in the exhibit, the KERP plan for Kmart was massive and contemplated the payment of almost $300 million to 9,705 key employees over and above their regular pay. The reader is reminded that these payments have administrative claim priority and thus also come out of the hide of unsecured creditors. In contrast, and to gain some perspective on the disproportionate size and scope of the Kmart KERP plan, World-Com's KERP plan contemplated only the payment of $25 million to 395 key employees.

The 2005 BAPCPA amendments attempted to curb these types of clear abuses, but as was discussed in Chapter 1 and Chapter 9, even with the more stringent requirements set out in the new Section 503(c) of the bankruptcy code, managements have managed to keep control over their compensation by reworking their traditional KERPs into incentive plans instead.

FRAUDULENT TRANSFERS

From 1998 to 2000, Kmart Corporation transferred operating assets, including real estate, inventory, and certain distribution centers, to the following Kmart subsidiaries: Kmart of Indiana, Kmart of Michigan, Kmart of North Carolina LLC, Kmart of Pennsylvania LP, and Kmart of Texas LP (these will be identified as "the subsidiaries"). In exchange for the transfers, Kmart Corporation became the owner of the subsidiaries, which owned approximately 20 percent of the aggregate real estate and inventory at the time of filing. Not only did the subsidiaries own a substantial amount of assets, but they also had no trade debt since their inventory was purchased by Kmart Corporation and then sold to them and paid for on a daily basis through daily sweeps of their store deposit accounts. The only liabilities of the subsidiaries had arisen from guarantee agreements with Kmart prepetition lenders (i.e., the subsidiary guarantees).

One of the subsidiaries, Kmart of Michigan (KMI), also became the owner of all of the trademarks, service marks, and trade names used in the Kmart business pursuant to the transfers described earlier. KMI licensed these to Kmart and was paid approximately $300 million per year, which it in turn lent back to Kmart in the form of a royalty loan.

At filing, certain prepetition lenders had claims totaling approximately $1 billion. These lenders claimed that they were entitled to substantially all of the value of the subsidiaries pursuant to the subsidiary guarantees and that their claims had to be paid in full before any of the subsidiaries' value could be upstreamed to Kmart Corporation on account of their ownership interests.

This argument was contested by the unsecured creditors' committee and other creditors, who asserted that the transfer of Kmart's operating assets to the subsidiaries and the marks and trade names to KMI constituted fraudulent transfers that could be voided pursuant to Sections 544 and 548 of the bankruptcy code. If these challenges were successful, the value of such assets would then be available to all Kmart creditors and not just the prepetition lenders.

These challenges together with other challenges discussed in the next section led to a settlement with the various prepetition lenders, which will be discussed in the section about professional costs.

SUBSIDIARY GUARANTEES AND SUBSTANTIVE CONSOLIDATION

The unsecured creditors' committee posed a second challenge to the legal basis for certain prepetition lenders' entitlement to the value of the subsidiaries and to the enforceability of the subsidiaries' guarantees. The challenge was based on the idea of substantive consolidation. As explained in Chapter 12, substantive consolidation is the doctrine that pools the assets and liabilities of separate legal entities as if they were merged into a single surviving entity. The judicial criteria that are often used to establish whether the estates should be substantively consolidated were discussed in Chapter 12. One result clearly could have resulted from a substantive consolidation dispute involving the Kmart subsidiaries: substantial, costly, lengthy, and contested litigation.

A creative solution to this problem was devised to avoid protracted and costly litigation. The debtors proposed a global settlement of their claims, embodied by the plan of reorganization, which provided distributions to their constituencies commensurate with the risks of their litigation positions. As part of the plan, the debtors' estates were deemed substantively consolidated. Deemed consolidation is a surrogate of substantive consolidation whereby for purposes of voting and making distributions, claims are estimated as if the distinct entities were consolidated even though the reorganized entity that emerges from bankruptcy is not consolidated and it may preserve its prepetition corporate structure. Although the settlement did not guarantee the best possible recovery to any particular constituency, it afforded recoveries that fell within a reasonable range of litigation possibilities.

Absent this global settlement, the prospects of lengthy and costly litigation would have significantly reduced the value of Kmart as a going concern.

CHAPTER 11 COMMITTEES AND OUT-OF-CONTROL PROFESSIONAL COSTS

As explained in Chapter 6, the estate pays the administrative expenses of a Chapter 11 case. These administrative expenses are largely comprised of fees and expenses paid out to professionals, mainly attorneys and financial advisers who will perform services for the debtor in possession (DIP) and any other committees appointed by the U.S. Trustee. In the Kmart case there were three such committees: the official committee of unsecured creditors, the financial institutions' committee, and the equity committee. Each of these committees hired attorneys and financial advisers that were paid by the estate, and these expenses were paid in cash with administrative expense priority. Exhibit 16.5 shows a detailed list of professionals involved in the Kmart case, their roles, and the fees and expenses that they charged to the estate.[3]

Professionals in the case were billing the estate at an approximate rate of $10 million a month. The prospect of protracted and contested litigation that arose as a consequence of potential challenges to the validity of asset transfers and subsidiaries' guarantees posed the threat that professional fees and expenses would materially reduce the potential recoveries of all of the claimants in the case, with the exception, of course, of the professionals. Another year in Chapter 11 would have cost the estate another $120 million in professional fees and expenses.

BLOCKING POSITIONS

As discussed in Chapter 12, the statutory rules for plan approval set out in Section 1112 of the bankruptcy code give rise to leverage factors that may benefit certain parties. Only impaired classes will vote on a plan of reorganization, and to achieve a consensual approval, each impaired class that receives less than full value for its claim must approve the plan by at least one-half in number and two-thirds in amount of the allowed claims actually voting on the plan. These requisite majorities create the situation where either a large holder or a few large holders of claims acting in concert, holding slightly more than one-third in amount, have what in effect is a blocking position for that class. Holders with blocking positions could also have a seat in the relevant committees. These blocking positions allow their

EXHIBIT 16.5 Administrative Costs Related to Professionals Employed in the Kmart Case as of May 2003

Professional Firm Retained	Fees	Expenses
Skadden, Arps, Slate, Meagher and Flom		
Attorneys for the Debtor	$ 53,745,000	$4,670,500
Dewey Ballantine LLP		
Special Counsel to Independent Members of Kmart Board of Directors	$ 897,237	$ 59,135
KPMG LLP		
Financial Advisers to the Official Committee of Unsecured Creditors	$ 9,190,391	$ 713,554
Otterbourg, Steindler, Houston & Rosen, P.C.		
Attorneys for the Official Committee of Unsecured Trade Creditors	$ 6,665,592	$ 297,585
FTI Policano & Manzo		
Financial Advisers to Financial Institutions' Committee	$ 7,783,472	$ 416,162
Jones, Day, Reavis & Pogue		
Attorneys for the Financial Institutions' Committee	$ 3,774,396	$ 389,854
Traub, Bonacquist & Fox LLP		
Co-Counsel to the Official Committee of Equity Security Holders	$ 1,116,832	$ 59,362
Goldberg, Kohn, Bell, Black, Rosenbloom & Moritz Ltd.		
Co-Counsel to the Official Committee of Equity Security Holders	$ 1,114,662	$ 202,538
Ernst & Young Corporate Finance LLC		
Financial Advisers for the Debtor	$ 1,112,551	$ 110,388
Stuart, Maue, Mitchell & James, Ltd.		
Fee Examiner to the Joint Fee Review Committee	$ 528,434	$ 4,495
Winston & Strawn		
Attorneys for the Official Committee of Unsecured Creditors	$ 2,373,287	$ 257,057
Saybrook Capital LLC		
Financial Advisers to the Official Committee of Equity Security Holders	$ 1,192,258	$ 93,504
PricewaterhouseCoopers LLP		
Financial Advisers for the Debtor	$ 11,984,452	$1,131,957
Rockwood Gemini Advisors		
Real Estate Adviser to the Debtor	$ 2,851,571	$ 517,288
Miller Buckfire & Lewis Co.		
Investment Banker to the Debtor	$ 1,575,000	$ 335,847

EXHIBIT 16.5 (*Continued*)

Professional Firm Retained	Fees	Expenses
Abacus Advisory & Consulting Corp.		
Corp./Inventory and Valuation Consultant	$ 664,513	$ 52,744
Members of the Official Committee of Equity Security Holders		$ 75,195
Members of the Official Committee of Unsecured Creditors		$ 172,247
Members of the Official Financial Institutions' Committee		$ 11,581
Total	$106,569,648	$9,570,993

holders to prevent the consensual approval of a plan and give them considerable leverage over the potential shape of the plan of reorganization, even though the benefits may be potentially limited by the threat of a cram-down plan.

In the Kmart case, ESL Investments, Inc. had such a position in two plan classes (the note claims class and the lender claims class). Both ESL and Third Avenue also had seats on both the official financial institutions' committee and the official unsecured creditors' committee.

As shown in Exhibit 16.6, ESL and Third Avenue controlled 55.3 percent of the note class and ESL controlled 35.6 percent of the lender class, giving them blocking positions in both classes.

One of the goals of these two parties was to take Kmart out of Chapter 11 as quickly as possible to reduce the erosion of value brought about by the many administrative costs of the case. Their leverage as blocking holders and members of two official creditors' committees was used to that effect.

EXHIBIT 16.6   Blocking Positions in the Kmart Case

Class	ESL 000's	Third Avenue 000's	Entire Class 000's	ESL+Third Avenue % of Class
Lender Claims	$ 383,514	$ 0	$1,076,156	35.6
Notes/Debentures	$1,161,175	$98,860	$2,277,385	55.3
Trade/Lease Rejection	$ 60,799	$79,251	$4,300,000	3.2
Preferred Obligations	$1,434,100	$ 0	$ 648,043	0.2

Information gathered from the disclosure statement with respect to the first amended joint plan of reorganization of Kmart.

BUYING CLAIMS IN CHAPTER 11

Strategic investors like ESL and Third Avenue frequently seek to influence the reorganization process. In order to do this they will seek to hold large amounts of the fulcrum security (i.e., the claims or interests that will be the most senior issue to participate in a reorganization). This poses two problems: (1) identifying the fulcrum security, which may largely depend on the specifics of the proposed plan of reorganization, and (2) purchasing large enough amounts to either control or significantly influence the reorganization process (i.e., a controlling or blocking position). As previously shown in Exhibit 16.6, ESL had blocking positions in both the potential fulcrum claims: the lender claims and the notes/debentures claims. This eliminated the first problem.

Accumulating a large position in specific claims is generally done after the debtor files for Chapter 11. This was the case in the Kmart case, where the acquisition of blocking positions in both the lender and the notes/debentures claims classes was completed while the debtor was in bankruptcy.

An issue that a claims purchaser needs to contend with is dealing with parties with informational advantages. Members of official committees have access to nonpublic information about the debtor and owe fiduciary responsibility to the constituents whom they represent. Their trading of securities is restricted pursuant to securities laws. With respect to the trading of claims that are not securities (bank debt, trade claims), in some cases the U.S. Trustee may require that committee members do not trade; but when they are not restricted and they do sell their nonsecurity claims, they will seek to protect themselves from liability by contract, by executing what are known as big boy letters. In a big boy letter, the parties to a transaction agree that the counterparty may have nonpublic information but will hold the counterparty harmless for failure to disclose such information. Strategic buyers seeking to influence the reorganization by attempting to buy blocking positions will have to contend with this problem. Further, if the strategic buyer seeks to become a member of an official committee also, the buyer may need to purchase the claims before joining the committee if members are restricted from trading in the types of claims held by the strategic buyer.

Can we track these claims' transfers? The short answer is: to a limited extent. When a claim that has already been filed is transferred, the transferee must file a notice of transfer with the court pursuant to Federal Bankruptcy Rule 3001(e)(2). This rule is meant to keep track of claim holders for purposes of distribution and voting. These transfers can be tracked by periodically examining the court docket.

The rule does not apply to claims arising from securities (i.e., publicly traded notes, debentures, or bonds). In these cases an indenture trustee represents the holders, and a transfer agent keeps the indenture trustee apprised of who owns what and when. Tracking changes in the ownership of these types of claims may be more difficult. One knows of a large holder when such owner seeks representation in the official creditors' committee. Since the indenture trustee will be a member of the official creditors' committee on behalf of all the holders, if a large holder wishes to have a seat at the committee, it will have make the request to the U.S. Trustee. One way of identifying large holders is through regulatory filings by insurance companies (Schedule D) and investment companies, including mutual funds (Schedule 13F). Bloomberg terminals provide a simple command (HDS) that will list all institutional holders of debt sorted by the size of their holdings.

Throughout the Chapter 11 case, the debtor must file monthly operating reports. These reports include unaudited monthly statements of cash receipts and disbursements, which give a good picture of how much cash is being generated by the business, how it is used, and whether the debtor is burning cash faster than it generates it. For a strategic investor, deterioration of the debtor's cash position can represent buying opportunities. As shown in Exhibit 16.7, while gearing up for the 2002 holiday season, Kmart experienced deterioration in its cash balances that had to be supplemented by borrowing under the DIP loan agreement. At the time this was happening, both lender claims and notes/debentures claims were selling for half or less what they had been selling for up until June.

DEBTOR-IN-POSSESSION FINANCING

Although the automatic stay provided to a debtor in Chapter 11 generates spontaneous additional financing through the suspension of payments to trade vendors for their prepetition claims, as well as payments of interest and principal to other unsecured creditors, there are offsets to these additional funds. In the Kmart case, the additional spontaneous financing paled in comparison with the large disbursements represented by roughly $300 million in critical vendor payments that had to be made shortly after the petition date, $200 million to $300 million in KERP payments, and nearly $120 million (per year) in professional costs. As a result, Kmart estimated that it needed additional financing to effect a reorganization and filed a first-day motion requesting court approval for debtor-in-possession (DIP) financing under Section 364(c) of the bankruptcy code.[4] Section 364(c) provides that if the debtor in possession is unable to obtain unsecured credit, the court may authorize, after notice and hearing, the obtaining of credit or the incurring of debt (1) with priority over any or all administrative expenses, (2) secured by a lien on property of the estate that is not otherwise

EXHIBIT 16.7 Cash Receipts, Disbursements, Cash, and Cash Equivalents Available and Prices for Distress Claims for Kmart during Chapter 11

	2002												2003		
	Jan*	Feb	Mar	Apr	May	Jun	Jul	Aug	Sep	Oct	Nov	Dec	Jan	Feb	Mar
Cash Receipts															
Store	$ 751	$2,429	$2,286	$3,324	$2,612	$2,344	$2,628	$2,122	$1,977	$2,670	$2,478	$4,758	$1,682	$2,191	$1,975
Other	$ 59	$ 180	$ 179	$ 187	$ 187	$ 151	$ 175	$ 141	$ 158	$ 224	$ 184	$ 176	$ 246	$ 209	$ 152
Operating Cash Flows	$ 810	$2,609	$2,465	$3,511	$2,799	$2,495	$2,803	$2,263	$2,135	$2,894	$2,662	$4,934	$1,928	$2,400	$2,127
Cash Disbursements															
Taxes	$ 194	$ 223	$ 148	$ 127	$ 136	$ 126	$ 124	$ 112	$ 94	$ 96	$ 121	$ 147	$ 147	$ 114	$ 102
Accounts Payable	$ 158	$1,141	$1,695	$2,331	$1,920	$1,965	$2,467	$1,753	$1,931	$2,429	$1,945	$2,470	$1,661	$1,352	$1,546
Fleming			$ 290	$ 352	$ 286	$ 275	$ 321	$ 245	$ 311	$ 419	$ 391	$ 409	$ 235	$ 218	$ 131
Payroll and Benefits	$ 126	$ 275	$ 280	$ 489	$ 364	$ 376	$ 440	$ 314	$ 319	$ 429	$ 327	$ 432	$ 354	$ 302	$ 295
Lease Departments	$ 73	$ 200	$ 97	$ 23	$ 77	$ 13	$ 33	$ 10	$ 11	$ 16	$ 14	$ 20	$ 13	$ 20	$ 15
Restructuring Expenses	$ 46														
Other											$ 5	$ 5	$ 20	$—	$ 1
Operating Cash Outflows	$ 597	$1,839	$2,510	$3,322	$2,783	$2,755	$3,385	$2,434	$2,666	$3,389	$2,803	$3,483	$2,430	$2,006	$2,090
Total Operating Cash Flows	$ 213	$ 770	$ (45)	$ 189	$ 16	$ (260)	$ (582)	$ (171)	$ (531)	$ (495)	$ (141)	$1,451	$ (502)	$ 394	$ 37

DIP Loan Borrowings (Repayments)	$ 330	$ (330)	$—	$—	$—	$—	$—	$—	$ 35	$ 540	$ 202	$ (777)	$—	$—	$—
Net Cash Inflows (Outflows)	$ 543	$ 440	$ (45)	$ 189	$ 16	$ (260)	$ (582)	$ (171)	$ (496)	$ 45	$ 61	$ 674	$ (502)	$ 394	$ 37
Cash and Cash Equivalents	$1,245	$1,685	$1,640	$1,829	$1,845	$1,585	$1,003	$ 832	$ 336	$ 381	$ 442	$1,116	$ 614	$1,008	$1,045
Lender Claims Prices	$ 49	$ 62	$ 66	$ 68	$ 70	$ 67	$ 58	$ 41	$ 31	$ 25	$ 29	$ 26	$ 37	$ 38	$ 39
Notes/Debentures Claims Prices	$ 45	$ 41	$ 50	$ 48	$ 45	$ 42	$ 33	$ 28	$ 20	$ 20	$ 22	$ 14	$ 15	$ 15	$ 15

*The figures for January 2002 are for a nine-day period.

subject to a lien, or (3) secured by a junior lien on property of the estate that is subject to a lien. The court authorized borrowings for an amount of $1.15 billion from the secured super-priority credit facility (the DIP facility) in January and approved the full $2.0 billion by March 2002. The direct costs associated with the issuance of the DIP facility were $71 million or 3.5 percent of the $2 billion limit.[5] A few of the postpetition lenders were also prepetition lenders who might have offset some of their claim losses by participating in this very lucrative and safe DIP facility. Borrowings from and repayments to the facility are shown in Exhibit 16.7.

KMART'S PLAN OF REORGANIZATION AND PLAN INVESTORS

At the time Kmart Corporation filed for Chapter 11 bankruptcy protection, the structure of its claims and interests looked approximately like the one presented in Exhibit 16.8.

Roughly a year after Kmart filed for bankruptcy protection, it proposed a plan of reorganization. Under the plan, Kmart would emerge from Chapter 11 on April 30, 2003. The financial advisers to Kmart had calculated that the reorganization value of the reorganized debtors would be in the range of $2.25 billion to $3.0 billion with a midpoint of $2.625 billion.

EXHIBIT 16.8 Kmart Corporation Approximate Structure of Claims and Interests as of the Time of Filing for Chapter 11, January 22, 2002

Claim or Interest	Amount or Value 000's	Approx. Price, 11/01	Approx. Price, 2/02
Secured Claims	$ 61,000	100	100
Lender Claims	$1,077,000	90	60
Notes/Debentures Claims	$2,280,000	85	40
Trade and Lease Rejection Claims*	$4,300,000	75	30
Trust Preferred	$ 648,000	—	—
Common Stock (519,050,664 Shares)	$ 519,051	5	—
Total	$8,885,051	$8,788,553	$2,909,200

*Trade and lease rejection claims are postpetition estimates and not knowable at the time of filing.

EXHIBIT 16.9 Classification and Treatment of Claims and Interests under the Kmart Plan of Reorganization

Class	Amount	Status	Recovery	Consideration
Class 1 Secured Claims	$ 61,000,000	Unimpaired	100.00%	Reinstated
Class 2 Other Priority Claims	$ 0	N/A	N/A	N/A
Class 3 Prepetition Lender Claims	$1,076,156,647	Impaired	40.00%	Cash
Class 4 Prepetition Note Claims	$2,277,384,987	Impaired	14.40%	Common stock
Class 5 Trade Vendor/Lease Rejection Claims	$4,300,000,000	Impaired	9.70%	Common stock
Class 6 Other Unsecured Claims	$ 200,000,000	Impaired	9.70%	Common stock
Class 7 Unsecured Convenience Claims	$ 5,000,000	Impaired	6.25%	Cash
Class 8 Preferred Obligations	$ 648,043,500	Impaired	N/A	
Class 9 Intercompany Claims	N/A	N/A	N/A	
Class 10 Subordinated Securities Claims	N/A	N/A	N/A	
Class 11 Existing Common Stock	N/A	N/A	N/A	
Class 12 Other Interests	N/A	N/A	N/A	

This value represented roughly six times the pro forma EBITDA for 2004. The equity value represented by the difference between the reorganization value and the estimated total amount of long-term debt to be outstanding after giving effect to the plan ranged between $753 million and $1,503 million, with a midpoint of $1,128 million.

The classification of claims and interests and their treatment under the plan of reorganization are summarized in Exhibit 16.9.

Cash in an amount of 40 percent of their prepetition claims would be paid to certain prepetition lenders (holders of unsecured bank debt) as a result of a compromise and settlement reached with them that included their claims related to guarantees provided by certain affiliate debtors of Kmart and issues related to substantive consolidation. ESL Investments, Inc., which held 35.6 percent of the prepetition lenders' claims, elected to be deemed to have contributed back to Kmart the cash that ESL would have otherwise received under the plan. In exchange for the cash, ESL would get common stock in the reorganized Kmart. Since the equity value of the reorganized Kmart was $1,218 million and ESL's deemed cash contribution was roughly $154 million, ESL got 13.6 percent of the common stock of the reorganized company on account of its prepetition lender claims.

To raise enough cash to pay for the remaining prepetition lender claims, Kmart entered into an investment agreement with both ESL Investments, Inc. and Third Avenue Trust (the plan investors) whereby they would buy 14 million shares of common stock in the reorganized company for $140 million. ESL would purchase 78.21 percent of the 14 million shares and Third Avenue the remaining 21.79 percent. Pursuant to the agreement, ESL would then further increase its ownership of the reorganized company by another 9.7 percent, and Third Avenue by 2.7 percent. ESL also got up to an additional 7.62 percent of the common stock through the "ESL option" whereby the debtor granted ESL an unconditional and irrevocable right to purchase new common stock from the reorganized debtor at any time within two years of the closing of the investment agreement in the aggregate amount of $86 million.

Under the plan, note holders recovered 14.4 percent of their allowed claims or $328 million in the form of common stock. Note holders as a group ended up owning 29.07 percent of the common stock in the reorganized company, and ESL in particular picked up another 14.82 percent ownership stake through the conversion.

Trade and lease rejection claims as well as other unsecured claims, which are comprised of personal liability and other litigation claimants as well as claims by governmental entities, recovered 9.7 percent of their claims and also got shares of common stock as consideration for their recoveries.

Trust preferred obligations (Class 8) shared in any recoveries on account of claims by Kmart against certain former members of its senior management and other persons identified by Kmart in connection with its investigations into certain accounting and other matters pertaining to former management's stewardship of the company, including events immediately preceding Kmart's filing for Chapter 11. A creditors' litigation trust was set up as a means for resolving claims arising from these investigations. The trust preferred obligations would share pro rata in any of such recoveries with members of Classes 4, 5, and 6, but their recoveries were contingent on all those classes voting for the plan.

The subordinated securities claims (Class 10) and the existing common stock (Class 11) were entitled to receive their pro rata share of the right

EXHIBIT 16.10 Strategic Investors' Equity Stakes in the Reorganized Kmart

On Account of	$ Recovery	Shares	Percent of Equity
	ESL Investments, Inc.		
Lender Claims	$153,405,600	11,727,975	13.60%
Notes Claims	$167,209,200	12,783,270	14.82%
Trade Claims	$ 5,897,537	450,871	0.52%
Investment Agreement	$109,494,000	10,949,400	9.71%
ESL Option	$ 86,000,000	6,615,385	7.62%
Subtotal	$522,006,337	42,526,901	46.28%
	Third Avenue Trust		
Notes Claims	$ 14,235,840	1,088,341	1.26%
Trade Claims	$ 7,687,390	587,707	0.68%
Investment Agreement	$ 30,506,000	3,050,600	2.70%
Subtotal	$ 52,429,230	4,726,648	4.64%
Total	$574,435,567	47,253,549	50.92%

to recover 2.5 percent of the recoveries from the creditors' litigation trust. However, if any class of impaired claims voted against the plan, neither class would receive any property on account of their claims and would be crammed down.

The results of the operation of the plan of reorganization and the investment agreement on the two strategic investors are shown in Exhibit 16.10.

Pursuant to the plan of reorganization and the investment agreement, ESL and Third Avenue would end up controlling the reorganized debtor. As a result of the issuance of new holding company common stock to claim holders and the plan investors, the debtors would experience an ownership change (within the meaning of IRC Section 382).

As explained in Chapter 5, a change in ownership has the effect of limiting the amount of net operating losses (NOLs) that the company can use to offset its income at any post-effective date and since the debtor effected such an ownership change in bankruptcy, IRC Section 382(l)(5) would likely dictate the extent of the limitations. Furthermore, since ESL and Third Avenue held a significant amount of the equity in the reorganized debtor, their decision to dispose of a significant amount of their positions could also trigger another ownership change, which could further limit or eliminate the debtor's ability to use NOLs and other tax attributes.

The debtor would also experience large cancellation of debt (COD) income as a result of its reorganization. Although COD income was not taxable because it was generated while the debtor was in bankruptcy, it would still reduce other debtor's tax attributes, including NOLs.

INVESTMENT PERFORMANCE

On January 31, 2002, Martin J. Whitman wrote to shareholders of his Third Avenue Value Fund commenting on the underlying rationale and prospects for his Kmart investments:

> *"The investment in Kmart Senior Notes and Kmart Trade Claims is in the nature of a risk arbitrage, i.e. there ought to be reasonably determinant workout scenarios in reasonably determinant periods of time. Early in the quarter, the Fund acquired Kmart Trade Claims at a price of around 79% of claim. If Kmart had not filed for Chapter 11 relief, the yield to maturity for this investment would have been around 53%. Kmart, however, did file and the Fund continued to acquire Senior Notes and Trade Claims at prices as low as 38% of claim. On an all-in basis, it appears as if the Fund had a cost basis for its entire Kmart position as of January 31, 2002 of around 57% of claim. The odds seem much better than 50–50, say 2/3–1/3, that Kmart will be reorganized, or liquidated, on a basis that will be profitable for the Fund. Kmart is a huge empire of 2,100 big boxes (stores) that ought to be valuable, if not to Kmart, then to other leading retailers, whether Wal-Mart, Home Depot, Lowe's or even Hutchinson Whampoa. In Chapter 11, Kmart has the option of rejecting leases on poorly performing, or poorly located, stores with a maximum liability to landlords of three years' unpaid rent. Given a two- to three-year case, the Internal Rate of Return ("IRR") to the Fund ought to be anywhere from 12% (a reorganization value of 80 after three years) to 42% (principal plus interest in reorganization value after two years). In a worst-case scenario, though, the Fund as a senior lender is extremely unlikely to be wiped out. In this regard, being a senior lender is quite different than being a common stockholder. On a reasonable worst-case basis where Kmart as an operation becomes an absolute disaster, Fund Management estimates that it could experience a negative IRR of 10% to 15%."*

EXHIBIT 16.11 Chronology of Purchases, Cost Bases, and Dollar Recoveries on Claims Held by Third Avenue Value Fund

Item	Jan 2002	Apr 2002	Oct 2002	May 2003
Notes Claims at Period's End	$ 87,454,000	$ 96,549,000	$ 98,860,000	$ 98,860,000
Trade Claims at Period's End	$ 66,000,000	$ 66,000,000	$ 79,251,449	$ 79,251,449
Total Claims	$153,454,000	$162,549,000	$178,111,449	$178,111,449
Dollar Cost	$ 87,468,780	$ 91,743,430	$ 93,530,775	$ 93,530,775
Value of Claims	$ 87,468,780	$ 70,206,122	$ 29,032,125	$ 21,923,231
Cost Basis (% of Claim)	57.00%	56.44%	52.51%	52.51%
Value of Claims (%)	57.00%	43.19%	16.30%	12.31%
Unrealized Gain/Loss	0.00%	−23.48%	−68.96%	−76.56%
Recovery under Plan				$ 21,923,231
Shares				1,676,047
Price per Share				$ 13.08
Cost Basis for Those Shares				$ 55.80
Investment Agreement[a]				$ 30,506,000
Shares				3,050,600
Price per Share				$ 10.00
Weighted Value of Shares[b]				$ 11.09
Cost Basis for All Shares[b]				$ 26.24

[a]Dollar investment pursuant to the investment agreement with the debtor.
[b]Total shares equal to 1,676,047 + 3,050,600 = 4,726,647.

Based on the public record, one can build an approximate picture of the Third Avenue Value Fund's Kmart investment record. Exhibit 16.11 presents a chronology of claim purchases, claim cost bases, and recoveries under the plan for claims held by Third Avenue Value Fund.

The Fund had purchased slightly more than 85 percent of its total Kmart claims (notes and trade claims) before the company filed for Chapter 11 relief on the idea that if the company did not file and claims remained performing, the Fund would stand to make a reasonable IRR in either two or three years. After the company filed, the market prices for all claims decreased steadily throughout the pendency of the case.

As of the end of October the Fund had purchased an extra $25 million in claims at better prices that had the effect of slightly reducing its cost basis from 57 percent to 52.51 percent of claim. Under the plan, notes would recover 14.4 percent of claim, and trade 9.7 percent of claim. On account of its claims, the Fund would recover $21,923,231 or 1,676,047 shares valued at $13.08 per share, compared to a cost basis per share of $55.80. Key in reducing the Fund's cost basis was its participation, together with ESL Investments, Inc., in the investment agreement with the debtor. Pursuant to this agreement, the Fund purchased 3,050,000 shares at $10 per share, thus reducing the Fund's cost basis per share to $26.24, less than half its original cost basis. Two years after emerging from Chapter 11 (three years after the original investment), the reorganized debtor's shares were trading in the public markets at $100 per share or roughly a 56 percent annual IRR over the period. One year after emerging, the shares traded in the public market at $40 per share or a 26 percent IRR.

The point, however, is not that the investment worked out better than expected, but that by having control, both ESL and Third Avenue did not necessarily need a public market-out. As long as the business generated reasonable returns on equity going forward, their investment would grow in value over time. Further, Kmart emerged from Chapter 11 with very little debt, allowing control investors to pursue other alternatives to monetize their gains (if they wished to do so), like pursuing a recapitalization, a leveraged buyout (LBO), or a sale to a strategic buyer. As it turned out, the rich pricing of Kmart common stock became the currency with which Kmart ultimately was able to effect its merger with Sears.

17

An Ideal Restructuring System

The goal of an ideal restructuring system is twofold. First, the reorganization ought to make the debtor feasible (i.e., financed well enough so that the debtor is unlikely to have to either go through the reorganization process again or be liquidated). Second, and at the same time, the creditors, insofar as possible, ought to receive a net present value for their claims as close as possible to the value of their claims, all in accordance with a strict rule of absolute priority where no creditors in the given class receive a preference over other creditors in the same class. There can be a conflict between the dual goals. Insofar as the senior creditor receives a net present value in the form of cash and/or well-covenanted senior securities, rather than ownership interests, this can, and frequently does, detract from debtor feasibility. From a societal or national productivity point of view, there are six topics germane to understanding an idealized restructuring system for distressed companies that have issued publicly traded securities and will participate in a reorganization.

1. Restructured companies need feasibility; creditors and parties in interest who are passive, noncontrol investors without a continuing business relationship with the debtor need a cash bailout.
2. Creditors ought to receive maximum net present value in accordance with a rule of absolute priority modified by the standard that the debtor ought to be made feasible.
3. We are really not discussing an ideal restructuring system here; we are discussing a good enough restructuring system.
4. Certain things about the U.S. restructuring system seem to be highly beneficial.
5. The sometimes-conflicting goals ought to be resolved from a theoretical, optimal restructuring system.
6. We suggest reforms for the present U.S. restructuring system.

FEASIBILITY AND CASH BAILOUTS

In the financial restructuring of basically viable business enterprises, there are the needs and benefits of two broad constituencies to consider: on the one hand the business enterprise itself, and on the other hand, claimants and parties in interest. These two broad constituencies, in their relationships with each other, combine communities of interest and conflicts of interest. For the business enterprise, its needs and benefits revolve around one concept: *feasibility*. For claimants and parties in interest that are not going to have any elements of control or specific future commercial relationships with the business enterprise (e.g., trade creditors or government regulators), their needs and benefits also revolve around one concept: *a cash bailout*. This cash bailout for noncontrol claimants and parties in interest can come from only two sources: payments by the business enterprise, especially in the form of cash payments in compliance with the contractual terms contained in loan agreements, and/or the ability of the holder to sell securities (or securities equivalents) to a market. A market, again, is defined as any financial or commercial arena in which participants reach agreement as to price and other terms that each participant believes are the best reasonably achievable under the circumstances.

GOOD ENOUGH RATHER THAN IDEAL

As practical people with an involvement in restructuring troubled companies, we all know, at least instinctively, that there can no more be an ideal restructuring system than there can be an ideal income tax system or ideal generally accepted accounting principles (GAAP). The restructuring field is just too complex to suppose that any one restructuring system won't have very particular shortcomings in any given situation, simply because every case of which we are aware is governed, in part, by a unique set of facts peculiar to that restructuring. Rather than an ideal restructuring system, we are really talking about a good enough system. For example, take the trade-off between a secured creditor's rights to seize collateral in the event of a money default and the contribution to ultimate reorganization value if a financially troubled debtor can use that collateral to continue as a going concern. No set of rules, and no system, ever will be ideal enough so that this trade-off is maximized in each case. Let's settle for good enough.

HIGHLY BENEFICIAL ELEMENTS IN THE U.S. RESTRUCTURING SYSTEM

Before addressing the theoretical components of an ideal or good enough restructuring system, let us address the current environment, which seems to raise publicly aired questions as to the utility, or futility, of Chapter 11. The gravamen of this outcry is that Chapter 11 ought to be abolished because:

- Professional fees and expenses are too high.
- The process takes too long.
- Management entrenchment is too deep.
- Adequately secured creditors in particular are short-changed.
- Very few of the companies being reorganized are being fixed via the restructuring process.

However, none of the critics seem to comment much on the things that come out of the U.S. restructuring system that, if not ideal, certainly at least seem to be good enough—much, much better that what the authors think occur in other industrial countries with other restructuring systems, which focus more than the United States on the rights of adequately secured creditors. Indeed, other countries (e.g., Canada, Great Britain, and China) are increasingly emulating the U.S. preference, embodied in Chapter 11, for reorganization rather than liquidation. For example, both Great Britain and China have in recent years passed new insolvency statutes that ought to encourage reorganization rather than liquidation.

Put succinctly, there are three areas in restructuring where we in the United States seem to be head and shoulders over most other countries, except perhaps Canada.

1. Preserving reorganization value for larger business entities.
2. Distinguishing between companies that are reorganizable and those that ought to cease operations and go out of business.
3. Providing relatively efficient markets that noncontrol claimants and parties in interest can use to effectuate cash bailouts.

Three elements seem to result in a preservation of reorganization values whether the restructuring takes place in court or out of court. Because there is the availability of court relief under Chapter 11, a corporate debtor has an ability to obtain financing, at least on an interim basis, to alleviate cash shortages—assuming that the relative lack of debtor in possession (DIP) financing in late 2008 is a temporary phenomenon triggered by a freeze-up of all credit markets. The existence, present or potential, of the automatic stay keeps claimants and potential claimants at bay. Secured creditors, through a trustee or otherwise, are seriously proscribed from seizing their collateral if doing so arguably interferes with the debtor's going-concern operations.

Most companies in need of restructuring probably are also in need of trade credit and/or cash infusions. The existence of Chapter 11, with its provisions making postpetition financing an administrative claim, seems to us to set up a pretty good market test in normal times (not like 2008) that help distinguish between debtors that ought to be reorganized and debtors that ought to go out of business. If a company cannot obtain needed financing from very sophisticated, experienced sources—to wit, the trade and DIP lenders—under conditions where structurally these entities are providing new credit on a supersafe basis, this suggests strongly overall that the most relevant decision of the marketplace is that these particular operations should not survive.

We in the United States benefit from having the most efficient, deepest, best informed, most honest capital markets, both credit and equity, that have ever existed in the history of mankind. This is certainly true for passive investors and creditors who don't have any elements of control over the issuer of the securities and claims that they own. We, as a nation, probably never meant it to turn out that way, but the U.S. capital markets are a tremendous national resource, which tends, among other things, to give participants in U.S. restructurings market-outs in cash before, during, and after restructurings that seem largely unavailable elsewhere in the world.

GOALS OF AN IDEAL RESTRUCTURING SYSTEM

Theoretically, an ideal restructuring system ought to have seven elements. It should:

1. Be administratively fast and inexpensive.
2. In the treatment of claimants and parties in interest, cause those who made bad credit and investment decisions (especially depository institutions and insurance companies) to suffer the consequences of their bad decisions, but not suffer so much that their solvency and the essential fabric of the economy are threatened.
3. Treat claimants and parties in interest, insofar as they are noncontrol persons; insofar as they do have a necessary, continuing, commercial, or governmental relationship with the debtor; and insofar as they participate in a reorganization so that they get reasonable prospects of a cash bailout, through obtaining either performing loans or access to capital markets, or both.
4. Meet a standard of fairness and equity so that reorganization or liquidation claimants receive treatment in accordance with some sort of rule of absolute priority.
5. Require reorganized firms to meet a standard of feasibility.

6. Distinguish between those troubled debtors that should be reorganized and those that should go out of business.
7. Create good enough values and uses for assets of reorganized and reorganizing companies, but not create so many advantages for such companies that there is no longer a relatively level playing field vis-à-vis competitors.

SUGGESTED REFORMS

In an article in the January/February (1993) edition of the *Journal of Bankruptcy Law and Practice* entitled "A Rejoinder to the Untenable Case for Chapter 11," one of the authors suggested that restructuring troubled companies, either in court or out of court, could be made more productive if three general things were accomplished in amending the bankruptcy code:

1. There ought to be an end to having the estate subsidize the professional fees and expenses of the various constituencies involved in reorganization proceedings. Indeed, the only payments to professionals by a debtor would be for its own professionals, and at the end of a case to professionals representing claimants and parties in interest, and then only, and strictly for, substantial contributions to corporate feasibility. Any participants in a restructuring would remain free to hire, and pay for, any professionals they chose themselves.
2. Management entrenchment ought to be diminished in terms of managing the reorganization process. To wit, there should be strict limits on the period of exclusivity (which was accomplished in the 2005 BAPCPA amendments to the bankruptcy act) plus the mandatory appointment of a shadow trustee by the creditor group with the most apparent stake in the outcome; this shadow trustee would become the trustee if the company were not successfully restructured during the period of exclusivity. Plus, postreorganization, there ought to be a model charter and bylaws that would cede large elements of corporate control to postreorganization holders of common stock. One year after reorganization, there would be a requirement that a new board of directors be elected and any groups holding 20 percent or more of the voting power could have their proxy solicitations financed by the company.
3. Whatever steps could be taken to encourage corporate feasibility and cash bailouts to recipients of postreorganization interests by sales to a

market, ought to be taken. Here is a laundry list of factors that would abet feasibility:

- Encourage (or even require) low reorganization values.
- Educate holders of claims and other interests to want more present value in terms of total return from a feasible company rather than less present value from cash returns required to be paid out by a less feasible company.
- Amend the Internal Revenue Code to encourage companies reorganizing to seek strong capitalizations with large equity components while at the same time enhancing the value of NOLs for the company, limiting COD income for the company further than is now the case.
- From a creditor's point of view, either eliminate original issue discount (OID) or make it less punitive.
- Change the prevailing concepts that bank and insurance regulators—which are properly concerned with capital adequacy—use to value junior securities, which after a restructuring become part of bank and insurance company portfolios.
- Amend mark to market accounting rules where appropriate, so that their application more accurately reflects the true economics of the business. This is particularly important where GAAP numbers are used for purposes of determining regulatory capital and where the business as a going concern depends on the performance of its assets, not their market value. For these types of companies management should have the option to report the value of their assets using amortized cost and be required to disclose the effects of the fair value method in the footnotes.
- Amend the bankruptcy code and the securities laws so that recipients of postreorganization interests have convenient market-outs.
- Eliminate the distinction in the Internal Revenue Code between "old and cold" and "hot and new" recipients of a reorganized company's common stock.
- Ban bankruptcy courts from preventing trading in securities post-bankruptcy.

We are not seeking to create a drastic reduction in professional compensation. This is only true in the sense that we think time spent on restructurings ought to be drastically reduced. Rather, the main point of our suggestions about the role of professionals revolves around a belief that in restructuring cases, either in court or out of court, no one is representing the companies' compelling interest in achieving feasibility. Companies, viewed as companies, have a combination of communities of interest and conflicts of interest with claimants and parties in interest during the restructuring process. Every constituency that will remain as an interest holder in a company benefits from feasibility. However, every claimant and party in interest has a conflict with the company in that the vast majority of senior creditors want cash, near-cash instruments, and tough covenants, which detract from feasibility. Junior constituencies want large reorganization values so that they have either participation in reorganizations or enlarged participation in reorganizations. The large reorganization values are achieved mostly by using inflated estimates of cash flow or earnings. Based on such optimistic estimates, the company is permitted to have a capital structure that actual future events will prove to have been not feasible. The corporate feasibility constituency ought to get better professional representation than it now seems to be getting. If it got that, it would contribute to making our restructuring system better than "good enough."

By far the largest single problem that we see with our restructuring system today revolves around actually fixing the companies. The great growth industry over the next few years may well be Chapter 22.

Notes

CHAPTER 1   The Changed Environment

1. Federal Reserve, Flow of Funds Accounts, Table F.102.
2. Rule 144A was adopted in 1990.
3. Steven N. Kaplan and Jeremy C. Stein, "The Evolution of Buyout Pricing and Financial Structure in the 1980s," *Quarterly Journal of Economics* 108, no. 2 (May 1993): 313–357; also "The Evolution of Buyout Pricing and Financial Structure (or, What Went Wrong?) in the 1980s," *Journal of Applied Corporate Finance* (Spring 1993): 72–88.
4. See Robert N. McCauley, Judith R. Ruud, and Frank Iacono, *Dodging Bullets: Changing U.S. Corporate Capital Structure in the 1980s and 1990s* (MIT Press, 1999).
5. Default data from Professor Edward Altman, NYU Stern School of Business.
6. Steven Miller, "The Development of the Leveraged Loan Asset Class," in *The Handbook of Corporate Debt Instruments*, ed. Frank Fabozzi (New York: John Wiley & Sons, 1998).
7. K. Barnish, S. Miller, and M. Rushmore, "The New Leveraged Loan Syndication Market," *Journal of Applied Corporate Finance* (Spring 1997): 79–88.
8. Other reference rates like the federal funds rate or Euribor are also used.
9. For an in-depth review of the syndicated loan market see G. Yago and D. McCarthy, "The U.S. Leveraged Loan Market: A Primer," Milken Institute Research Report, October 2004.
10. National Shared Credit Program, press release, September 2007.
11. Joint press release, September 25, 2007, National Shared Credit Program, Federal Reserve Board, and leveraged loans par outstanding at nonbank institutions from S&P LCD.

CHAPTER 2   The Theoretical Underpinning

1. William F. Sharpe, *Investments*, 3rd ed. (Upper Saddle River, NJ: Prentice Hall, 1985), 67.
2. For a detailed discussion of capital structure from a corporate perspective, see Chapter 7 in *Value Investing: A Balanced Approach*, by M. J. Whitman (New York: John Wiley & Sons, 1999).

3. Known as the "cram down" section with respect to the confirmation of a Chapter 11 plan of reorganization.

CHAPTER 3   The Causes of Financial Distress

1. This is not an unusual corporate structure for broker-dealers and insurance companies.
2. A very high-profile LBO transaction at the time.
3. The High-Grade Structured Credit Enhanced Leverage Fund, also managed by Bear Stearns Asset Management.
4. Home Products International, Inc. is used later in the book as an example case of a prepackaged Chapter 11 bankruptcy.
5. Although focused on MBIA, Inc., much of the discussion applies to other very well capitalized financial guarantors like Ambac Financial Group, Inc., for example. The discussion draws heavily on public disclosures and presentations made by the company.
6. Such modifications can be found in both the schedule to the International Swaps and Derivatives Association (ISDA) master agreement and the confirmation letter for the specific transaction.
7. These contracts do not qualify for the financial guarantee scope exception under Statement of Financial Accounting Standards (SFAS) 133.
8. The volatility of these estimates of fair value can be material, as evidenced by the following company disclosure in its 2006 10-K: "The fair value of the Company's derivative portfolio may be materially affected by changes in existing market data, the availability of new or improved market data, changes in specific contract data, or enhancements to the Company's valuation models resulting from new market practices."
9. These estimates are expressed as additions to loss reserves or impairments, depending on whether the contract was a financial guarantee or a CDS. The estimated credit impairment on insured derivatives was $1.03 per share as of December 31, 2007.
10. In a reorganization context, the fulcrum security is defined as the most senior security that will participate in the reorganization, where participation means that the security will likely convert to equity ownership in the restructuring.
11. State insurance regulators allow insurance companies to classify the capital raised through surplus notes as surplus, the statutory equivalent to equity capital.
12. SEC 8-K filing, June 28, 2001.

CHAPTER 4   Deal Expenses and Who Bears Them

1. We are grateful to Professor Lynn M. LoPucki for providing the fee and expense data.
2. The size factor has been used extensively in the academic literature on this subject.

3. These are the results of a study that we performed using Professor LoPucki's data and data that we collected to measure the complexity of a case for each of the cases included in the database.
4. See "The Professional Costs of Chapter 11: A Different View," by Fernando Diz and Martin J. Whitman, *Journal of Bankruptcy Law and Practice* 14 (2005): 3–27.
5. *In re Fleming Companies, Inc.*, 304 B.R. 85 (Bankr. D. Del. 2003).
6. Lynn M. LoPucki and Joseph W. Doherty, "The Determinants of Professional Fees in Large Reorganization Cases," *Journal of Empirical Studies* (January 2004).

CHAPTER 5   Other Important Issues

1. See "The Professional Costs of Chapter 11: A Different View," by Fernando Diz and Martin J. Whitman, *Journal of Bankruptcy Law and Practice* 14 (2005): 3–27, and Chapter 4 of this book.
2. M. J. Whitman et al., "A Rejoinder to the Untenable Case for Chapter 11," *Journal of Bankruptcy Law and Practice* (January–February 1993): 839–848.
3. See discussion of the stock-for-debt exception later in this chapter.
4. There are exceptions to the creation of COD income from debt cancellation whose discussion is beyond the scope of this book.
5. A loss corporation is defined in IRC Section 382(k)(1), but it is a corporation either entitled to use a net operating loss carryover or that has a net operating loss for the current taxable year.

CHAPTER 6   The Five Basic Truths of Distress Investing

1. The prepackaged Chapter 11 reorganization of Home Products International is the subject of Chapter 15 in this book.

CHAPTER 7   Voluntary Exchanges

1. Good source material on the subject of taxation includes *Bankruptcy and Insolvency Taxation*, by Grant W. Newton and Robert Liquerman (Hoboken, NJ: John Wiley & Sons, 2006).

CHAPTER 8   A Brief Review of Chapter 11

1. Medium-size to large companies that have more than 12 creditors.
2. See Vern Countryman, "Executory Contracts in Bankruptcy, Part I," *Minnesota Law Review* 57 (1973): 439, 460; and "Executory Contracts in Bankruptcy, Part II," *Minnesota Law Review* 58 (1974): 479.
3. Reclamation of goods under Section 546(c), for example.

4. Which according to the Seventh Circuit Court of Appeals is just a fancy name for a power to depart from the bankruptcy code.

CHAPTER 9   The Workout Process

1. See Supreme Court decision in *Associates Commercial Corp. v. Rash* (1997).

CHAPTER 12   Distress Investing Risks

1. *Mobile Steel Co.*, 563 F.2d 692 (5th Cir. 1977)
2. *Enron Corp. v. Springfield Associates, L.L.C.*, No. 05-01025 (S.D.N.Y. filed August 27, 2007).
3. *In re Autotrain Corp.*, 810 F.2d 270, 276 (D.C. Cir. 1987).
4. *In re Augie/Restivo Baking Co., Ltd.*, 860 F.2d 515 (2d Cir. 1988).
5. See Andrew Basher, "Substantive Consolidation: A critical examination," Harvard Law School (2006), for an in-depth discussion of the three alternative tests.
6. *In re Owens Corning*, 419 F.3d 195 (3rd Cir. 2005).
7. Section 548(a)(1)(A) of the bankruptcy code deals with transfers with the actual intent to hinder, delay, or defraud (i.e., intentionally fraudulent).
8. *In re Jim Ross Tires Inc. d/b/a HTC Tires & Automotive Centers*, 379 B.R. 670 (Bankr. S.D. Texas 2007) was a case where the secured portion of the claim was not allowed as a secured claim, and *In re First Community Bank of East Tennessee v. Jones* (Bankr. E.D. Tenn. 2008) was a case where the secured portion was avoided as a preference.
9. Fernando Diz and Martin J. Whitman, "The Professional Costs of Chapter 11: A Different View," *Journal of Bankruptcy Law and Practice* 14 (2005): 3–27.

CHAPTER 14   Brief Case Studies of Distressed Securities, 2008–2009

1. Chapter 15 of this volume presents the Chapter 11 case of Home Products International, Inc.

CHAPTER 15   A Small Case: Home Products International

1. Chase Venture Capital Associates, L.P., whose general partner is Chase Capital Partners.
2. Samstock, LLC's sole member is SZ Investments, LLC, whose managing member is Zell General Partnership, Inc., whose sole shareholder is Samuel Zell as trustee of the Sam Zell Revocable Trust. Rod Dammeyer, an executive officer of Samstock, LLC, has sole voting power of 150,000 shares of HPI common, which are deemed beneficially owned by Samstock, LLC.
3. 8-K report for 2/28/97, Exhibit 99.1 and Note 15 of the 10-K405 report for 12/28/96.

4. Seymour was purchased from Chase Venture Capital Associates.
5. Exhibit 10.10 to the 10-K report for 12/27/97 and Exhibit 2.1 to the 8-K report for 12/30/97.
6. Exhibit 10.11 to the 10-K report for 12/27/97.
7. 10-Q filing on 3/28/98.
8. Exhibit 10.1.1 on the S-4 report of 6/11/98.
9. The excess of the purchase price over the estimated fair value of the acquired net assets of Tenex and Newell was $13.2 million and $59.8 million respectively (Note 2 to the financial statements of the 10-K report of 12/26/98).
10. Exhibit 10.1 to the 10-Q report of 9/23/2000.
11. Third Avenue Value Fund letter to shareholders, first quarter report, January 31, 2001.
12. 8-K report from 1/30/2006.

CHAPTER 16   A Large Reorganization Case: Kmart Corporation

1. Kmart 2001 and 2002 10-K reports.
2. For details on the limits on such claims, see Section 365 of the bankruptcy code.
3. Data obtained from interim fee applications and hearings on final fee applications available through PACER.
4. From motion filed by Kmart Corporation et al. on January 22, 2002.
5. Kmart Corporation 10-K report for fiscal year ended 1/29/2003.

About the Authors

MARTIN J. WHITMAN is Chairman and Co-Chief Investment Officer of Third Avenue Management LLC, the investment adviser to the Third Avenue Funds, as well as to private and institutional clients. Mr. Whitman has a long, distinguished history as a control investor and is a recognized expert in the field of bankruptcy. He has successfully identified value in distressed securities for more than 50 years. He is the author of *The Aggressive Conservative Investor, Value Investing: A Balanced Approach*, and *Dear Fellow Shareholders...* as well as of a number of articles on security analysis and investment banking. He has lectured on value investing and distress investing in various forums, including the American Management Association, Columbia University School of Law, New York University School of Law, the Wharton School of the University of Pennsylvania, Yale University's School of Management, and Syracuse University's Whitman School of Management, which is named in his honor. Mr. Whitman graduated from Syracuse University magna cum laude in 1949, with a bachelor of science degree. He received a master's degree in economics from the New School for Social Research in 1958, has received honorary degrees from Syracuse University and Tel Aviv University, and is a CFA charter holder.

FERNANDO DIZ is the Martin J. Whitman Associate Professor of Finance and Director of the Ballentine Investment Institute at Syracuse University's Whitman School of Management. After earning his Ph.D. from Cornell University in 1989, Diz joined the Syracuse University faculty to offer courses on value and distress investing and derivative securities. Dr. Diz acts as a designated manager and faculty adviser to the Orange Value Fund, LLC, a private investment vehicle created by its members to offer a selected cadre of Whitman undergraduate students the opportunity to learn and apply "safe and cheap" investing. Together with Martin J. Whitman, Dr. Diz created and has been co-teaching the Distress Investing Seminar at the Whitman School for the past seven years.

Index

Printed in the USA
CPSIA information can be obtained
at www.ICGtesting.com
LVHW020308110923
757813LV00004B/9

9 780470 117675